CONTROL AND POWER IN
GOVERNMENT RELATIONS

To: CMR, thank you.

Control and Power in Central–Local Government Relations

Second Edition

R.A.W. RHODES
University of Newcastle

Routledge
Taylor & Francis Group

LONDON AND NEW YORK

First published 1999 by Ashgate Publishing

Reissued 2018 by Routledge
2 Park Square, Milton Park, Abingdon, Oxon OX14 4RN
711 Third Avenue, New York, NY 10017

Routledge is an imprint of the Taylor & Francis Group, an informa business

A Library of Congress record exists under LC control number: 99015646

Typeset by Manton Typesetters, Louth, Lincolnshire, UK.

ISBN 13: 978-1-138-61221-1 (hbk)
ISBN 13: 978-1-138-61223-5 (pbk)
ISBN 13: 978-0-429-46351-8 (ebk)

Contents

List of Figures and Tables

Figures

Tables

Preface to the 1981 Publication

This book attempts to provide a reinterpretation of central–local relations in Britain. To be precise, it has four objectives.

(i)   To identify the strengths and weaknesses of the existing literature and to provide a bibliographical guide for both students and those who might wish to carry out research in the field in the future.

(ii) To demonstrate that a focus on the links between central departments and local authorities is restrictive. The subject needs to be redefined as 'intergovernmental relations' in order to encompass the range of relationships between the various units of government.

(iii) To develop a theory of intergovernmental relations which not only raises interesting questions about the specific topic but also relates the study of intergovernmental relations to broader issues in the study of British government.

(iv) To identify a coherent programme of future research.

The book has had a somewhat unusual history and a brief note on its conception and gestation will help to explain the form of its birth. Its conception lies in a commissioned paper for the Committee of Inquiry into Local Government Finance (Layfield) published in 1976. Subsequently, I presented papers on future research into central–local relations to the Social Science Research Council's (SSRC) Panel on Research into Local Government (April 1977) and to a Public Administration Committee Working Group on Research into Central–Local Relations (November 1977). In January 1978, I was invited to join the SSRC Panel on Central–Local Government Relationships and I was asked to produce a review of the existing literature on the subject and to develop the analytical framework outlined in the foregoing papers. My paper for the Panel was completed in May 1978 and the Panel's own report was produced in January 1979. The Panel's recommendations were accepted by the Research Initiatives Board of the SSRC and, as part of the continuing effort to stimulate research into central–local relations, the SSRC decided to sponsor the publication of a number of the papers commissioned by the Panel. This book is a revision of the full-length version of my paper for the Panel.

In revising the original paper, I have not attempted to provide a guide to recent changes in the system of central–local relations. Rather the emphasis has remained on reviewing existing literature and research and as yet there has been little research on current developments. Accordingly, I have concentrated on providing a perspective for the *future* study of central–local relations and the revisions have taken the form of clarifying the argument and effecting a reduction in the length of the original SSRC paper.

I was greatly aided in the process of revisions by the critical comments of my colleagues on the Panel. Early drafts of various sections of the paper were presented to a number of conferences and seminars. I would like to thank the Department of Politics (Aberdeen); the Department of Politics (Strathclyde); the Royal Institute of Public Administration (Edinburgh and East of Scotland Branch); the Institute of Local Government Studies (Birmingham); the Local Politics Group of the Political Studies Association (Birmingham and London); and the participants of the Public Administration Committee Annual Conference (York) and the Policy Studies Conference (Birmingham) for their patient and friendly criticism.

A number of individuals have also commented, either in whole or in part, on various drafts. My thanks to Doug Pitt (Strathclyde), Barbara Webster (Inlogov), Ed Page (Strathclyde), Ken Benson (Missouri–Columbia), Mike Goldsmith (Salford) and Bob Goodin (Essex). The first draft was written while I was a member of the Department of Administration, University of Strathclyde, and I must thank Lewis Gunn for his help and support. At different times, Ed Page and Kevin Pudney expedited the compilation and checking of the bibliography and Brian Hardy provided invaluable assistance at every stage in the preparation of the final manuscript. Maureen Russell (Strathclyde), Pat Caplin (Essex) and Desne Harrington (Essex) have patiently typed and retyped the various drafts. Finally, George Jones (LSE) and John Stewart (Inlogov) have been endless sources of criticism and encouragement and I owe both of them a special debt of gratitude. As ever, the responsibility for the remaining shortcomings is mine alone.

The author and publisher would like to thank the following who kindly gave permission for quotations to be included from their publications: The Clarendon Press for R.J. May, *Federalism and Fiscal Adjustment*; *Town Planning Review* for R.A.W. Rhodes, 'Some Myths in Central–local Relations'; G.W. Jones for *Responsibility and Government*; American Elsevier and the *European Journal of Political Research* for R.A.W. Rhodes, 'Understanding Intergovernmental Relations'.

Rod Rhodes
Colchester,
March 1980.

Preface and Acknowledgements

I was weaned on the American behavioural political science of the 1960s. Until I was 50, I had never read R.G. Collingwood or Hayden White. Their blend of philosophy and history was a revelation. I became enamoured of Collingwood. As Stephen Toulmin describes him, he was 'a lone wolf'; 'one of those English nonconformists who are fated to end up creating a party of one member' (Collingwood, 1978). Pigeon-holed as an 'idealist', he forswore the 'occasional remonstrance'; 'I became used to it: otherwise I might have been too much annoyed to keep that rule against answering critics which every one must keep who has work of his own to do' (ibid., p.56). But, and the reason for this excursion, his advice on critics for the 'more mature' scholar was sound:

> I am nearly fifty, and cannot in any case hope for more than a few years in which I can do my best work. I take this opportunity, therefore, of saying that I will not be drawn in to discussion of what I write. Some readers may wish to convince me that it is all nonsense. I know how they would do it; I could invent their criticisms for myself. Some may wish to show me that on this or that detail I am wrong. Perhaps I am: if they are in a position to prove it, let them write not about me but about the subject, showing that they can write about it better than I can; and I will read them gladly. And if any think my work good, let them show their approval of it by attention to their own. (Ibid., pp.118–19)

I intend to listen to Collingwood and concentrate on what I want to say. This book reprints the complete text of *Control and Power in Central–Local Government Relations*, minus the long bibliography. This Preface discusses why the book remains of interest.

The original manuscript was a report to the (then) Social Science Research Council (Rhodes, 1978). A new edition written 20 years later would be a different book and that would defeat the object of the exercise. The aims of this reprinted version of the book remain as for the original version (see above, p.ix), although the emphasis now falls on developing theory.

It is unnerving to reread a book written some 20 years ago. Inevitably much has changed since publication in 1981, so this book has a new Part II which reprints two essays criticizing the original theoretical framework, with a new chapter updating the story to 1999. Although there is no longer a select annotated bibliography, Chapter 8 provides a guide to the recent literature and there is an extensive list of references. I have made no changes of substance to the reprinted material. Any changes are limited to spelling and other typographical errors and standardizing the references by employing the author-date system throughout.

The aim of this Preface is to revisit briefly the individual chapters and discuss the continuing relevance of the book. It does so under the headings of theory, not trends; intergovernmental relations, not central–local relations; politics, not management; and policy, not institutions.

Theory, not Trends

Chapter 2 discusses the literature on central–local relations in Britain and is clearly out of date. Much has happened since 1979. I do not propose to write a history, however brief, of changes in central–local relations between 1979 and 1998,[1] or of the literature about those changes (see Stoker, 1995). However, the original version strove hard to escape the confines of a narrow focus on trends in central–local relations. A central objective of the original book was to develop a theory of intergovernmental relations (IGR) which related the subject to broader issues in the study of British government (see above, p.ix).

I argued that the study of IGR 'can only develop if it becomes consciously theoretical and encompasses issues and problems traditionally ignored or eschewed in the literature on central–local relations'. I also claimed that 'theories of advanced industrial society raise issues of direct relevance to the study of central–local relations' (pp.3–4 below), giving Daniel Bell's post-industrial society thesis and corporatist theory as examples. Of course, I would appeal to neither theory today, but my general point remains valid: the study of central–local relations is not a cosy little corner of Public Administration divorced from the rest of the social or human sciences; it is a subject to be interpreted through various theoretical spectacles, including rational choice and fashionable versions of state theory such as regulation theory.[2]

My main theoretical contribution can be found in Chapter 5 of the 1981 book, where I used the power-dependence framework and the concepts of networks and policy communities to analyse IGR (see next section). The continuing relevance of these ideas is the reason for reprinting the book.[3] In

Part II, I show how the debate around these ideas unfolded. Chapter 6, published in 1986, addresses several weaknesses in the original formulation, most notably such theoretical issues as the inadequacies of corporatist theory and my failure to distinguish clearly between the different levels of analysis. The chapter develops the notion of policy community, proposing a definition and typology of networks that were to become known as the 'Rhodes model'. Chapter 7, published in 1992, then offers a critical review of this model, posing seven questions; for example, 'how and why do networks change' and 'which interests dominate in networks'? Finally, Chapter 8, published for the first time, surveys the 1990s and offers a critical account of that literature rooted in an anti-foundational epistemology. I argue for an ethnographic approach which shifts the locus of analysis from institutions and policy to individuals and their narratives of life in networks. In short, therefore, Part II carries forward the story from 1981 and power-dependence in policy communities to 1998 and narratives of networks as governance. Whatever the quality of the work, the original framework started a protracted and at times heated debate about networks in British government.

Intergovernmental Relations, not Central–Local Relations

This phrase refers to the interactions between government units of all types and levels. However, in the UK, the common terminology is 'central–local relations', which refers to the links between central government departments and local authorities. Even in the 1970s, this use was far too narrow. In the 1981 volume I reviewed the North American literature on intergovernmental relations (Chapter 4 below) to show its relevance to the United Kingdom, arguing that the 'network of intergovernmental relations is far broader than central–local relations' and 'The complexity of the institutional environment must be recognised and analysis extended to include all public bodies' (see pp.22–3, 27–8; and p.71 below), although 'for ease of presentation' I focused on central–local relations, recognizing that 'The framework could be extended to cover the range of public sector organizations' (pp.53 and 78 below see also Rhodes, 1976, pp.196–8; 1978, pp.211–12).

The intervening years serve only to strengthen this argument because the Conservative government of the 1980s bypassed local government, preferring to use special-purpose bodies and fragment service delivery systems. There was a shift from local government to local governance. Service delivery now involves the private sector and voluntary bodies and IGR must encompass such developments as contracting out and public–private partnerships. The phrase 'local *governance*' captures the range of organizations, drawn from the public, private and voluntary sectors, involved in delivering local services (see, for example, Rhodes, 1997a; ch.3; and 1999). It also encompasses the increasing influence of the European Union (EU) on UK policy making and the multi-level links between local–regional governments, national government and supranational government (Rhodes, 1997a, ch.7). Institutional differentiation and pluralization characterize British government. The centres factored problems into manageable bits and fragmented government institutions, so governance maps the multiplying networks, their increasingly diverse membership and the effects on policy making and implementation. It explores the self-organizing capacity of networks and the inability of the centre to steer; that is, to coordinate policy horizontally across centres, vertically between levels of government in a network and across the boundaries of networks. Such ideas gain popular currency not only under the governance label but also through such nostrums as joined-up government and holistic government.

The relevance of the IGR prism to British government is obvious. It was always my aim to show that IGR existed in unitary as well as federal systems (for an up-to-date review of the American IGR literature, see Wright, 1988). Rhodes (1988, pp.2–3, 69–70 and 407–13; 1997a: ch.1) counters the image of the directive, all-pervasive, unitary centre with that of a differentiated polity characterized by a maze of networks. Britain is a 'centreless society', meaning there is no one centre but multiple centres or policy networks. Central to the metaphor of the differentiated polity are the notions of the fragmentation of institutions and policy between networks; the interdependence of actors within networks; and imperfect control of the centres over service delivery. These ideas are central to understanding the unintended consequences of central policies and the control deficits in policy implementation, deficits which all too often take the form of policy disasters like the poll tax. The metaphor of the differentiated polity and its IGR will become even more relevant when the Scottish Parliament and the Welsh and Northern Ireland Assemblies begin to flex their muscles.

Politics, not Management

The original framework was devised against the backcloth of an earlier era of management reform and its ideas about corporate management (see Stewart, 1972). Organization theory was the height of fashion in the study of public administration (see Rhodes, 1997, pp.168–70). I sought to blend organization theory and political science in the study of central–local relations (see p.55, n.1 below), to put management reform in its political context and to politicize organization theory. Unfortunately, the 'mutual disregard' continues to this day (Olsen, 1991) but the framework still shows its origins.

It emphasizes goal setting as a political process (see pp.37–40, 53–4 and 82–3); game playing (ibid., pp.43–6) and the rules of the bargaining game (ibid., pp.84–5 and 105–7). I agree with those colleagues who seek to develop this approach to intraorganizational political processes (Social Science Research Council, 1979, App.II; Dowding, 1991; 1995).

If the basic model needs developing, nonetheless it remains relevant for three reasons. First, any understanding of IGR and governance needs an analysis of bargaining as rule-governed interactions in and between organizations. Politics, whether party politics or bureaucratic politics, is ubiquitous in governance. Second, organization theory has parallel concerns to political science in the analysis of such processes and remains a source of theoretical insights (see, for example, March and Olsen 1989). Third, any account of the management of networks is necessarily about politics. The reforms of the 1980s, whether labelled managerialism or marketization, did not provide a tool kit for the manager to repair his or her organization. The reforms were variously understood and hotly contested. Research on the changes must seek to understand and compare the several stories. Chapter 8 of the present volume develops an actor-centred, or decentred, account of networks which seeks to build on my earlier account of organizational politics by exploring the competing stories people tell each other as they try to make sense of their changing organizational worlds.

Policy, not Institutions

Both Chapters 3 and 4 focus on organizational relationships and the literature on interorganizational analysis was a major influence on the power-dependence framework. That literature has increasingly focused on networks (see, for example, Clegg, 1990) and their management (see, for example, Ferlie and Pettigrew, 1996; Kickert *et al.*, 1997; Rockart and Short, 1991). But I became uneasy about this focus on institutional relationships, arguing for the analysis of policy areas over time (see, p.106) and for the primacy of networks over institutional links:

> The phrase 'central–local relations' suggests a bias towards the analysis of *institutional* relationships. Such an analysis does not always provide an adequate account of policy systems. To focus on policy communities is to assert the primacy of policy networks and policy content over the relationships between particular types of institutions. The phrase 'central–local relations' is, therefore, an inappropriate definition of the subject. 'Intergovernmental theory' with its emphasis on fragmentation, professionalisation and policy networks is more appropriate. (p.135)

This shift from institutions to policy, redefining central–local relations as networks, was a first step in changing the way I approached the study of British government. It foreshadowed a further shift, this time from policy to individuals. In effect, Part II maps the transition from institutions to policy to individuals and their beliefs. Openness is one criterion for judging a theory. It means taking criticism seriously and preferring positive speculative theories which open new avenues of research and make new predictions supported by the agreed facts (Bevir, 1994). My critical reassessment of the policy networks idea led to an exploration of the way they are constructed.

A constructivist approach to networks differs markedly from current approaches in two main ways. First, and most obvious, the social science approach adopts a positivist epistemology which leads its proponents to treat networks as social structures from which we can read off the beliefs, interests and actions of individuals. The network is given priority over the individual, determining actors' beliefs. In contrast, a constructivist approach regards networks as enacted by individuals. The beliefs and actions of individuals are not determined by their 'objective' position in an organization or network.

Second, the network literature is characterized by typologies. For example, van Waarden (1992, pp.39–41) provides the most daunting example. Over three closely printed pages, he identifies 11 network types which differ along seven dimensions encompassing 37 characteristics (see also Marsh and Rhodes, 1992, p.251). This butterfly collecting or Casauban approach to networks just assumes that they can be counted and classified. A constructivist approach does not treat network dimensions and characteristics as given. The 'facts' about networks are not 'given' to us. Individuals construct networks through the stories they hand down to one another. The study of networks, therefore, is inextricably bound up with interpreting the narratives on which they are based. This approach is explained and defended in more detail in Chapter 8.

Closing Remarks

If the review of the literature is now out of date, if the account of trends in central–local relations has been overtaken by events, the book's broad themes remain relevant. Theory underpins all the stories we tell ourselves about British government. Networks continue to be a prominent feature of policy making in British government. The debate on governance has picked up the theme of the organizational complexity of IGR. Present-day concerns about policy coordination reflect the complexities of managing IGR. The differentiated polity metaphor directs attention to the unintended consequences of policy. The analysis of bargaining as rule-governed interactions is central to understanding governance and unintended consequences. Policy network theory opened many new avenues of theory and research, shifting its focus from institutions, to policy, to individuals. The constructivist approach turns networks on their head by insisting they are enacted by individuals through the stories they tell one another and cannot be treated as given facts. So where does the study of networks go from here? I pick up that story in Chapter 8. Here I am content to show that the 1981 framework continues to be relevant, not least because it still prompts new ideas and avenues of exploration about British government.

Acknowledgements

I must thank Janice McMillan for her help in preparing this book for publication; she retyped the manuscript, standardized the references and prepared the index. Gerry Stoker provided helpful advice on what I should and should not do in preparing this version. The original version of Chapter 6 was published in M. Goldsmith (ed.), *New Research In Central–Local Relations* (Aldershot, Gower 1986) and is reprinted with permission. The original version of Chapter 7 was written with David Marsh and I thank him and Kluwer publications for permission to reprint. It was originally published in the *European Journal of Political Research*, 21, 1992, pp.181–205. My thanks also to Mark Bevir for his help in writing Chapter 8, which is published for the first time. Several colleagues provided advice and criticism on the chapters in Part II and their contribution is noted in the respective endnotes. Finally, I want to thank Janice McMillan and Vincent Wright for their ever-present support and help.

Notes

1   I have regularly updated the story. See Dunleavy and Rhodes (1983, 1986 and 1988), Rhodes (1984, 1988, 1991, 1992 and 1997a, ch.6). Chapter 5, pp.98–9 below, predicts some of the key trends of the 1980s, namely, bypassing local government, local government vulnerability to central intervention and the decline of political accountability.
2   Chapter 1, p.12, n.1 identifies state theory as an important theoretical approach to central–local relations. Chapter 6, pp.122–5 discusses Peter Saunders' 'dual state theory' in detail (for his response to the critics, see Saunders, 1986). There is still an extensive state theory literature, although it does not focus on central–local relations. On regulation theory and the transition from Fordism to Post-Fordism and its implications for the state, see Jessop (1990). For other relevant examples, see Judge *et al.* (1995) and Stoker (1995).
3   On the lineage of the model and a reply to my critics, see Rhodes (1997a, pp.8–13 and

24, n.1). My main publications on policy networks are Marsh and Rhodes (1992) and Rhodes (1986, 1988, 1990 and 1997a). The 'Rhodes model' is widely discussed in the literature. See, for example, Börzel (1998), Dowding (1995), Jordan (1990), LeGales and Thatcher (1995), Marsh (1998) and Marsh and Smith (1995). For additional references, see Rhodes (1997a, chs 1 and 2). The model has also acquired textbook status. See, for example, Chandler (1991), Cochrane (1993), Elcock (1994), Stoker (1991) and Wilson and Game (1994).

ROD RHODES
Newcastle-upon-Tyne
September 1998

PART I
CONTROL AND POWER IN
CENTRAL–LOCAL
GOVERNMENT RELATIONS

1 Introduction

The subject of central–local relations has been of peripheral interest to social scientists. The topic has been seen as within the province of public administration, with an attendant fixation on the legal–institutional aspects of the relationship. Recently, this situation has been changing. First, central government has become increasingly concerned about its perceived inability to control local authority expenditure. The most obvious manifestation of this concern was the appointment and report of the Committee of Inquiry into Local Government Finance (1976). Second, there has been a growing realization that, in spite of the many changes in the system of central–local relations over the last decade and a half, there have been virtually no academic studies of either the changes or the way the system actually works (a major research study is Griffith, 1966; on the limited amount of research, see Barker, 1978).

One of the major objectives of this book is to take stock of that research which has been published on central–local relations and to identify some of the possible directions for future research. The review covers the post-war period but, and the qualification is an important one, it is not limited to central–local relations narrowly defined. Perhaps one of the major problems associated with the study of central–local relations is the preoccupation with a narrow range of issues. This book argues that central–local relations is but one facet of a larger system of intergovernmental relations which encompasses both links between the UK government and the so-called peripheral areas of Wales and Northern Ireland and the links between the various central governments and other subnational units of government.

The scope of this review is broader, however, than the system of intergovernmental relations in Britain. Not only has the literature on central–local relations been preoccupied with a limited number of governmental institutions but it has also demonstrated a marked aversion to theory. It will be argued that the study of intergovernmental relations is important not just because it is currently deemed to be a policy problem but because it can illuminate facets of modern government of concern to social scientists. A number of theories of advanced industrial society raise issues of direct relevance to the study of central–local relations. The bulk of this chapter will review, albeit briefly, some of those macro theories capable of informing the study of central–local relations. Subsequent chapters will review in more detail some of the theoretical work on interorganizational analysis and intergovernmental relations which modify these general considerations for application in specific contexts. And the argument linking these, at times, disparate contributions is that the study of intergovernmental relations can only develop if it becomes consciously theoretical and encompasses issues and problems traditionally ignored or eschewed in the literature on central–local relations.

The pleas for theory and for a wider definition of the subject matter than a focus on central–local relations are, of course, easy to make. The problems of developing such a theory are far greater. However, if this review is to identify future areas of research, it is essential to move beyond exhortation and provide a framework for the analysis of intergovernmental relations in Britain. In the absence of such a framework, there is a danger that one compiles a list or shopping bag of 'interesting' projects. These projects can have no overall rationale and could bear little relationship to each other. A framework of analysis is essential if such fragmentation is to be avoided.

The justification for a theoretical framework does not lie, however, either in the inadequacies of previous work or in the need to identify a coherent group of projects. It lies in the ability of that framework to identify issues and problems previously ignored, to raise new questions and to provide a distinctive reinterpretation of the subject. The 'power-dependence' model of intergovernmental relations developed in this book suggests that these relations are simultaneously rational, ambiguous and confused. In other words, the functional links between national and subnational units of government are rational within a given policy area. Actors in the same policy area at different levels of government share common interests in the development of that policy area. However, the links between policy areas are ambiguous and, when the system is viewed as a whole, as is the case for public expenditure decisions, the pattern of relationships is confused. The framework presented in this book attempts to explain why the system is rational, ambiguous and confused. However, this statement anticipates future chapters. Recently, emphasis has been placed upon the problems associated with central–local relations, especially the failure of central government to control the level of local expenditure (Social Science Research Council, 1979, p.5). In these circumstances, it is particularly important to demonstrate that the study of intergovernmental relations can shed light on matters of more general concern in the social sciences.

The Context of Intergovernmental Relations: Some Theoretical Issues

Phrases such as the 'contract state', 'the new industrial state', 'turbulent environments' and 'organized social complexity' occur with increasing frequency in both academic and more popular literature, along with expressions of concern about the growing lack of accountability in modern government (Smith and Hague, 1971; Jones, 1977; Galbraith, 1972; Emery and Trist, 1965; La Porte, 1974; Toffler, 1971). They have not been missing from interpretations on British government. For example, Tony King (1975, p.168) has argued: 'If Britain is becoming harder to govern, it is partly because the number of dependency relationships in which government is involved has increased substantially, and because the incidence of acts of non-compliance by the other participants in these relationships has also increased substantially.'

In a similar vein, Richard Rose has suggested: 'The growing complexity of government tends to make government over complex, reducing its efficiency and upon occasion, its effectiveness. ... Today, the chief policies of government depend for success upon the results of complex processes of interaction that can be influenced but not controlled by government.'

This 'ungovernability' or 'overload' thesis has been widely discussed and it is not without its problems. As Richard Rose has pointed out, 'ungovernability' is a term 'that is ill-defined, variously defined or never defined at all' (1978, pp.15, 16, 1). Its status as a theory is similarly elusive. Only limited attention is paid to why governments have increasingly intervened in the economy. Explanations of ungovernability stress the level of electoral expectations, complexity, competition between interest groups, scarcity of resources or some combination of all these factors for explaining policy failure (Brittan, 1975; Douglas, 1976; Scharpf, 1977; Rose, 1978; King, 1975). A more adequate theory would explain why, for example, organized social complexity was a feature of British society in particular and advanced industrial societies in general. In fact, the 'ungovernability' thesis draws together in varying mixtures elements from the numerous theories of post-industrial society without explicitly demonstrating its links to that theory (in whatever version) or explicating the causal connections between the selected elements. Or to make the same point a different way, the ungovernability thesis explores the consequences for government of changes in its power and in the distribution of power in society without explaining the causes of those changes. For a broader ranging analysis, it is necessary to turn to theories of 'corporatism' and 'post-industrial society'.

Winkler (1976, p.103) defines corporatism in the following terms: 'Corporatism is an economic system in which the state directs and controls predominantly privately-owned business according to four principles: unity, order, nationalism and success.' In this definition, control refers to 'control over the internal decision *making* of privately owned business' (ibid., p.104). To the extent that corporatism stresses the interdependence of government and business, therefore, there is a marked parallel with the relationships between central and local government.

Winkler (1976, p.117) identifies four structural causes of corporatism: 'industrial concentration, declining profitability, technological development and international competition'. Corporatism is a response to long-standing basic trends in the British economy. The principles underlying the administration of the corporatist economy are: 'antinomianism, inquisitorial justice, strategic control, delegated enforcement, mediated enforcement and extra-legal power' (Winkler 1977, p.50). The state avoids formal operating procedures; uses the courts to sustain and restore order and cooperation; regulates national economic performance through control of a few, large organizations; uses private organizations to administer policy; conducts public administration through autonomous, intermediary institutions such as quasi-non-governmental and quasi-governmental organizations (collectively termed 'quangos'); and uses private coercion in support of public policy (ibid., pp.50–55).

This sketch of corporatist theory indicates its relevance to the study of intergovernmental relations. First, corporatist theory emphasizes the allocation of functions not only between government and industry but also between the various units of government. A key element in the theory can be assessed, therefore, by exploring the efficacy of central control over quangos as compared to local authorities. Apart from administrative and financial economy, Winkler argues that the state resorts to 'mediated enforcement' 'to conceal potentially contentious state activities'. In other words, quangos are 'indirect, concealed forms of administration' (ibid., pp.54 and 55). Accordingly, one would predict that quangos were less likely to be called to account for their actions (either by elected representatives or by the electorate) than local authorities. In more general terms, corporatist theory suggests that differences between the different institutional forms of state actions should be analysed. What difference does it make that a service or policy is entrusted to a local authority rather than a quango?

Second, the corporatist state may well view local authorities as means for legitimating its decisions and for coopting potential dissidents; that is, as part of the machinery of delegated enforcement. For example, the creation of the Consultative Council on Local Government Finance enables local authorities to 'participate' in making public expenditure decisions. This cooption could be described as a form of social control, a way of defusing opposition to cuts in public expenditure and of turning the opponents of cuts into agents for implementing central government policy. Certainly, corporatist theory raises interesting questions about the roles of the national institutions of local government.

It is possible, of course, to identify additional, specific themes in corporatist theory which could be explored in the context of intergovernmental relations. For example, the relationships between local authorities, the Home Office and the police could be explored in the light of the (alleged) growth in the use of private coercion to support public policy. However, the most interesting feature of corporatist theory is the exploration of changing (and increasing) state power. Winkler (1976, pp.134–6) argues that the state has some degree of autonomy and then focuses on the causes of the interdependence of government and industry and the consequences of this interdependence for the form, extent and autonomy of state action. The consequences of this focus for the study of intergovernmental relations can be illustrated by a brief examination of local government finance, the study of which typically takes the form of either straightforward descriptions of the system or analyses of changing patterns of grant and expenditure (see, for example, Hepworth, 1976; Boaden, 1971). There have been few analyses of the development of the system and the main preoccupation has been the effects upon local authorities of increasing dependence on central grant (one of the exceptions is G. Rhodes, 1976).

Corporatist theory suggests that central government's policy on local government finance will be an integral part of its economic policy: that is, just as the principles of corporatist administration are a response to the structural problems of the British economy so changes in local government finance reflect these problems. Moreover, as these problems intensify, so will central government's attempts to control local finance. Accordingly, there is need for a historical study of local government finance relating changes not only to the specific financial problems of local authorities but also to the fluctuating fortunes of the British economy. Within such a broad study a number of specific issues can be explored. Trends in local government finance could be compared with trends in the financing of other subnational units in order to assess whether the centre's need to control both the economy and local authorities has led it to bypass local authorities and resort to 'mediated enforcement'. The analysis could include also changes in the form of financing and explore the extent to which the centre became involved in the budgetary process of subnational units. The changing scope of central government's involvement in the finance of local government throughout the post-war period provides a setting for the exploration of many of the themes of corporatist theory. And casting the study of local government finance in this form provides a necessary corrective to the concern with the details of the system by emphasizing the evolving form of the system and its relationship to the economic context of British government.

The theory of corporatism does not just assume that there is a growing interdependence between the state and industry, it also attempts to explore the causes of this interdependence and its consequences for the state. It provides an interpretive framework within which the study of intergovernmental relations can be located.

However, there are problems with corporatist theory. As applied to Britain, analysis has been limited to the fields of economic policy and industrial relations. Nor is it clear that the state is able to maintain unity – a key corporatist notion – in these fields. Marsh and Grant argue that the government, the Trades Union Congress (TUC) and the Confederation of British Industry (CBI) have not been able to evolve an agreed industrial and economic policy, that there is no basic consensus underpinning the system and that the decisions of the leadership of the CBI and the TUC are not accepted as authoritative by the membership (Marsh and Grant, 1977). And yet these features would seem to be essential for unity in the field of economic policy.

There are also problems with the analysis of the long-term structural changes in the British economy (see, for example, Jessop, 1979) and there are ambiguities in the concept of corporatism. For example, Winkler does not distinguish between state corporatism in which 'the state plays a directive role in the establishment of class harmony' and societal corporatism where 'the representative organisations are autonomous but co-operate with the state and each other because they recognise that they are mutually interdependent' (Marsh and Grant, 1977, pp.195–6). And yet such a distinction would seem to be particularly appropriate to an analysis of, for example, the Labour government's 'social contract'.

Corporatist theory is, therefore, only one of a number of possible interpretive frameworks for the study of intergovernmental relations. But its major themes command attention. The interdependence of organizations, the power of the state and the broad socioeconomic context of government policy are issues which cannot be ignored. Indeed, they are not the exclusive preserve of corporatist theory.

The theory of 'post-industrial society' has appeared in many variants and this profusion no doubt accounts for the popularity and pervasiveness of a number of its central tenets. Daniel Bell defines the concept of post-industrial society as follows:

1   Economic sector: the change from a goods producing to a service economy;
2   Occupational distribution: the pre-eminence of the professional and technical class;
3   Axial principle: the centrality of theoretical knowledge as the source of innovation and of policy formulation for the society;

4 Future orientation: the control of technology and technological assessment;
5 Decision-making: the creation of a new 'intellectual technology'. (Bell, 1976, p.14)

These 'tendencies' are reflected in, and reinforced by, three major processes in western industrial society:

> the transformation of the industrial enterprise by the emergence of managers as controllers of the organisation; the changing composition of the occupational structure by the relative shrinkage of the industrial proletariat and the expansion of a new technical and professional stratum; and the transformation of the political system through the extension of the state bureaucracy and the rise of political technocrats. (Ibid., p.99)

For Bell, 'the major source of structural change in society ... is the change in the character of knowledge' (ibid., p.144) and one of the major structural changes is the spread of bureaucracy. 'In the mid-twentieth century, bureaucracy has become the central problem for all societies' (p.80) and we live in an 'organizational society' where the complex web of organizations provide the 'locus of one's life' (p.162). The problem is to manage this organized complexity or networks of interdependence and this task is conceptualized in terms of 'games against nature and games between persons' (pp.28, 127, 468). The conflict between the professional and populace in the locus of the organization is seen as the distinctive form of conflict of post-industrial society (pp.128–9). Quite clearly, the theory of post-industrial society treats interorganizational dependence as one of the defining characteristics of the new era.

Obviously, this summary neither does justice to Bell's argument, although it introduces his major themes, nor reflects the variety of approaches (see also Etzioni, 1968; Touraine, 1974; Vickers, 1972). However, it will suffice for a discussion of the theory's relevance to the study of intergovernmental relations.

Perhaps the single most suggestive theme in Bell's analysis concerns changes in the class structure of industrial society and the consequences for the distribution of power. With the divorce of ownership and control and the growing primacy of knowledge for the process of production, the professional and technical class and the political technocrats – the 'technostructure' in Galbraith's (1972, pp.59–71) terms – have risen to pre-eminence. In the context of intergovernmental relations, this argument suggests an analysis focusing on the roles of professional local government officers and civil servants and on their power in relation to the elected representatives, interest groups and citizens. To what extent do the professionals in, for example, education constitute a group of political technocrats spanning both levels of government? Are intergovernmental relations structured around professional policy communities? To what extent is the power of the professional limited by 'the cantankerousness of politics'? Does 'the conception of a rational organization of society' stand confounded with the professionals adhering to rationality having to rethink their premises (Bell, 1976, p.366) or has this rationality so permeated society that it legitimates the decisions of the technostructure? Moreover, such questions involve both trends and effects. How has the power of the professional waxed and waned over the years? An analysis of the rise of the social work profession in the post-war period should prove of interest in charting the processes underlying 'the professionalisation of everyone' (Wilensky, 1970). What kinds of decisions are made by the political technocrats employing what criteria? Do different professional policy communities have differing ideologies or are they linked by a common adherence to the norms of rationality? To what extent do they define the needs of clients for the clients? This list of questions is not exhaustive but illustrates the kinds of issues which the 'post-industrial society' thesis raises for the study of intergovernmental relations.

As with corporatism, there is no suggestion that the 'post-industrial society' thesis is without its weaknesses. As Burns (1974) has pointed out, the label is a nonsense because the key features of 'post-industrial society' are all present in industrial society. The description of 'super-industrial' is to be preferred, if only to emphasize the continuities with industrial society rather than the discontinuities. A number of the key characteristics of post-industrial society are hotly disputed. The divorce between ownership and control and the emergence of a managerial elite concerned with 'social responsibility' as much as profit has been asserted rather than documented (see, for example, Nichols, 1969; Blackburn, 1972). In fact, the major problems with the 'post-industrial society' thesis are the varying emphases of its proponents and the claims made for it. The claim that we are entering a new era should be disregarded. The theory should be viewed as a heuristic tool which identifies important changes in the nature of industrial society; changes ignored or slighted in many accounts of industrialism and which will repay further study. And considerably more care should be exercised in defining the content of the theory. For example, it is not uncommon for Bell and Touraine to be discussed together as if their versions of post-industrial society were similar, if not identical. In fact, Touraine's (1974, ch.1) analysis of 'the programmed society' emphasizes the continued importance of class conflict and he attempts to map the changing dimensions of this conflict. But the key feature of the theory for this discussion is its ability to locate intergovernmental relations within a broader framework. The treatment of bureaucracy as a central feature of post-industrial society, the focus on the complex web of organizations and the analysis of the role of political technocrats and of 'rational' decision making all demonstrate that the study of intergovernmental relations need not be pursued in splendid isolation. It can, and indeed must, be related to broader theoretical issues.

These brief discussions of corporatism and post-industrial society have done no more than introduce a number of themes which could be explored in future research.[1] As described above and, for the most part, as discussed by their respective authors, these themes are extremely general. They need to be translated into the specific context of intergovernmental relations in Britain. The remainder of the book is devoted to this task.

Summary of Part I

In Chapter 2, the existing literature on intergovernmental relations is reviewed. Employing the expository devices of the 'conventional wisdom' and the 'conventional critique', it is argued that the study of this topic has been confined to a narrow range of issues. Five 'forgotten dimensions' of intergovernmental relations are identified: the need for theory, variations in local discretion, the variety of relationships, the influence of political factors and the role of the professional. The preoccupation with central control and the financial aspects of the relationship between the various levels of government has led to the relative neglect of these dimensions.

In Chapters 3 and 4, attention is focused on the need to develop a theory of intergovernmental relations. However, this search is not conducted at the macro level. The literature on interorganizational analysis and intergovernmental relations is explored to see what contribution they can make to repairing the defects of the existing literature on intergovernmental relations in Britain. In addition, the relationship between these 'middle-range' theories and the macro theories discussed above are briefly explored. In the case of interorganizational analysis, it is argued that the analysis of interdependence is far more precise than that contained in either corporatism or the 'post-industrial society' thesis. However, this literature has become preoccupied with the measurement of interactions or exchanges and it will not facilitate the analysis of intergovernmental relations unless it is located within a theory on intra- and interorganizational *power*. In the case of the literature on intergovernmental relations, there is much of value in the analyses of the micropolitics of the relationships between the various tiers of government. With a few notable exceptions, however, the descriptions of intergovernmental relations have not been located within any explanatory framework. An explanation of the strategies and games of the actors presupposes a theory of the relative power of the various units of government.

In Chapter 5, a power-dependence framework for the analysis of intergovernmental relations is presented. It is argued that the discretion and the relative power of the various tiers of government are a product of their resources, the rules of the game and the values and interests supporting both the rules and the existing distribution of resources. The interactions between the units of government are analysed as if they were a 'game' in which the participants employ strategies within known rules. In the light of this analysis, a number of suggestions are made for future research into intergovernmental relations in Britain.

Note

1   One theory not explored in this book is Marxism. Various discussions of the 'local state' can be found in Pickvance (1976). At the time of writing, it is difficult to evaluate the utility of this work for the study of intergovernmental relations, especially as it tends to remain highly abstract, not to say abstruse. For a preliminary attempt to demonstrate the relevance of this approach to the study of intergovernmental relations, see Dunleavy (1980a). At least three problems can be identified which would appear to limit the applicability of the approach. First, the theory of the state proposed by Poulantzas and Castells would seem to be both tautological and teleological. For a discussion of these points, see Saunders (1980, pp.180–89). Second, considerable confusion appears to surround the concept of the 'relative autonomy of the state'. One of the few applications of Marxist theories of the state to British local government. Cockburn (1977, p.47) defines the state (including local authorities) as having 'a basic unity': 'All its parts work *fundamentally* as one.' The extent to which the various institutions of the state are unified would seem to be a matter for investigation and not for definition. On this point see Pickvance (1976), and Perrow (1979). Finally, it is misleading, in all probability, to talk as if there were *a* theory of the state. There are *major* differences between the various contributors within this tradition and to subsume them all under a single label is to conceal as much as it reveals. For example, compare the work of Miliband (1969) with Poulantzas (1973). Such contrasts exist also in the study of British government. Compare, for example, Cockburn (1977) with Dearlove (1979), with Jessop (1980). To date, the contribution of this tradition has been negative rather than positive: it has highlighted the defects of conventional forms of analysis rather than providing a redefinition of the subject matter of research with supporting empirical investigations.

2   Some Myths in Central–Local Relations

On a bitter winter's day, two porcupines moved together to keep warm, soon hurt each other with their quills, so they moved apart, only to find themselves freezing again. The poor porcupines moved back and forth freezing and hurting until they finally found the optimum distance at which they could huddle in warmth and yet not pain each other, too much.

    Have central and local government yet found the optimum distance?

The study of central–local relations is largely allegorical. The literature abounds with myths embodying popular ideas on social phenomena and parables of imagined events. To foster an understanding of central–local relations, therefore, it is necessary to unpick the traditional tapestry: to separate fact from fiction. The tools for this exercise are provided by the expository devices of the 'conventional wisdom' and the 'conventional critique'.

The 'Conventional Wisdom'

At the risk of some oversimplification, it can be argued that discussions of central–local relations in the 1950s and 1960s were based on the distinction between the agent and the partnership models (see Hartley, 1971). In the agent model, local authorities implement national policies under the supervision of central departments. Local authorities have little or no discretion. In the partnership model, local authorities and central departments are co-equals under Parliament. Local authorities have considerable discretion in designing and implementing their own policies. It is argued that local government is moving from being a partner to being an agent. This centralization has come about for two reasons. First, central government exercises increasingly tight control over capital expenditure whilst, at the same time, local authorities have become increasingly dependent upon central grant.

Second, central departments have acquired more powers of detailed control. These are the myths which accord central government a supernatural role. Moreover, advocates of the partnership model are great believers in local autonomy and, as a result, the trend for local authorities to become mere agents of central government justifies pleas for a return to the golden era of local autonomy. Myths and parable are thus entwined.

Such a brief description of the 'conventional wisdom' verges on caricature, but it is nonetheless easy to illustrate the main tenets of this view of central–local relations. Thus the Maud Report concluded:

> We are clear that there is a tendency for control and direction by the central government to increase, and for the financial independence of local authorities to decline still further and that both these tendencies weaken local government and detract from its effectiveness. (Committee on the Management of Local Government, 1967, p.76)

The Redcliffe-Maud Report was similarly of the opinion that 'there are strong centralising influences at work'. Central government was said to be 'less willing to leave local problems to local solutions'. Three reasons were advanced for this state of affairs in addition to 'the weaknesses inherent in the present structure of local government'. First, the 'national insistence on a high level of services'; second, 'national restriction of the level of capital expenditure'; and third, 'the growing proportion of [local] funds found by the central government' (Royal Commission on Local Government in England, 1969, pp.12, 133).

The Wheatley Report was equally critical: 'From the *practical* point of view, we have come to the conclusion that the kinds of control exercised by central government have in total a damaging effect on the independence and initiative of local authorities' (Royal Commission on Local Government in Scotland, 1969, p.243). And, as with the English report, financial independence figures prominently in the recommendations for change (ibid., p.246; and Royal Commission on Local Government in England, 1969, pp.133–4).

Official reports are not the only source of such criticisms. For example, Professor W.A. Robson (1966, p.53) was a long-standing and vehement critic of increasing central control: 'Can anyone seriously doubt that, as the Treasury comes to provide more and more money for the local councils, the voices of Whitehall will speak more often and with greater insistence?' And in more apocalyptic vein, Edmund Dell (1960, p.335) writes:

> Local government as it exists in this country today is far too dependent on Whitehall to be capable of being significantly responsive to local interests or to local public opinion when it does exist, if the Government rules otherwise ... Local government continues as a matter of tradition: but it is a dying tradition.

The central government's victory over local government is complete. Political power in this country has never been more centralised.

Nor is this diagnosis of recent origin. In 1956, a West Midlands Study Group employed the metaphor of 'the local authority ... being ground smaller and smaller between two millstones' to describe the relationship and one of the stones was central government 'armed with more and more pervasive control, reaching into the determination of local policy' (West Midlands Study Group, 1956, p.244). The second stone was professionalism. Twenty-one years later, the Society of Local Authority Chief Executives similarly criticized the extent of detailed controls, unnecessary advice and duplication of effort. Their examples ranged from Transport Policies and Programmes/Transport Supplementary Grant and the Community Land Act to the length of grass after cutting and how to measure it (Expenditure Committee, 1977, p.1085; see also Association of County Councils *et al.*, 1979).

It is possible to continue quoting from official reports, books and articles throughout the post-war period, all of which mine a similar vein (see, among others, Chester, 1951, p.337; Birley, 1970, p.30; Green, 1959, p.156; Hill, 1966, pp.169–79; Redcliffe-Maud and Wood, 1974, pp.24, 135, 160; Richards, 1973, pp.165–70; Sharp 1962, pp.375–86; Swaffield, 1970, pp.310–11). Developments in central–local relations in Britain since the Second World War have been seen as a process of centralization based on ever more pervasive central control and the erosion of local government's independent financial base. As Jeffrey Stanyer (1976, p.211) has argued, this diagnosis has achieved the status of a 'conventional wisdom':

> For over forty years W.A. Robson has been writing of 'the centralising tendency which is undermining local government', 'the subordination of local autonomy to the dictates of central power ... their [local authorities'] transformation into mere receptacles for government policy', and his judgements have been taken over by virtually every textbook, Royal Commission and committee of enquiry, and the local government world itself. The central domination of local government and the reduction of local authorities to will-less agents of the Government is therefore a common theme of the discussion of local government and indeed part of a conventional wisdom.

However, Stanyer also provides an archetypal example of the 'conventional critique'.

The 'Conventional Critique'

The problem with the 'conventional wisdom' is that it is difficult to substantiate its factual statements. To continue Jeffrey Stanyer's quotation (1976, p.211): 'Such a view ... is misleading to a high degree and is based on a misunderstanding of local government behaviour, or rather an ignorance of what happens in local government.' The arguments of the critics on the effects of financial dependence and central controls can be briefly summarized.

Whilst it is indisputable that local authorities have received an increasing proportion of their total *expenditure*[1] from central government, it is difficult to identify the consequences of this trend. If 'he who pays the piper calls the tune', one would expect dependence on central grant to limit variations between local authorities in their patterns of expenditure and to standardize the proportion of resources allocated to the various services within local authority budgets. In fact, irrespective of the size or wealth of local authorities, there is enormous variation in the patterns of expenditure (see Boaden, 1971, chs 1 and 2). Moreover, with the partial exception of the education service, increasing financial dependence did not affect the rates of change of the patterns of choice within local authority budgets (see Ashford, 1974). This evidence has prompted the conclusion by critics of the 'conventional wisdom' that local authorities should be seen as political systems in their own right. They do not simply follow central direction: they make their own decisions about their level and pattern of expenditure.

It is also argued that, although central government has an impressive list of controls at its disposal, they constitute only a potential for control. Included among the available controls are general statutory provisions; circulars, departmental letters and other forms of advice; confirmatory and appellate functions; adjudicatory functions; inspection; default powers; audit; control over the appointment, dismissal, discipline, pay and conditions of work of some local authority staff; and control over local bills (Griffith, 1966, pp.54–62). It is important to investigate how these controls work in practice, To what extent do central departments use their powers and to what extent do local authorities accept such attempts to control them? For example, Professor J.A.G. Griffith (ibid., pp.515–28) has argued that central departments differ markedly in their willingness to exert control. He distinguishes between laissez-faire, regulatory and promotional departments. Developing this typology, David Regan (1977, pp.33–4) argues that the same distinctions can be drawn between different sections or divisions of the same department. Quite clearly, therefore, it is misleading to talk of central control. Rather, there are different types and degrees of control exerted by the various constituent units of central government.

Similarly, it is argued that local authorities vary in their willingness to accept control. A variety of studies show central departments striving year after year to cajole, bully and persuade local authorities to implement a policy. The examples include smoke control, comprehensive education, nursery education, parking meters, fluoridation, the introduction of insulin, building council houses and planning (see Blackstone, 1971; Brier, 1970; Dearlove, 1973; Hartley, 1971; Scarrow, 1971; Swann, 1972; Friend *et al.*, 1974; Isaac-Henry, 1970; and the various case studies of the reorganization of secondary education listed in Ribbins and Brown, 1979). Few of these examples could be described as extreme cases of conflict between the two levels of government, as for instance, could Poplar and Clay Cross (see Keith-Lucas, 1962; Mitchell, 1974; Skinner and Langdon, 1974). And even when local authorities have unequivocally broken the law, central departments can have great difficulty in exercising control. John Dearlove's (1973, p.20) conclusion that the Royal Borough of Kensington and Chelsea accepted or rejected central interventions in the light of its own political priorities has been seen as applicable to many other local authorities:

> The Royal Borough is prepared to stand out against the advice and direction contained in government White Papers, circulars, private meetings with ministers and personal letters directed solely to them, if their own view as to what should be the proper scope of government is challenged. At the same time ... a local authority may use the supposed obstacle of central control for the purposes of internal political defence ... the impact of the central government upon the day-to-day decisions of local authorities often depends on local responsiveness, and the preparedness of local authorities to accept advice or guidance which in law the central government has no strict authority to give and no legal power to enforce.

The 'Conventional Critique' Revisited

Ironically, this critique of the 'conventional wisdom' has become so prevalent that it too can be labelled 'conventional' (see the criticisms of literature on central–local relations in Boaden, 1971, chs 1 and 2; Dearlove, 1973, ch.1; Stanyer, 1976, ch.10; Smith, 1976, ch.7; Smith and Stanyer, 1976, pp.122–9). And this label is deserved because, although it serves to correct some of the grosser oversimplifications in the literature on central local relations, the 'conventional critique' has some marked weaknesses.

First, it presents an unsympathetic reading of the literature. The themes of the various books and reports are treated in isolation from the various qualifications made by their authors.[2] As a result, a number of suggestions or clues which could guide future research are ignored. For example, the

West Midlands Study Group adds to the usual complaints about central control some comments on the role of the professional local government officer. It is argued that one of the factors eroding local autonomy is

> a service professionalism divorced from the old conception of a local government service and finding its strongest links with the central government departments and, through it, with colleagues in other areas all over the country, rather than with councils and committees and colleagues in other departments. (West Midlands Study Group, 1956, p.244)

In the haste to remove the detritus of the past, the perceptive is discarded along with the irrelevant and the wrong-headed. A number of the 'forgotten dimensions' of central–local relations (discussed below) are mentioned but not amplified in that literature characterized as the 'conventional wisdom'.

Second, the 'conventional critique' focuses on the issues raised directly in the 'conventional wisdom'. Adopting this focus begs the question of whether these issues are the ones most deserving of attention. For example, there is an almost exclusive concern with the financial aspects of the relationship. Financial considerations, although important, are not the only relevant factors affecting central–local relations. The 'conventional wisdom' has been allowed to set the parameters of debate and analysis.

Third, the 'conventional critique' presents a one-sided description of the relationship through its emphasis on local authorities as political systems in their own right. Local authorities may vary in their willingness to accept central control, but not all local authorities resist central intervention or are successful in their resistance. Many local authorities comply with central instructions even when the policy is as contentious as, for example, comprehensive education. Effective non-compliance may depend on the obedience of the majority and the non-statutory basis of central government's intervention. Any satisfactory analysis of central–local relations must explain compliance as well as non-compliance with both central advice and statutory instructions.

There is an additional problem with the argument that local authorities should be viewed as political systems in their own right: the evidence from the analysis of local government's patterns of expenditure is inconclusive. For example, the variations in the patterns of expenditure could have been welcomed by central government, especially as it was encouraging the growth of local expenditure for much of the period under scrutiny. It is also possible that the 'needs element' of Rate Support Grant (RSG) itself contributed to the variations in expenditure.[3] In so far as central government defines local needs and provides grant on that basis, it encourages local variation and this variation cannot be said to provide evidence of local discretion. And, a last example of the limitations of the evidence used to support the 'conventional critique', the methods of analysis employed are insensitive. It is possible that central government's interventions are highly specific to particular services and particular authorities and, because such interventions either cancel each other out or do not in total constitute a significant shift in the direction of expenditure, they are not revealed by aggregate data analysis. Alternatively, central government could selectively distribute resources but, because of the inevitable lag in local budgetary responses and frequent policy changes at the centre, these selective controls do not have an effect in a consistent direction at the aggregate level. The evidence supporting the 'conventional critique' is not, therefore, without its ambiguities and uncertainties.

Finally, the literature reviewed by the 'conventional critique' is primarily the literature of the 1960s. It presents a static picture of the state of research and, with self-effacing modesty, ignores the extent to which its own criticisms have changed 'the name of the game'. The 1970s have seen a number of studies of central–local relations which present a different picture from that contained in the 'conventional wisdom'. A review of the literature must cover this recent work, including not only the academic work discussed above but also government reports and other official documents (for example, Layfield Report, 1976).

The 'conventional critique' has served its purpose of insisting that conclusions on central–local relations should be grounded in an understanding of the actual behaviour of the two levels of government rather than on a commitment to local autonomy, but in demonstrating the weaknesses of the 'conventional wisdom', the 'conventional critique' has focused on a narrow set of issues. It has demonstrated that the topic of central–local relations is dominated by myths. Central government is not all-powerful. Dependence on grant does not necessarily mean a decline in local discretion. The existence of controls does not mean either that they are used or, when they are used, that they are effective. But the 'conventional critique' has remained imprisoned by these myths because it has failed to redefine both the scope of research and the relevant questions.

Some Recent Developments

Any consideration of recent developments in the study of central–local relations must begin with the Layfield Report. Superficially, with its stress on the centralizing trend of recent years and its distinction between more central responsibility and more local responsibility, the Report seems to rehearse the agent and partnership arguments all over again. However, the

Report's diagnosis of the defects of the current relationships contains some distinctive emphases.

A threefold distinction is offered. The term 'partnership' is seen as a synonym for the confused sharing of responsibilities, in marked contrast to conventional usage. It is sharply distinguished from both central responsibility and local responsibility. The Report's list of defects in the relationship is worth quoting in full:

(i)   no firm guidelines have been available to local authorities either on the expenditure they should plan for in the medium term or in the grant they may expect;

(ii)   the government's efforts to control local authorities' expenditure in the short term have led to disruption;

(iii)   the true cost of expanding local government services has not been brought home to local councillors or the public;

(iv)   the arrangements for resource allocation, grant negotiation and loan sanction have not made clear where the responsibility rests for decisions affecting local authorities' expenditure;

(v)   the government puts conflicting pressures on local authorities;

(vi)   local authorities in England have felt out of touch with the government's arrangements for resource planning;

(vii)   the government's controls have been used for purposes for which they were not intended and were not suited. (Layfield Report, 1976, pp.45–6)

In other words, the Report does not indulge in wild diatribes about central control but attempts to describe precisely what is wrong with the relationship. The picture which emerges is less one of central control and more one of an *ambiguous and confused* relationship in which neither level of government is clear about its responsibilities.

The consequences of ambiguity and confusion are said to be a trend towards centralization: 'What has been clearly visible over recent years is a growing propensity for the government to determine, in increasing detail, the pace and direction in which local services should be developed, and the resources which should be devoted to them, and the priorities between them' (ibid., p.65).

Local authorities have been caught between the pressures of demand for improved local services, an inflexible tax base and the unpopularity of rate increases. As a result, expansion has been financed out of grants. 'Financial pressures seem to have been critical in tipping the balance of forces to the centre' (ibid., p.72) and with increasing dependence on central monies there has been increasing interference by central government in the level of local taxation and increasing guidance over the pattern of local expenditure. The Report (p.72) concludes: 'The increasingly detailed intervention by the government is incompatible with that measured consideration of local expenditure needs and priorities, judged by local conditions and requirements and with local taxation decisions reflecting local expenditure decisions, which lies at the heart of fully responsible local government.'

If confusion is to be overcome, the Report urges that a choice be made between locating responsibility firmly with central government and reversing the trend towards centralization and reviving local accountability. The key principle for obtaining some much-needed clarity is: 'whoever is responsible for deciding to spend more or less money on providing a service is also responsible for deciding whether to raise more or less taxation' (ibid., p.50). The application of this principle could lead to either more central accountability or more local accountability. Irrespective of which was adopted, the present confusions in the system would be removed and the principle of accountability would be satisfied. The consequence of the choice is the same in both cases: the restructuring of the pattern of central–local relations.

At first glance, this description of current trends seems remarkably similar to the conventional wisdom outlined and criticized above. There are, however, a number of important differences. First, the problem is not described as being one of financial dependence. The Report is perfectly explicit in its argument that confusion and ambiguity are the basic problems. These, allied to the financial problems, have brought about the trend towards centralization. Second, the Report (p.64) does not see the solution of these problems wholly in financial terms: 'no financial system can do more than create the conditions for the development of the desired relationship; other measures, including many important non-financial ones, are needed to give it practical expression'. Finally, the existing relationship is not analysed solely in legal–institutional terms. There are various references to the political factors which sustain the current confusion. The argument has been summarized by George Jones:

> Where grant is a preponderant and growing part of local revenue the government will seek to ensure that it is spent in accordance with national policies and priorities. The grant represents money that central departments have fought hard to obtain against the Treasury and other departments with their rival programmes. Each department seeks to advance the particular service it looks after ... Civil servants and ministers ... are not likely to relinquish their concern with the money once it is handed over to local authorities to spend. As custodians of taxpayers' money and as defenders and promoters of particular services they wish to ensure that the grant is spent on their services as they said it would be. Civil servants also wish to protect their minister from criticism in parliament about the poor performance or inadequacies of services. A high grant, therefore, pulls the central officials to involve themselves in local affairs ... local authority

officials and councillors, recognising the high level of grant, feel that they have little justification for resisting departments. The political consequences of a high grant are to increase the pressure for central involvement in local government. (Jones, 1977, p.11)[4]

Party politics and organizational politics rarely figure prominently in the analysis of financial dependence.

The conclusions of the Layfield Report are reinforced by the report of the Central Policy Review Staff (CPRS). The CPRS Report rejects the criticisms that central departments issue spectacularly inconsistent advice and that local authorities are ahead of central government in development of corporate planning. It suggests, however, that:

(i)   departments act in isolation from each other;
(ii)   the relationship is confused by uncertainties over each other's responsibilities;
(iii) there is a multiplicity of overlapping channels of communication;
    (a)   advice is offered in areas which are prima facie within local government's discretion;
    (b)   the status of advice is uncertain;
    (c)   the same channels of communication serve different purposes;
    (d)   advice is either too general or too specific;
(iv)   the distribution of functions at the subnational level is complex;
(v)   central government does not see local authorities 'in the round' as corporate entities trying to deal with interrelated problems;
(vi)   the information available on services is patchy; and
(vii) the controls on local authority capital expenditure are inflexible and reinforce compartmentalisation between programmes. (Central Policy Review Staff, 1977, pp.1–3)

The distinctive feature of the CPRS Report lies in its emphasis on the multiplicity of channels of communication involved in the relationship. Thus, in addition to such channels as legislation and circulars, they point to the important role of planning procedures, many of which are of recent origin, such as structure plans, transport policies and programmes, 10-year social service plans, comprehensive community programmes, regional reports, local corporate plans and housing investment programmes. The CPRS Report points to the difficulties which arise from the interrelationships of these plans (ibid., pp.12–15).

One of the curious features of the study of central–local relations is the title of the topic and the implication that intergovernmental relations in Britain are limited to links between central departments and local authorities. By default, many commentators equate local government in Britain with the English local government system. And yet there are quite different institutional arrangements for central–local relations in Scotland, Wales and Northern Ireland. Similarly, even in England, intergovernmental relations are not confined to links between central departments and local authorities. There are the links between local authorities and the regional offices of central departments and the plethora of 'fringe bodies' – the ubiquitous 'quango' under an even more opaque title. Some recognition of the complexity of intergovernmental relations can be found in the CPRS Report which notes the 'plural' nature of government and the 'multilateral' contacts of both levels of government (ibid., pp.15–18, 21–2, 24–5, 35–7, 40–41; for a discussion of the 'plural' nature of British government, see Chapter 4 of the present volume). In brief, recent official reports describe central–local relations as ambiguous, confused and complex: hardly the dominant language of the 1960s.

The problem with official reports is that, of all the reasons which lead to their being written, a concern for the state of academic research is conspicuous primarily for its absence. Thus the various features of central–local relations discussed in the Layfield and CPRS reports are not located within an explicit interpretive theoretical framework. Such reports are expected to reach conclusions, not to pioneer theoretical insights or to undertake field research to test their hypotheses. Fortunately, there are other sources of evidence supporting the picture of central–local relations in the 1970s presented in official reports.

John Friend and his colleagues at the Institute for Operational Research (now the Centre for Operational and Organizational Research) have conducted, over the years, a series of studies of planning under uncertainty (see Friend and Jessop, 1969; Friend *et al.*, 1974; Friend, 1976; 1977). Although they have not been specifically concerned with central–local relations, nonetheless their analysis contains many relevant insights, primarily because the most recent work has been concerned with 'multi-organizations' and the constraints upon planning created by the need for several organizations to work together.

The central concept from which the theoretical framework for the study of the expansion of Droitwich was developed is that of the 'multi-organization', or 'a union of parts of separate organisations formed by the interaction of individuals in the pursuance of some common task' (Friend *et al.*, 1974, p.42). Through a series of case studies, Friend and others demonstrate that complex linkages are required between organizations if effective action is to be taken. Although they focus on the planning problems created by such links, they offer a number of comments on central–local relations. Thus:

Even where the opportunities for joint exploration are clearly limited, as in the case of relationships between individual local authorities and government departments which are required to operate formal systems of external control over the activities of many such bodies, we found that a *significant degree* of informal exploration to alternatives sometimes took place. (Friend *et al.*, 1974, p.350; emphasis added)

Moreover, 'we sometimes found it necessary to look on certain actors from central departments as themselves forming a part of the local policy system, rather than simply as an external source of recognised policy guidelines' (ibid., p.351). In other words, Friend and others provide extensive evidence for the proposition that the relations between central and local government are complex, involving a range of governmental institutions and, more important, they demonstrate that ostensibly hierarchical relationships dissolve under the exigencies of implementing a policy. Central departments become but one of a number of actors, all facing a common problem. Finally, they show that these interactions have a number of consequences for policy making. These consequences include placing a premium on 'reticulist' (or networking) skills and the pre-eminence of 'partisan mutual adjustment' (or incremental decision making) over rational planning processes.

The utility of Friend's framework in the analysis of central–local government relations is limited by its specific concern with planning problems. The study does not specifically examine central–local relations and it does not compare and attempt to explain variations in interactions. More important, the theoretical framework limits any attempt at this kind of analysis. A multi-organization is defined in terms of the pursuit of a common objective or task. However, this form of relationship is highly specific. Organizations could interact with each other without pursuing a common task. Similarly, the forms of interaction between organizations need not be limited to partisan mutual adjustment and the construction of networks of communication. A range of strategies are available to organizations including, for example, disruption, manipulation, competition and, a particularly important strategy for central departments, the authoritative allocation of resources. Finally, even though only a limited number of strategies are examined, the study does not attempt to explain why some strategies are adopted and others rejected. Most of these limitations arise from the specific focus of the study on planning problems. Accordingly, it is more appropriate to emphasize the simple fact that Friend and others provide a picture of central–local relations very different from that prevalent in the 1960s. The starting point for studies of central–local relations can no longer be central controls. In future, the starting point must be the complexity of interactions and the constraints imposed thereby on both levels of government.

The study of local government finance is not immune to this redefinition of the field of central–local relations. The Consultative Council on Local

Government Finance was established, following the Chancellor of the Exchequer's Budget Speech of 15 April 1975, to promote regular consultation and cooperation between central and local government on major issues of common concern. To date, there have been only two short studies of an innovation which may be one of the most significant for central–local relations in recent years (brief background information on the Consultative Council is given in the Layfield Report, 1976, pp.408–9; the two studies referred to are Harris and Shipp, 1977; and Taylor, 1979). From these descriptions, it is clear that, although the local authority associations have become increasingly involved in the public expenditure survey (PES) at an early stage, this involvement is not without problems.

> There are two practical difficulties with the involvement of local authorities in PES: – the timetable of PES conflicts with that of RSG ... – the input of time and effort by the local authority associations and their representatives does not currently allow them to play much more than a reactive role ... In addition, central government departments are most unlikely to allow local authorities into the inner workings of the Survey and to upset the subtle balance of influence within Whitehall ... A possible role for the local authority associations within these constraints is to work with the government departments concerned and thence to influence PES by influencing the departments' own submissions within the Survey machinery. (Harris and Shipp, 1977, p.85; see also Taylor, 1979, pp.25–9, 30–31)

PES is a sensitive, interdepartmental political process and the local authority associations must influence the departmental contributions to the survey. In addition, Harris and Shipp (1977, p.88) argue that ambiguity in the communications from central government not only serves to reduce conflict but also may preserve the freedom of manoeuvre of local authorities to act as they see fit! The financial relationships between central and local government can also be characterized, therefore, as a complex set of interactions involving a range of government institutions and placing a premium on networking skills.

The study of central–local relations has been dominated by the myths of financial dependence and central control and the parable of local autonomy. This allegorical strain pervades the 'conventional wisdom', and even the 'conventional critique' is not immune in spite of the fact that recent research suggests that a more appropriate starting point for analysis would be an exploration of the ambiguity, confusion and complexity of the relationship. It is now time to draw this exercise in demythologizing to an end. A more constructive approach is required. What additional topics need to be explored? What are the 'forgotten dimensions' of central–local relations?

The 'Forgotten Dimensions' of Central–Local Relations

Without suggesting that the following list of topics is exhaustive, the discussion focuses on five 'forgotten dimensions': the need for theory; variation in local discretion; the variety of relationships; the influence of political factors; and the role of the professional.

The Need for Theory

Both the agent and partnership models provide an inadequate basis for the analysis of central–local relations: critics of the 'conventional wisdom' have shown both to be descriptively inaccurate. There remains a need for a theory which recognizes that the relationship can range from compliance to non-compliance; from a high degree of dependence, through interdependence, to a high degree of discretion. The vocabulary of central–local relations needs to be extended to admit the possibility of bargaining between the two levels of government as well as the fact of central control.

At least some of the existing literature does recognize the varying degrees of dependence. Thus Noel Hepworth (1977, p.16) argues: 'The "present confusion" of responsibilities to use Layfield's expression is an extremely convenient escape route for local politicians (and central politicians as well).' In a similar vein, the CPRS report points to the game-like qualities of central–local relations:

> In general, we believe that at least some complaints by local authorities (and others) about the non-corporateness of central government should be discounted. Local authorities and central government are engaged in a continual amicable struggle for advantage: and in an age of organisation it is no more than a conventional gambit to decry one's opponent as disorganised.
>
> It can be argued that complaints from local authorities about ambiguity (or anything else) are simply part of their continual political game with central government, and as such should not be taken too seriously. (Central Policy Review Staff, 1977, pp.43, 47)

However, the awareness has not been translated into explicit theories about intergovernmental relations in Britain. The study of central–local relations will develop as much from the improvement of our tools of analysis as it will from the description of previously neglected features.

Variation in Local Discretion

Any discussion of central–local relations quickly raises prescriptive issues and, most commonly, the issue of local autonomy. The concept of 'local autonomy' is both an elusive and an emotive one. On the one hand, autonomous local government can be seen as an essential bulwark against the tyranny of the centre. On the other hand, it can be seen as highly divisive: a way for parochial local elites to assert their own interests over those of the state (see Sharpe, 1970). Even without its prescriptive connotations there remains the problem of whether the term 'local autonomy' refers to local government or the local community. If the latter, analysis would have to cover the decisions of every major organization, governmental and non-governmental, to determine the extent to which they were constrained by extra-community factors. If the former, there is the problem of whether other governmental units are the only source of constraints. As Terry Clark (1974) has argued, local autonomy is a product of a range of factors (for example, national factors, natural physical resources, institutions supporting localism and loyal local elites). Intergovernmental links are but one among these factors. Too frequently the term 'local autonomy' is used loosely, with little recognition of these problems. A study which focuses on the links between central departments and local authorities cannot explain variations in local autonomy. It would be preferable if the term 'local discretion' were reserved for the extent to which the room for decisional manoeuvre of local government decision makers was constrained by other governmental units (modified from Jowell, 1973, p.179). 'Local discretion' is a component of, rather than a synonym for, 'local autonomy'.

Even if the narrower term 'local discretion' is employed, there remain inadequacies in the literature, notably a heavy emphasis on the impact of financial resources. And although other resources have been identified, including administrative, political, constitutional and professional resources, they are neither precisely defined nor discussed at length. The important questions concern the relative importance of these resources for local discretion. For example, can political influence compensate for financial dependence? Accordingly, there is a need to explore the *range of resources* which can influence the extent of local discretion.

The Variety of Relationships

As noted earlier, both central government and local authorities are plural, not unitary, entities. Not only can different sections of the same central department have different attitudes and behave differently towards local authorities but the converse may also be equally true. In addition, there are many other public sector organizations besides central departments and local authorities. Future research must recognize this variety.

First, it would be as well to confine the term 'central–local relations' to the links between central departments and local authorities, employing the term 'intergovernmental relations' to encompass the generality of relationships, that is the links between central government and other subnational public sector organizations, the links between subnational public sector organizations, and the links between the Scottish, Welsh and Northern Ireland governmental systems and both their own subnational public sector organizations and the British government (see Hogwood, 1979, especially pp.30–35). It would then be possible to compare different facets of the system of intergovernmental relations and explore the extent to which central–local relations were different both from other types of intergovernmental relations (such as 'fringe bodies') and between different parts of the United Kingdom (such as Scotland).

Second, there is a distinction to be drawn between individual local authorities and the national institutions of local government. There are numerous national institutions including the local authority associations (of both England and Wales, and Scotland) the various joint bodies (for example, LAMSAC, LACSAB, LGTB)[5] and the professional bodies (see below). The role(s) of these bodies is (are) shadowy. What are their links to their members? Do they represent local government's views to central departments or do they present the views of central departments to local authorities? For example, it could be argued that the cooption of the local authority associations into the public expenditure survey through the Consultative Council is a way of defusing opposition to expenditure cuts and legitimating central government's decisions. Do the various national institutions comprise a national local government community which provides an effective central bargaining capability for local authorities? There has been virtually no research on the national institutions of local government.[6]

Third, it cannot be assumed that there is a single pattern of links between central departments and local authorities. Are the links functional ones: that is, between the equivalent departments (or sections of departments) at the two levels of government? Is there a corporatist element in the pattern of links and, if so, how effective is this corporatist element?

Finally, there is the problem of measuring the alleged complexity of the relationships. Although a number of studies (see above) have described the complexity of central–local relations for specific policies or issues, no-one has attempted to map the interactions for a major part of the system. If the system is both a 'system' of relationships and complex, it would be as well to document the fact and, more important, to demonstrate that it is a problem. For example, do policies fail because they require the agreement and cooperation of too great a number of public sector organizations (see Pressman and Wildavsky, 1977; Hood, 1976, pp.17–20)?

The Influence of Political Factors

The 'conventional critique' has demonstrated that, at least for some issues, local authorities can be viewed as political systems in their own right and, as argued above, the effect of political resources on relationships needs to be considered along with the effect of financial resources. Little is known, however, about the political channels of influence between central and local government, with the minor exception of a few studies of the local government background of MPs. Such channels do exist and there are links between local and national political elites. Local politicians do have 'clout' at the national level. They are not necessarily retiring wallflowers who shy away from the media and are overawed by the national eminence of the minister. They can impose 'political costs' on a minister. A protracted fight with a local authority is costly to a minister in time, energy and his esteem in the eyes of colleagues and, possibly, the electorate. No minister actively seeks the sobriquet of 'national bully'. As Anthony Crosland recognized, there is a degree of ambivalence in the attitudes of ministers to central–local relations:

> All governments and Ministers are a bit schizophrenic about their relationship with local authorities. On the one hand they genuinely believe the ringing phrases they use about how local government should have more power and freedom ... On the other hand, a Labour government hates it when Tory councils pursue education or housing policies of which it disapproves, and exactly the same is true of a Tory government with Labour councils. This ambivalence exists in everybody I know who is concerned with relations between central and local government. (Boyle *et al.*, 1971, p.171)

A similar attitude can be found amongst local authorities. While they bemoan central interference in local affairs, they are still not above requesting specific policy guidance from central departments.

Potentially, there are many channels of influence, including party conferences, contact with MPs, delegations, personal friendships, telephone calls to ministers at home, representation on national bodies and even parties aboard yachts on the Thames.[7] But we do not know how extensive political contacts are or how important they are for particular decisions. Are formal links (such as delegations) more numerous and important than informal links? To what extent and under what conditions can local politicians embarrass national politicians and effect changes in policy? What is the influence of variations in party composition at the local level upon the relationship between the two levels of government? How significant are national party decisions on policies for the local party? Have local authorities been 'nationalized' in more than name? What are the roles of the Labour Party's

Local Government Section and the National Executive Committee's Regional–Local Government Committee, and how much influence do they have on local parties? The same questions can be asked of the Conservative Party's Local Government Department and National Local Government Advisory Committee. What are the links of individual local authorities and local authority associations with MPs and Parliament and how effective is this lobbying? These and similar questions can be raised but, given the existing evidence, they cannot be satisfactorily answered.

The Role of the Professional

The professional officers have many opportunities to exert influence on behalf of their employing authority, the local authority associations and their professional associations, although they are conspicuous for their absence in the literature on central–local relations. For the local authority they have one-to-one contacts with counterparts at the centre and, if necessary, they can lobby anyone who will listen on behalf of the local authority. In the capacity of advisers to the committees of local authority associations, they are part of the delegations to, and meetings with, central departments. Through the professional associations they can lobby or advise central departments about preserving or improving professional standards (see, for example, Lee *et al.*, 1974, pp.39–52, 75–84; Harris and Shipp, 1977, pp.19–21). But again the extent and consequences of this involvement remain obscure. Do they form part of a national professional community – a community including civil servants – which pursues its own professional interests? Does some legislation, although seen by some as yet another imposition on local government, have its origins in the aspirations of, and lobbying by, a profession? What is the relationship between the professional associations and other national institutions of local government? If the professionals are prominent in central–local relations, is it possible to identify, in Galbraith's terms, a 'technostructure' (Galbraith, 1972; see also the distinction between 'technocrats' and 'topocrats' discussed below in Chapter 4). Certainly, it is surprising that the concern about the power of the official in local government has not spread to an analysis of their role in central–local relations.

Conclusions: the Rationality of Ambiguous Confusion?

The normal description of central–local relations is dominated by the myths of financial dependence and detailed control and the parable of local autonomy. Even the 'conventional critique' falls victim to mythology by restricting its analysis to the subject matter of the 'conventional wisdom'.

However, more recent official reports and research studies suggest that there are a number of 'forgotten dimensions' in the study of central–local relations, including the game-like nature of relations, the variety of resources underpinning local discretion, the variety of relationships and the influence of political and professional factors. The 'problem' of central–local relations is not, therefore, one of central control but of ambiguity, confusion and complexity. This state of affairs means that attempts at control by central departments are irritating and frustrating for local authorities not because they are effective but because they are ad hoc, even random measures. And there are advantages for both parties in this situation. Ambiguity bestows room for manoeuvre. Freedom of action can be negotiated and renegotiated. Even the most stringent controls can be circumvented. It is possible that both parties have a vested interest in at least some degree of ambiguity, even confusion. The clarification of responsibilities could be a painful process. It is convenient to be able to blame central government for cuts in, for example, education. There is a rationality underlying the complex and ambiguous confusion: the rationality of the 'game'. The relations between central and local government are too often seen in an oversimplified light. The intricate pattern of linkages is both a constraint and a source of opportunities. Both the 'conventional wisdom' and the 'conventional critique' serve to obscure this fact.

However, the discussion of the 'forgotten dimensions' of central–local relations bears rather too close a resemblance to a shopping list of future research studies for comfort. It is important to indicate the range of questions which need to be answered, but it is equally important to develop the tools of analysis: to expand the vocabulary of central–local relations. A plethora of detailed, descriptive case studies, even if they are on the topics discussed above, will not necessarily advance the study of central–local relations. Barefooted empiricism needs the guidance and insight of a framework of analysis.

Allied to this point is the historical parochialism of the study of central–local relations. Too often the sole preserve of public administration, the subject needs to break out of these confines. It can illuminate facets of modern government of general concern to social scientists. It can provide a fruitful locus for the analysis of the power of the professional: for exploring the problems of accountability created by the interdependence of a multitude of complex governmental bureaucracies, and for the incidence and causes of policy failure. Building bridges between the study of central–local relations and theoretical issues in the study of western industrial society is an essential step in the development of an adequate framework of analysis. It cannot be achieved by the traditional methods of legal–institutional case studies.

Notes

1   The statistics supporting the argument that local authorities are financially dependent on central grant usually cite grant as a proportion of current relevant expenditure. These figures accentuate the degree of dependence. If grant is treated as a proportion of total local income, that is, if 'other income' (rents, trading income) is included, the increase in grant between 1949 and 1970 (the period covered by the quotation in the text) was 6 per cent. This increase is not a dramatic one when spread over 21 years. Between 1970 and 1974, the increase was 5 per cent and this increase is obviously more in line with the financial dependence thesis. Unfortunately, diagnosis preceded the symptoms. Figures are from the Committee of Inquiry into Local Government Finance (1976, p.384), hereafter referred to as the Layfield Report. For a detailed discussion of the financial statistics, see Crispin (1976).

2   For example, a number of writers with a clear legal–institutional focus recognize the 'informal pressures' in the relationship (see Cross, 1974, p.178). Also compare Chester (1951, p.121) with Hartley (1971, p.450). Both authors point to the problems created for central government by local authority inactivity.

3   At the time of writing, RSG contains three elements: the domestic element which provides rate relief for domestic ratepayers, the resources element which ensures that all local authorities have a minimum rateable value per head of population, and the needs element which 'compensates for differences between local authorities in the amount they need to spend per head of population'. For further details, see the Layfield Report (1976, pp.454–9 – the quotation is from p.456); also Hepworth (1976, chs 3, 12 and Appendix 3). However, the Local Government Planning and Land (No.2) Bill contains proposals to replace the needs and resources elements with a block grant.

4   The relevant sections of the Layfield Report are pp.65–8, 78 and 265. This discussion of the Layfield Report is concerned with its description of central–local relations and *not* its proposed reforms. For a discussion of the Reports' recommendations, compare Jones (1977, pp.8–20) with Cripps and Godley (1976).

5   This 'alphabet soup' refers the Local Authorities Management Services and Computer Committee, the Local Authorities Conditions of Service Advisory Board and the Local Government Training Board.

6   The major exception is Griffith (1966, pp.33–49) but this book is now out of date. A brief history of the associations can be found in Keith-Lucas and Richards (1978, ch.9). The role of the associations in the reorganization of local government is discussed in Wood (1976) and Isaac-Henry (1974, pp.1–12). The role of the associations in the negotiations over RSG is outlined in Harris and Shipp (1977) and Taylor (1979). It is important to note that the above studies refer to the local authority associations and not the national institutions of local government. There has been a marked increase in the number of joint bodies, and future research can no longer ignore their role(s) in central–local relations.

7   An interesting, anecdotal source of information is Crossman (1975, pp.39, pp.60–61, 352–3, 612). On the political influence of local authorities, Ashford concludes: 'The complex interactions of mayors, local and central officials and national politicians so common in France, is unknown in Britain' (Ashford 1977, p.489). Ashford overstates his case. Comparatively, such interactions may be less common, but they are not unknown in Britain. However, it is too early for this kind of generalization. The real distinction between Britain and France may reside in the greater importance of organizational (or small 'p') politics in British central–local relations whereas the local politician plays the more important role in French central–local relations. Whichever generalization is most appropriate, it would be as well to collect some evidence.

3 Interorganizational Analysis

Introduction

If the study of central–local relations in Britain has been preoccupied with the detailed description of a narrow range of topics and has demonstrated a marked aversion for theory; if recent theories of advanced industrial society are at a level of generality which does not admit of easy application to the study of facets of British government, the problem to be confronted in the following chapters can be succinctly stated. How can these two levels of analysis be reconciled? In the next two chapters, the literature on interorganizational analysis and intergovernmental relations will be examined to see if they are capable of effecting such a reconciliation and what light they can shed on the 'forgotten dimensions' of intergovernmental relations. Before turning to these particular tasks, however, one preliminary issue must be dealt with. What is the justification for applying theories developed by different disciplines and in different governmental contexts to the study of British government?

The relevance of the literature on intergovernmental relations seems obvious. It is exploring the equivalent of central–local relations in different governmental systems. Its importance does not reside solely in the fact of shared subject matter. Not only has there been a growing awareness of the 'plural' nature of British government (Rose, 1976) but a number of commentators have pointed to the parallels between allegedly 'unitary' systems and federal systems. Thus Jesse Burkhead (1974, p.64) reflects: 'It may be some comfort for students of federalism that unitary governments have problems of intergovernmental relations not unlike those that emerge in a formal system of national-state–local relationships.' In a similar vein, William Riker (1969, p.142) comments:

> it is clear that county councils in Britain can do about as much as local governments in the United States. Certainly dissident national groups in the peripheral provinces (e.g. Welsh and Scottish nationalists) probably feel no more put upon by central authority than do the states' rights partisans of the American South.

Unfortunately, the literature on central–local relations in Britain has had a marked parochial streak. At times, it seems as if any books or articles which lack the phrase 'central–local relations' in their titles are automatically deemed irrelevant. As a result, the parallels between intergovernmental relations in unitary and federal systems have not been explored in any detail. The next chapter takes at least a first step in repairing the omission.

The dangers of applying inappropriate theories to the study of British government seem most acute in the case of organization theory and its offspring interorganizational analysis. Although there is a shared concern with the interdependence of organizations, nonetheless organization theory has been frequently criticized for its management orientation. The alleged concern with questions of efficiency, with techniques and with the interests of managers does not seem a particularly promising starting point for the study of government. However, these criticisms reflect an unduly narrow conception of organization theory and a palpably inaccurate characterization of a great deal of research on organizations. Martin Albrow's (1973, p.412) distinction between organization theory and the sociology of organizations is useful in this context:

> The organization theorist is concerned to help managers and administrators. By contrast, the perspective of the sociologist is 'impractical'. His search is for understanding, untrammelled by the needs of men of affairs. Therefore he cannot accept the conceptual framework of the organization theorist as setting the limits to his research interests in organizations.

Instead the sociology of organizations is 'devoted to discovering the causes and consequences of various types and features of organizations' (ibid.). Accordingly, the term 'sociology of organizations' is to be preferred in order to emphasize that the literature discussed in this chapter is not exclusively management-oriented. In short, both literatures are concerned to explore the relationships between various types of organizations and, therefore, offer the prospect of insights into the relationship between central departments and local authorities. It is the task of the next two chapters to determine precisely what contribution they can make and the remainder of this chapter evaluates the literature on interorganizational analysis. The study of organizations has burgeoned in the post-war period and during the 1970s there was a growing interest in the relationship between organizations and their environments and, in particular, in the links between organizations. Interorganizational analysis has aroused considerable interest. Perrow (1979, p.239) describes it as 'exciting work' which is leading to the 'revitalisation of organisation theory'; Scharpf (1978) argues that the perspective is central to an understanding of policy failures and policy implementation;

and Elkin (1975, p.183) suggests that the perspective 'provides a language to handle some of the fundamental problems of comparative urban political inquiry'. Any attempt to assess the validity of such claims is hampered, however, by the lack of agreement on either the key concepts or their definition. At its simplest, interorganizational analysis suggests that within the environment of an organization are other organizations upon which it is dependent and with which it interacts. This environment has manifold consequences for the structure of, behaviour in, and performance of, an organization. A typical summary of this complex of interactions is provided by Elkin (ibid., pp.175–6):

> At the same time as the focal organisation attempts to manage its dependencies by employing one or more strategies, other organisations in the network are similarly engaged. The consequence is that behaviour within the network is complex and dynamic: there are multiple, over-lapping relationships, each one of which is to a greater or lesser degree dependent on the state of others.

But once analysis proceeds beyond this general picture, there is considerable diversity in approaches to the topic, a diversity which can be best understood by examining those issues which divide the various contributors: the nature of the environment, the appropriate unit of analysis, organizational goals, power and exchange and the consequences of the interactions. The following assessment suggests the conclusion that the literature on interorganizational analysis has become preoccupied with classification and with methodological questions and does not facilitate the analysis of intergovernmental relations. However, it is not the sole, or even the main, objective of this chapter to itemize the inadequacies of interorganizational analysis. Rather the intention is to argue that, if the emphasis is placed on intra- and interorganizational power, interorganizational analysis can provide a series of concepts of considerable value.[1]

The Nature of the Environment

A basic assumption in the literature on interorganizational analysis is that the organization is an open system. Emery and Trist (1969, p.281) have pointed out that 'there has been something of a tendency to continue thinking in terms of a "closed" system, that is, to regard the enterprise as sufficiently independent to allow most of its problems to be analysed with reference to its internal structure and without reference to its external environment'. Instead they argue for recognition of the 'mutual permeation of an organisation and its environment' and suggest that environmental changes are a major source of uncertainty for organizations (ibid., p.282). They identify four types of 'causal texture of organisational environments': placid, randomized environment; placid, clustered environment; disturbed–reactive environment; and turbulent fields (ibid., pp.245–9). The first three types correspond to, respectively, the economist's classical market, imperfect competition and the oligarchic market. Finally, the turbulent field involves an increase in the area of 'relevant uncertainty': that is, it is both complex and rapidly changing. This formulation has been influential and the study of organizations has been dominated by open system models (see, for example, Katz and Kahn, 1966; Terreberry, 1968). However, it is important to know which aspects of the environment are 'relevant' since an organization will probably be confronted by several environments.

Aldrich and Pfeffer (1976, pp.79–105) have suggested that there are two views of the link between the organization and its environment. The first view sees the link as an exchange of resources. Thus a particular organization needs resources, for example money, raw materials. The environment is a stock of these needed resources. Consequently, an organization bargains for its share of these resources. The second view sees the link in terms of information rather than resources; uncertainty is the most important feature of the environment; complexity and instability generate uncertainty which the organization acts to reduce or remove. Unfortunately, the problems associated with the concept of environment cannot be reduced to a choice between competing definitions. As Karpik (1978, p.9) has argued, the words 'system' and 'environment' are ambiguous: both terms having a 'semi-descriptive, semi-theoretic status'. He phrases the problem as follows: 'the systemic approach ... is only capable of setting up a standard of judgement in the sociological community provided it is founded upon a parallel theory that constructs the object of study, states its particularities, and shows how it fits into society as a whole'.

In other words, some rationale has to be found for focusing on the environment. A study interested in the process of managing structural change and the development of interorganizational learning processes would ask different questions from a study interested in the legitimation of the power of administrative and managerial personnel in society (compare, for example, Metcalfe, 1978, with Habermas, 1971). The inadequacies of systems theory are too well known to warrant detailed repetition (see Silverman, 1970, chs 2 and 3) but the consequences of these weaknesses for interorganizational analysis are severe because they mean that there are no internally generated criteria for defining the relevant aspects of the environment.

The Unit of Analysis

The introduction of the concept of 'organization set' was central to the development of interorganizational analysis. This phrase was used to describe the environment of organizations by Blau and Scott (1963, p.195). Credit for its development is usually accorded to Evan (1966), who defined the organization set as 'an organisation or a class of organisations' and its 'interactions with the network of organisations in its environment'. He refers to the organization that is the point of reference as the 'focal organisation'. The external environment is treated as a series of discrete units to be mapped and analysed from the standpoint of one particular unit. Some of these other organizations provide inputs of resources to the focal organization – the input set. Others consume the output of the focal organization – the output set.

However, the focal organization and its organization set has limitations as the unit of analysis. The links with other organizations are seen as an extension of intraorganizational characteristics and processes. But the links between a variety of organizations may have characteristics completely different from the characteristics of any one, or even every single, organization involved in those interactions. The network of linkages may have characteristics in its own right. The concept of the organization set arbitrarily limits the analysis. It would be preferable to focus on the network or the patterns of direct and indirect linkages between organizations. In this way, the extent to which the links are an extension of intraorganizational processes can be explored rather than asserted. The problem is to limit the number of links to be studied. Ultimately, a large number, if not all organizations, could be linked directly and indirectly. The network has to be bounded, but if the analysis is grounded in systems theory, there are no clear criteria for specifying these boundaries. The concept of network warns of the dangers of arbitrarily limiting the number of links to be studied but it raises again the problem of selecting and defining the object of study.

Organizational Goals

To complicate the picture further, there is the thorny issue of organizational goals, because the goals of the organization will influence the resources it needs to acquire and the uncertainties to which it responds. It is common practice to talk of the goals or the mission of the organization; in fact, the pursuit of goals continues to be seen as a defining characteristic of organizations. However, a number of objections have been raised to the use of the concept (see, for example, Gross, 1969; Mohr, 1973; Perrow, 1970). First, it is argued that organizations do not have goals. To explain organizational activities in terms of the organization's goals is to reify the organization, that is to imply that it has the power of thought and action. Second, when the formal goals of an organization are studied, either they are found to be inoperative or the organization seems ineffective because it does not achieve the stated goals. Finally, it is difficult to distinguish between goals and means. One person's goal can be another's means en route to another, 'higher' goal.

These difficulties led Etzioni (1960, pp.257–78) to reject the 'goal model' and to suggest that a 'systems model' should be adopted. Rather than judging an organization by its success or failure in achieving stated goals, it should be evaluated by its capacity to find an optimal allocation of resources to ensure its survival. Alternatively, Yuchtman and Seashore (1967, pp.891–903) suggest that an organization's effectiveness should be evaluated by its capacity to acquire resources.

However, neither of these formulations offers a satisfactory solution to the problem. In order to find an optimal balance of resources, the criteria for determining the optimal balance have to be specified. Similarly, criteria for determining the resources to be acquired have to be stated. These criteria can be specified by appealing either to the stated goals of the organization or to system needs; that is, the optimal balance or resources required are determined by the need for system self-regulation and survival. But, as Silverman (1970, p.4) has pointed out, the concept of self-regulating activities also implies that the power of thought and action lies in social constructs. An air of philosophic resignation pervades much of the discussion of goals.

Such resignation seems premature. Thompson's work on organizational goals suggests a way of resolving at least some of the difficulties. He uses the term 'domain' to define 'needed' or 'relevant' resources. Domain refers to the claims which an organization makes for itself in terms of the services provided and the population served. The goals an organization pursues will determine which other organizations it will interact with. However, these goals are themselves a product of the relationship of an organization to other organizations. Unless domain consensus is established, that is, unless there is some agreement that the goals an organization pursues are legitimate, that organization will be in a state of conflict with other organizations. To avoid this conflict an organization will negotiate with other organizations about its goals. Thus the needed resources and the relevant uncertainty are defined by the goals of the organization and the domain consensus (see Thompson, 1967, pp.27–9; Levine and White, 1961; Thompson and McEwen, 1958).

Just as domain consensus is negotiated, so the goals of a particular organization are the product of a political process. Thompson (1967, pp.127–

30) suggests that goals be seen as the product of an internal process of negotiation and bargaining between groups. Out of this process there will emerge a dominant coalition with an agreed set of temporary goals (ibid.; see also Cyert and March, 1963). Over time, however, an organization has multiple and conflicting goals. Formal statements of the mission of an organization are replaced by a focus on the identification of the goals of specific groups and on descriptions of the process of goal setting.

This approach avoids the twin problems of reification and formalism. The merit of Thompson's approach resides in the emphasis on negotiation. The goals of a particular organization are the outcome not only of politics within the organization but also of bargaining between organizations. Moreover, the stress on the negotiation of goals implies that the perceptions of the dominant coalition are important to an understanding of an organization's response to changes in its environment. In other words, the environment is both constitutive and constituted (Ranson *et al.*, 1980, pp.1–17). This approach differs markedly from the dominant view of the environment, which emphasizes its importance as a source of constraints upon the organization. For example, Pugh and Hickson (1976) emphasize the effects of size, dependence and technology on the organization's structure. Similarly, Lawrence and Lorsch (1967) argue that the structure of the organization is shaped by environmental constraints. These writers invoke a form of environmental determinism to explain changes in organization structure. The organization does not shape its environment but is shaped by it.

Thompson's analysis of the relationship between the organization and the environment suggests that it is by no means clear that the environment exercises such a determinant influence. A number of studies have developed his suggestions. Child (1973, p.98) suggests that decision makers can choose which aspects of the environment they will respond to: 'The critical link lies in the decision makers' evaluation of the organisation's position in the environmental areas they regard as important.' The power of the dominant coalition is seen as crucial to an understanding of the relationship between an organization and its environment. Chandler (1962, p.15) has shown in a study of some 70 American corporations, that structure follows strategy: 'Strategic growth resulted from an awareness of the opportunities and needs ... to employ existing or expanding resources more profitably. A new strategy required a new or at least refashioned structure if the enlarged enterprise was to be operated efficiently.'

Perrow (1972b, p.199) has reversed the determinist argument. He suggests that the most significant failure of organization theory is 'the failure to see *society* as adaptive to *organisations*'. The position is trenchantly stated: 'To see ... organisations as adaptive to a "turbulent", dynamic ever-changing environment is to indulge in fantasy. The environment of most powerful organisations is well controlled by them, quite stable, and made up of other organisations with similar interests, or ones they control.' In a later edition of the same book, he distinguishes between ground and figure, suggesting that organizations and the links between organizations are the figure and that values and power distribution are the ground which give the figure definition. He sketches a theory of the role of organizations in society in which the state is not primarily a 'tool' of the capitalist class, but 'an independent entity with organisational needs of its own, thus serving as a broker between the capitalist class and other classes, and meeting its own needs for growth and power in the process' (Perrow, 1979, p.215).

The theme common to these studies is that the relationship between the organization and its environment can only be understood by exploring the intra- and interorganizational distribution of power. Systems theory cannot specify the 'relevant' aspects of the environment, provide the criteria for bounding the network or define goals without reifying the organization. Karpik (1978, p.9) has argued that systems theory has to appeal to a 'parallel theory' in order to overcome these problems. Thompson and others have identified one form of such a parallel theory. In the next section, the concept of organizational power will be explored in some detail.

Power and Exchange

Dependence is the key concept in the analysis of power and exchange. Its origins lie in exchange theory and the analysis of the processes which govern the relationships between individuals. Thus Blau (1964, p.118) defines dependence in the following terms:

> By supplying services in demand to others, a person establishes power over them. If he regularly renders needed services they cannot readily obtain elsewhere, others become dependent on and obligated to him for these services, and unless they can furnish other benefits to him that produce interdependence by making him equally dependent on them, their unilateral dependence obligates them to comply with his requests lest he cease to continue to meet their needs.

The most important single statement of the concept of dependence in the context of interorganizational analysis is that by Thompson. He suggests that any given organization is dependent upon other organizations: '(1) in proportion to the organization's need for resources or performance which that element can provide, and (2) in inverse proportion to the ability of other elements to provide the same resource or performance'; and dependence is the obverse of power: 'an organization has power, relative to an element of its task environment, to the extent that the organization has the capacity to satisfy needs of that element and to the extent that the organization monopolizes that capacity' (Thompson, 1967, pp.30–31; see also Emerson, 1962).

The importance of the concept of dependence, and the reason that it is stressed more than the concept of power, lies in the fact that it admits of reciprocity. Thus dependence is a source of constraints upon an organization but, at the same time, an organization can act to loosen those constraints. An organization can be both dependent upon another organization and have power over that organization. As Crozier and Thoenig (1976, p.562) point out: 'Even if one partner appears to completely dominate the other, the dependence remains reciprocal.'

Many problems surround the concept of dependence. In the first instance, and to set the context for the rest of the discussion, the ways in which the concept is deployed in the literature on interorganizational analysis will be criticized. Subsequently, three approaches to the complexities of the concepts of power and dependence are explored: power as resources, power as rule-governed interaction, and power as the mobilization of bias. It is argued that the analysis of organizational power cannot be restricted to any one of these approaches but must encompass all three.

The Classification and Measurement of Interactions

For the most part, writers on interorganizational analysis have not been preoccupied with the concepts of power and dependence. There is a marked tendency simply to cite Thompson's definition and then get on with the business of classifying and measuring interactions. There are disagreements, of course, about the best way of pursuing this activity. For example, should the analysis focus on the exchange of resources or adapting to uncertainty? And the dichotomy between resources and uncertainty does not exhaust the possible contents of exchanges. Litwak and Hylton (1962) measure dependence using the indicators of awareness of other organizations, acquaintances and interactions between organizations and written agreements. Thompson and McEwen (1958, pp.25–8) stress resource exchanges, overlapping board membership and joint programmes. Benson (1975, p.231) has criticized the measurement of dependence by the examination of interactions as putting the cart before the horse: 'interactions at the service delivery are ultimately dependent on resource acquisition'; and two resources are said to be basic – money and authority. One final example of this particular preoccupation with measuring interactions is Klonglan *et al.*'s (1976) 'cumulative index of co-operative inter-organisational relations'. Moving from low intensity to high intensity, it contains the following items: director awareness of the existence of other organizations, director acquaintance between organizations, director interaction between organizations, information exchange, resource exchange, overlapping board membership, joint programmes and written agreements. The proliferation of measures of interorganizational relations is symptomatic of a literature too often dominated by methodological refinement at the expense of research into substantive problems.[2] Thus Crozier and Thoenig (1976, pp.562, 548) comment:

> organisational students tend either to try to build an abstract theory from which they deduce from [*sic*] a set of cybernetic axioms and derive normative prescriptions or to measure those empirical relationships about which one can get reliable data even if they are meaningless for understanding how the system really functions ... And even when such empirical analyses are set forth, they are comparatively weak and quite inadequate in view of the scientific objectives stated.

Thus Levine and White (1961, pp.585, 589) investigated 22 health organizations in New England and reported their initial impressions on unanalysed data from some 55 other health organizations. Links were measured by examining referrals between agencies, the transfer of labour services, the transfer of resources, written communications and joint activities (see also Evan, 1976; Turk, 1970). And yet it is quite common for essentially limited studies to begin with grandiose assertions that networks are a fundamental feature of modern industrial society (see, for example, Turk, 1977, ch.1).

The attempt to develop measures of dependence is not itself a foolish or irrelevant expenditure of effort. The problem is the extent of this preoccupation. It has led to a focus on the structure of interactions and consequently important issues have been ignored. What is the relationship between resources and power? To what extent are interactions constrained by pre-existing rules of the game? To what extent is the distribution of power between organizations sustained by shared values? It is as important to examine these questions as it is to measure the amount and classify the types of interaction.

'Structuralist' v. 'Game' Approaches

Although Thompson's formulation of the concept of interorganizational dependence has been influential, it is not without problems. Because its origins lie in exchange theory, there is the problem of explaining why a given distribution of power exists. Only if it is assumed that there is a given distribution of power can exchange theory explain the relationships between the various parties.

Birnbaum (1976, p.29) has criticized Blau in these terms: 'the structural distribution of resources can often give rise to opposition directed against the beneficiaries of social organisation when their power does not result from the previous, exchange relationship. But he does not investigate the origin of this unequal distribution of resources.' There has been some recognition of this problem in the literature on interorganizational analysis. For example, Benson (1975, p.233) has argued that 'inter-organisational power relations cannot be fully understood without attention to the larger patterns of societal dominance'. Similarly, there are ambiguities in Thompson's discussion of goal setting as a political process. He draws heavily on the work of Cyert and March (1963) but their account does not discuss the origins of the goals of the contending parties within the organization; does not explore explicitly the effects of inequalities in the distribution of power for goal setting; and tends to focus only on those goals relevant to the formal structure and to ignore the range of individual commitments to the organization (for a more detailed critique, see Burns, 1969; Pettigrew, 1973 chs 1 and 2). It is necessary, therefore, to treat Thompson's formulation as a starting point and to pursue in more detail some of the objections which have been raised.

Recently, the discussion of the concepts of power and dependence has polarized between 'structuralist' and 'game' approaches. A detailed exploration of this debate will serve, incidentally, to demonstrate the inadequacy of the distinction and, more important, to identify the ways in which the study of organizational power needs to be developed if it is to become an adequate alternative to systemic approaches. The difference between structuralist and game approaches is summarized as follows by Crozier (1976, p.195). In the structuralist approach, 'some environmental variables or problems determine the structure of an organisation, and the structure of an organisation or the fit between the structure and the problem determine its effectiveness'. On the other hand, the game approach analyses the behaviour of individuals in organizations as:

> the result of the strategy each one of them has adopted in the one or several games in which he participates ... These games are played according to some informal rules which cannot easily be predicted from the prescribed roles of the formal structure. One can discover, however, these rules, as well as the pay-offs and the possible rational strategies of the participants, by analysing the players' recurrent behaviour.

Crozier (ibid., p.196) is one of the major contributors to the study of intra and interorganizational power 'games'. He argues: 'The literature has rightly underscored the fact that the relation of the organisation to its environment is a relationship of dependence. Yet studies usually describe and classify the resources of power employed in this relation more than show the mechanisms of the game between the partners.' The starting point for Crozier's analysis of the game rather than the structure of interactions is the power relations within the organization.[3] Every organization has areas of uncertainty within it and power lies in the ability to control this uncertainty: 'Each participant in an organisation, in an organised system ... wields power over the system he belongs to and over the members of this system insofar as he occupies a strategically favourable position as regards the problems on which the success of the system depends' (Crozier, 1973, pp 220–21).

Control over such uncertainty places a participant in a favourable position with other members of the organization: he can blackmail them. 'It is anyway impossible to eliminate blackmail ("chantage"), since it is related to the perennial need for adjustment and innovation. No human enterprise can adapt to its environment if it is reduced to its formal power, to the theoretical pact which defines it' (ibid., p.223).

However, anyone who has control over uncertainty is at one and the same time dependent upon others within the organization. His ability to use 'chantage' is, therefore, limited. He is forced to bargain and negotiate with other members of the organization. Crozier stresses the ways in which participants experience their participation. The contrasting perceptions of the participants enable the researcher to identify their strategies and the rules under which they are deployed (for a detailed description of his methods, see Crozier, 1972). In this scheme resources are not 'objective', but are defined by the participants, and control of a resource does not necessarily confer power on the controller. They only become important when so perceived by the participants and deployed in support of strategies (Crozier and Friedberg, 1977, p.71). The constraints under which 'chantage' takes place and the strategies used are described as a game: 'The terms of the exchange result neither from chance nor from some abstract and theoretical balance of power. They are the result of a game whose constraints create compulsory hurdles and opportunities for manipulation for the players, and therefore determine their strategy' (Crozier, 1973, p.219).

Crozier does not, therefore, classify the resources available to the various participants or measure the amount and type of interactions between them. Rather, he focuses on the relationships between the various participants and, in particular, on the strategies they employ: 'The nature of the relationship does not depend upon the resource of each player, but on the powers which they use in the game ... Power in the relationship cannot be deduced by an objective analysis of opposing forces' (Crozier and Thoenig, 1976, p.563).

Nor is the game confined to relationships within the organization. It can be applied to relations between organizations:

Regulation is the basic mechanism of organisations. From that point of view, there is no difference in kind, but only a difference in degree between an organisation and an inter-organisational network. Both are social and human systems, more or less stable and structured, integrating various units, regulating their behaviours, and imposing a collective game on their members. (Ibid., p.562)

The 'games' in French local government involving the prefect and local notables (especially mayors) provides a striking illustration of Crozier's thesis. Conventionally, the prefect has always been regarded as representing the interests of the 'state' and the 'notable' as the defender of local interests. Yet both are interdependent: the success of one depends upon the other. The prefect will be concerned that no strong local interests oppose central policies and thus reduce his efficacy as a prefect. The mayor derives his power in his relationship with the prefect from his claim to represent 'the whole community'. Both have an interest in 'bending the rules'. The prefect does not want to appear as merely the executor of decisions taken at the centre, but he will have to secure the complicity of the notables, since such rule bending is potentially open to criticism. Conversely, the notables have an interest in the bending of rules since they derive status within the local community from getting 'something special' for the community (see also Becquart-Leclerq, 1978; Kesselman, 1967; Worms, 1966).

Thoenig (1978b, pp.167–97) has extended the concept of the game to the whole structure of 'territorial administration' in France. At each level there exist relations of dependence around which games evolve. He identifies two separate channels of territorial administration, the elected and the administrative. There are areas of common interest between members of each of the channels and within each channel. But communication is not structured vertically or horizontally. Rather the system is one of 'cross-regulation'. Each member of a channel tries to have his interests favoured by members of the other channels upon whom they are dependent. The complexity of these interactions places a premium on playing several roles. It is an enormous advantage to be involved in more than one game. Thus mayors become general councilmen and deputies. In spite of the complexity of this 'honeycomb' pattern of relations, however, the game is remarkably stable because it provides benefits to each participant. All have a vested interest in preserving the status quo (Crozier and Thoenig, 1976 p.559; see also Thoenig, 1978a; 1978b).

Crozier's 'game' model of interorganizational relations leads to a reinterpretation of central–local relations in France – one which lays considerably less emphasis than usual on central direction and hierarchical control. Moreover, its emphasis on the strategies of participants in a game appears to be different from those studies which focus on measuring the resources of organizations and the structure of interactions. This 'structuralist' approach is illustrated by the work of Scharpf and his colleagues.

In their analysis of policy making in the Federal Republic of Germany, they focus on the ways in which the structure of interactions contributes to policy failure. They argue that the welfare state has failed in three ways:

- the failure of *effectiveness* in the management of the economy,
- the failure of *efficiency* in the management of the social service sector, and
- the failure of *responsiveness* to differentiated, qualitative demands in the performance of all government functions. (Scharpf, 1977, p.343)

This 'crisis of ungovernability' requires that policy analysis relate public sector structures and processes to substantive policy outcomes (as in Mayntz and Scharpf, 1975). How does the fragmented decision-making structure of the Federal Republic affect policy outcomes? Central to their answer is the analysis of empirical networks of interorganizational dependence. The various studies emphasize the 'goodness of fit' between prescriptive policy networks – the 'objective' policy problem and the feasible alternatives within given constraints – and empirical networks: that is, actual policy performance (see Scharpf *et al.*, 1976; 1978). Any 'mismatch' is seen as an important predictor of policy failure.

The analysis of the networks focuses on the structure of interactions, an approach explicitly defended by Scharpf (1977, p.353):

At this time, it is still an open question whether the attempts by Michel Crozier and his group ... to develop a theory of intra- and inter-organisational 'games' will eventually succeed in identifying a limited number of relatively stable, recurring game patterns which would help to reduce (and thus explain) the bewildering variety of observable interactions.

As long as the empirical–theoretical breakthrough of a 'transactional' sociology of organisations is still uncertain, however, inter-organisational policy studies might do well to follow a 'structuralist' approach that focuses upon the more stable ('structural') factors facilitating or impeding the employment of specific influence strategies.

The 'semi-permanent relationships of unilateral and mutual dependence' are discussed in terms of resource acquisition (ibid., p.366) and they are explored in a series of case studies in such policy areas as modernizing the dairy industry, pollution, urban renewal, federal highway construction and regional industrial policy.

Scharpf's (ibid., p.354) theory of interorganizational relations is based on the 'classic' resource dependence model with the definition of resources 'extended to cover the range of all Laswellian values, including such intangibles as "respect", "affection" and "rectitude"'. The discussion focuses on the exchange and substitutability of resources. In brief, the concept of power is defined in terms of the resources of participants.

At first glance, these summaries of the work of Crozier and Scharpf would seem to reveal a marked difference in approach. Important differences certainly exist, but the distinction between structuralist and game approaches serves only to obscure them. The problem with virtually all dichotomies is the implication that the alternatives are mutually exclusive. It is as misleading for Scharpf to label Crozier's work 'transactional' as it is for Crozier to assert that studies focusing on resource acquisition have ignored the strategies of participants. Crozier identifies a range of constraints on the 'game' and specifically recognizes the importance of structural constraints (Crozier, 1973, p.214). Conversely, Scharpf *et al.* (1976, pp.100–106) describe explicitly the strategies deployed by decision makers in the government of the Federal Republic of Germany. Similarly, various authors have essayed lists of strategies that decision makers can employ (see, for example, Elkin, 1975, p.175; Selznick, 1949, p.13; Thompson, 1967, pp.134–7; Thompson and McEwen, 1958, pp.159–63). Many of these authors may list hypothetical strategies rather than documenting the strategies employed in particular circumstances, but this is *not* Crozier's complaint. The distinction between game and structuralist approaches polarizes the field when the differences are only ones of relative emphasis. And, in the process, some important differences are obscured.

First, it is inaccurate to suggest that the structuralist approach is necessarily concerned to measure the resources available to the interacting organization. A distinction needs to be drawn between those studies which classify and measure the interactions between organizations and those which focus on the prior question of resource acquisition (Benson, 1975, p.231).

Second, those studies which do concentrate on resource acquisition tend to define power in terms of the resources commanded by decision makers. Such a conception of power is unduly limited. For example, there is no guarantee that the researcher's list of resources would correspond to that of the participants, that the same resource would be of equal use in a variety of situations, or that the various resources can be compared. Such limitations underlie Crozier's critique of structuralist approaches, his stress on perceptions of power and his denial that resources are 'objective'. And, at this point, the major difference between proponents in the field of interorganizational analysis can be specified. The structuralist/game dichotomy obscures the fact that the difference concerns the concept of power, and whether it derives from and consists of command over resources or whether it derives from perceptions of power and consists of rule-governed interactions.

Replacing one dichotomy with another, however, does little to advance the analysis. By emphasizing that the differences lie in the concept of power, the objective is not to argue in favour of one or other conception but to suggest that both facets of power are relevant to an understanding of interorganizational linkages. Although a focus on power as resources is limited, it is not thereby rendered irrelevant. Similarly, perceptions of power can be an unreliable guide. An actor's (perceived) power may stem from his command of resources and the conditions under which the various resources can be effectively deployed may influence the choice of strategies. The precise nature of the relationship between resources and strategies cannot be explored by a focus on perceptions alone. In Britain, central departments control far greater financial resources than local authorities. It is important to find out when and how the control of financial resources provides support for, and affects the choice of, strategies by central departments. As Benson has argued, the choice of strategies is a function of the amount and distribution of resources. For example, authoritative strategies are said to require a dominant position in the flow of resources, whereas cooperative strategies require some minimal degree of equality in the distribution of resources (Benson, 1975, pp.241–6). It would be misleading to suggest that Crozier is unaware of the intricacies of the relationship between resources and strategies. He points to the constraints of technology, law, formal organizational structure and other elements of the environment on the participants in the game. The emphasis on perceptions reflects, therefore, his desire to avoid the determinism associated with many conceptions of the organization–environment link and to show that the rules of the game are only partially governed by technical, historical and environmental constraints.

This ability of participants to make and remake the rules of the game introduces a third aspect of the concept of power. Clegg (1975, p.49), reviewing Crozier's earlier work, has argued that the power of many of the lower participants in the organizational game is power at the margin, that is, it is restricted in scope. In a similar vein, Fox (1973, p.217) remarks that union or worker representatives 'have already been socialised, indoctrinated and trained by a multiplicity of influences to accept and legitimise most aspects of their work situation: a situation designed in the light of the values and purposes of the major power holders'. As a result, the power of the worker is limited not only by inequality in the distribution of resources within the organization but also by a consensus which limits the area of negotiation to issues which do not threaten the values and purposes of major power holders – that is, management.

In other words, it is possible to distinguish between power as resources, power as rule-governed interactions and power as the 'mobilization of bias'. Although each group may control some resources, although there may be scope for 'chantage' within and between organizations, this bargaining does not necessarily mean there is equality in the distribution of power. The existence of shared values may limit the bargaining to a narrow range of issues and stipulate rules of the game which favour one of the contending parties.

The major problem with this third aspect of power lies in the assumption by some writers that such inequalities in the distribution of power can be identified with the domination of the organization by one group – management. Both Clegg and Fox are criticizing the assumption in some versions of pluralism that there is an equal distribution of power in organizations. It does not follow, however, that an assumption of strict equality is an essential component of a pluralist approach, or that the consensus is designed by and for one specific group of participants. In arguing for a recognition of the plurality of social systems within the organization, the intention is to explore the relative power of the participants, the bases of their power, the ways, if any, in which the rules of the game are 'negotiated' (see Strauss *et al.*, 1963) and the pervasiveness of unobtrusive controls or control of decision premises (Perrow, 1972b, pp.149–53). As Crozier and Friedberg (1977, p.70) argue, although social and economic inequalities are important in the game and managers have greater room for manoeuvre, nonetheless management cannot ignore the rules of the game (see also Burns, 1977, p.86). All participants are constrained by the rules. They are not unilaterally determined by any one group, nor are they determined equally by all groups. Nonetheless, the critique suggests that the ways in which the rules of the game are negotiated and have evolved over time is a key area of investigation. Much of the so-called 'pluralist' literature on organizational power has focused on issues and power resources (or bases) to the exclusion of other facets of power (see, for example, Hickson *et al.*, 1971; for critiques, see Clegg, 1975, pp.43–53; Bachrach and Baratz, 1962; Lukes, 1974).

The concept of the 'mobilization of bias' is a product of the community power debate in political science and, to date, it has not figured prominently in the analysis of organizational power.[4] Bachrach and Baratz (1963, p.641) discuss the 'mobilization of bias' (and the allied concept of 'non-decisions') as follows:

> When the dominant values, the accepted rules of the game, the existing power relations among groups, and the instruments of force, singly or in combination, effectively prevent certain grievances from developing into full-fledged issues which call for decisions, it can be said that a non-decision-making situation exists.

As interpreted by Parry and Morriss (1974, pp.317–36), this critique requires that we distinguish between the many kinds of decisions, whether they be 'key issues' or routine, administrative decisions and, for each kind of decision, between the types of power involved. Three types of power are discussed: the power to initiate a routine, the power by which a routine is maintained and the distribution of power following the performance of a routine. Of particular relevance in this formulation is the focus on routines, and the values and power distribution sustaining them. It is precisely this focus which is required in the study of organizational and interorganizational power and which is so prominent in Crozier's work. However, it is not simply a matter of describing the rules of the game operative at a given point in time. Clegg (1975, chs 4 and 5) distinguishes between power, rules and domination, arguing that pluralist theory has focused on the surface manifestations of power – participation in key issues. He argues for an analysis of the rules supporting and constraining such participation and for an analysis of the structure of domination which supports the rules. The analysis of power must explore the origins of the rules, the values and distribution of power supporting them and the pressures changing them. At this juncture, the limits of Crozier's analysis can be specified more precisely. He focuses on power and, more important, the rules underlying the exercise of power, but he does not analyse the generation of rules. He explains why actors continue to support pre-existing rules of the game, but he does not explore variations in the degree of commitment to these rules. Shared values can limit not only the scope of 'chantage' but also the form of the rules. The basis of support for the rules thus becomes of central importance.

There have been few studies of this aspect of organizational power (but see Perrow, 1972b, pp.59–68; Bendix, 1956). In the context of interorganizational analysis, the value of exploring power as the mobilization of bias has been demonstrated by the study by Warren et al., 1974, pp.19–25) of 'institutionalised thought structure', and its effect on the pattern of relationships between organizations involved in the Model Cities programme. The existence of shared values is said to explain the lack of competition and even contact between the organizations involved, and yet the lack of coordination between agencies was assumed to be a major contributory factor to the failure to solve urban problems. Moreover, the new agencies of the Model Cities programme were quickly assimilated to the shared values. Not surprisingly, they record little evidence of innovative attacks on problems. The 'institutionalised thought structure' was, to employ Perrow's (1972b, p.236) term, the 'ground' against which the 'figure' of organizational interactions had to be viewed. Warren and others document the ways in which the rules of the game and the distribution of power between organizations are sustained by the shared values of the organizational network.

The analysis of the concepts of power and exchange in the literature on interorganizational analysis cannot be adequately summarized by distinguishing between structures and games. The major distinctions reside in the differing approaches to the concept of power. However, these approaches are not mutually exclusive. It needs to be more readily appreciated that power can no more be reduced to the sum of each participant's resources than it can be viewed solely in terms of each actor's perceptions; that the rules governing interactions cannot be treated as given, nor can they be viewed in a deterministic manner as the product of the values and interests of any one group. Power is a multifaceted concept and its utility in the analysis of the relationships between organizations will not be improved if it is arbitrarily limited to but one of the facets.

Consequences

Given that organizations are interdependent and employ strategies to manage their dependence, what are the consequences of this activity? This question has not figured prominently in the interorganizational analysis literature. Some attention has been given to the structural consequences of dependence. For example, networks have been compared by size, compactness, density and diversity (see Evan, 1976, Part IV; Mitchell, 1969). Some attention has also been paid to the interorganizational decision-making process, and these studies are often concerned to prescribe for improved decision making (see, for example, Friend *et al.*, 1974; Tuite *et al.*, 1972, and the various publications of Fritz Scharpf and his colleagues). In its preoccupation with measuring interactions, the literature has omitted to ask why such networks matter. Indeed, Perrow (1972b, p.193) argues that far too much time has been devoted to the study of 'trivial organisations'. There would be little point in studying organizational networks if, as much of the literature implies by default, little of consequence follows from their existence. The roots of this literature often lie in some version of the post-industrial society thesis, but only rarely are the links between the macro theory and the specific studies of networks clearly articulated. The location of empirical work within a broader, interpretive framework is not a feature of interorganizational analysis – a point discussed in more detail below. Fortunately, clues about the importance of networks can be culled from other sources.

For example, a number of studies have pointed to the problems created for the implementation of a policy by the need to work with and through a large number of separate organizations. Each organization has its own interests and commands resources of its own. Compliance or cooperation is not automatically forthcoming and in negotiating agreement the original policy can be changed (see, for example, Bardach, 1977; Hanf and Scharpf, 1978, chs 8 and 12; Hood, 1976; Pressman and Wildavsky, 1973). Similarly, Sampson (1974) has documented the activities of ITT, demonstrating that the actions of large multinational companies are not necessarily benevolent, that they are by no means the passive victims of a turbulent environment and that governments experience major problems in controlling them. These and other sources suggest that the relative power of organizations in a network has crucial effects on both the process of policy making and political accountability (see also Bailey, 1979; Galbraith, 1973; Perrow, 1972a; Sampson, 1976).

Although the interactions between organizations are not the only influence upon policy making, it is clear that they are sufficiently important on a range of issues to warrant far more attention than they have received to date. The failure of the literature on interorganizational analysis to explore such consequences can be numbered amongst its greatest failings.

Conclusions

Models in the social sciences are never wholly satisfactory; they are more or less useful. This chapter has reviewed the literature on interorganizational analysis and in so doing it has criticized the bulk of the contributions. The objective has not been to demonstrate the truism that all models are incomplete but to identify the ways in which the existing models can be developed. As Karl Weick (1979) has argued, much criticism in the sociology of organizations is not balanced by a concern with affirmation: with the need to enlarge our understanding of the phenomenon of organizing in the act of criticizing. This chapter has at least attempted to approach its subject matter in a constructive manner.

To recap, it has been suggested that the systems approach to the study of the link between organizations and their environment is inadequate because the theory cannot specify the 'relevant' aspects of the environment, or provide the criteria for bounding the network, or define goals without reifying the organization. Moreover, there is no one theory of interorganizational analysis. The field has been described as a set of issues. Building upon the work of Thompson, it has been argued that a focus on intra- and interorganizational power can provide both the analytical cutting edge lacking in systems theory and a coherent perspective. Thus the goals of the organization are described as the outcome of an intra- and interorganizational political process: they are negotiated. The environment does not determine the goals and decisions of an 'organization'. The environment is constitutive but it is also constituted by the dominant coalition. However, much of the literature on interorganizational analysis has adopted a deterministic or constitutive position on the effects of the environment on organizational decision makers. There has been a preoccupation with classifying and measuring interactions. Even those authors who have built upon Thompson's work have tended to adopt a narrow conception of the exchanges with the environment. A review of structuralist and game approaches to the study of organizational links suggests that it is necessary to distinguish three facets of organizational power: power as resources, power as rule-governed interactions and power as the mobilization of bias. None of these aspects of power is adequate if examined in isolation from the others. To comprehend the links between organizations, analysis has to encompass all three facets of power. And the concern with intra- and interorganizational power is also a concern with the consequences which arise from the activities of organizations, whether these consequences take the form either of frustrating the implementation of policy or of obscuring the accountability of organizations for their actions.

The discussion of interorganizational analysis in this chapter forms part of the search for a more adequate theoretical framework for analysing intergovernmental relations and to assess the contribution which recent theoretical developments in the field of interorganizational analysis might make to an understanding of such relations. Criticism of the interorganizational literature has not sought, therefore, to expose inherent weaknesses but to highlight key common concerns and potential areas of development. It has been argued that the literature contains a number of useful concepts and it is appropriate to ask what contribution they can make to the study of the 'forgotten dimensions' of British central–local relations.

First, the concept of organizational *networks* draws attention to the variety of relationships in which a central department or a local authority could be engaged. It is no longer adequate to limit analysis to the central department–local authority link. At the very least, the concept of networks enjoins the analysis of links between public sector organizations in all their guises and there is no necessary reason why analysis could not be extended to private sector organizations also. The view that Britain is a unitary state has worked against recognition of the fact that its intergovernmental relations are complex. And, equally important, the literature on interorganizational analysis provides tools for measuring and comparing networks. If intergovernmental relations in Britain are complex, it would be as well to document this ostensibly simple point as precisely as possible.

Second, the concept of *goals* as the outcome of a political process within and between organizations acts as a corrective to the 'top-down' view of intergovernmental relations; for example, the view that goals are determined by central departments and implemented by local authorities. There are many prescriptions in the literature on central–local relations for central departments to make their policy explicit (Griffith, 1966, pp.537–9). The view of goals as temporary and the product of bargaining suggests that it would be more profitable to explore the process of goal setting in public sector organizations to identify the constraints on making explicit policy settlements. Indeed, it is relevant to ask if goals are determined at the centre: to what extent is there a 'bottom-up' dimension to goal setting? Moreover, this perspective suggests that there will be a variety of competing goals. Accordingly, it is important to compare different policy areas and to ask if they have distinct organizational networks.

Third, the concepts of *power and exchange* emphasize that the relationship between centre and periphery is not a 'control' relationship. Rather, central departments and subnational public sector organizations are interdependent. Recognition of this point opens up a series of questions about intergovernmental relations which until recently have been conspicuous only by their absence. To what extent do the participants control different amounts and types of resources? To what extent do they recognize and work within agreed rules of the game? Do they employ strategies to manage their relationships? Do they compete for discretion in designing and implementing policies? To what extent do the participants share values which limit the scope of negotiations? In addition, within these general areas, a number of more specific questions can be raised. For example, attention is focused on the identification of the rules of the game: describing how they are applied in specific situations, analysing how they are adjusted to meet changed situations, and, most important, exploring their origins.

Finally, the interorganizational model suggests that institutional complexity can have marked *consequences* for governmental effectiveness and accountability. Crozier and Thoenig (1976, p.556) describe French central–local relations as a 'game' that is 'closed and secret' in which the participants 'fear public opinion and hide from the sanctions of electoral suffrage' (and c.f. pp.20 and 26 above). It is certainly relevant to ask if the ambiguity and confusion of British central–local relations has similar consequences.[5] But the discussion in this chapter has directly confronted the relationship between interorganizational analysis and theories of advanced industrial society only in brief. The relationship between these two levels of analysis must now be explored in a little more detail.

As already noted, interorganizational analysis tends to adopt some version of the post-industrial society thesis, albeit implicitly. The focus on the complex web of organizations, the analysis of interdependence, the separation of ownership and control and the stress on the power of large-scale organizations in modern society are shared themes. Similarly, corporatist theory stresses interdependence between organizations and, in Winkler's (1976) case, specifically appeals to Thompson's (1967) analysis of organizational interdependence.

On the face of it, therefore, there would appear to be marked affinities between the two levels of analysis. But in this case appearances are deceptive. The argument that interorganizational analysis needs to be located within a theory of inter- and intraorganizational power is but one way of saying that it has become divorced from any broader interpretive framework. Whatever the roots of interorganizational analysis, those roots do not inform the interpretation of empirical results. In other words, interorganizational analysis is capable of informing the analysis of the 'figure' or the surface level of interactions between the various units of government but it is not able to explore the 'ground' or the deep structures of power, values and interests which support and sustain those interactions. Appearances to the contrary, interorganizational analysis does not affect a reconciliation between levels of analysis (see Clegg, 1975, pp.70–79; and Chapter 5 below). Not that this problem is peculiar to interorganizational analysis in particular or even the sociology of organizations in general. It will be considered again in the discussion of the literature on intergovernmental relations.

Notes

1 A subsidiary objective of this chapter is to draw the attention of political scientists to the literature on the sociology of organizations. Compared to, for example, the literature on intergovernmental relations, this literature is relatively unknown to British political scientists. It is hoped that this chapter will persuade them that it will repay exploration.
2 See, for example, the debate over the Aston measure of dependence. The measure includes items both on other organizations and on relations to the owning group. See Pugh and Hinings (1976, pp.23–4). Mindlin and Aldrich (1975) point out that the items on relations to the owning group skew the dependency measure. To conclude a typical exchange, Pugh and Hinings (1976, p.174) reply: 'We consider this criticism to be very well taken conceptually and that the distinction between inter- and intraorganizational dependence needs to be refined and developed in future work.'
3 I would like to thank Ed Page (University of Strathclyde) for his assistance with, and translations of, various passages in books and articles by Michel Crozier not available in English. Where possible, I have referred to translated work only.
4 One of the major charges levelled against critics of the pluralist literature is their inability to specify satisfactory methods for the study of the 'mobilizations of bias'. Ignoring the easy retort that methods should not dictate the subject matter of research, a number of studies have begun to develop an appropriate methodology. Some of the relevant issues can be seen by comparing Crenson (1971) with Polsby (1979). For further discussion, see Chapter 5 below.
5 The description 'game' is potentially misleading. Although it is a striking metaphor

which serves admirably to highlight the differences between interorganizational and traditional approaches to the study of intergovernmental relations, it is only a shorthand expression covering situations in which decision makers employ strategies within known rules of the game to pursue their goals. However, it can all too easily be taken to refer to certain theories of transactional psychology (see, for example, Berne, 1968) or it can obscure the differences between games proper and social interaction (Silverman, 1970, pp.210–22). Finally, continual reference to 'the game' can serve to obscure the point that there is an 'ecology of games' (Long, 1958, pp.251–61). In an effort to avoid some of these misleading connotations, the more prosaic term 'rule-governed interactions' has occasionally been substituted for the 'game' metaphor.

4   Intergovernmental Relations

Introduction

The literature on intergovernmental relations (IGR) is extensive and, since
no short review could possibly draw together all the disparate threads, this
chapter does not attempt to provide a detailed survey or to describe IGR in
particular countries. Rather, it emphasizes the various theoretical models
which have been used to analyse variations in the relationships between
tiers of government and, in particular, those research studies which suggest
potentially fruitful approaches to the study of British central–local relations.
As with the literature on interorganizational analysis, however, it will be
argued that there is no ready-made theory which can simply be transposed
to the British context.

A number of additional themes will also be explored. First, it will be
argued that the IGR literature can shed light on the 'forgotten dimensions'
of British central–local relations because it has focused increasingly on the
complex interdependencies of levels of government and because discussions
of the politics of IGR have stressed the prevalence of bargaining, the strategies of participants and the importance of the rules of the game. Second, and
in sharp contrast to the interorganizational analysis literature, there have
been a few systematic attempts to explain the origins of, and changes in, the
rules of the game. In other words, the relationship between the 'ground', or
the underlying distribution of power, and the 'figure', or the interactions of
participants, has been explored. However, in spite of this concern with the
distribution of power between levels of government, it will be argued that
the analysis is limited partly because it is country-specific. Finally, the
contrasts and parallels between the IGR and the interorganizational analysis
literature will be explored to determine whether or not the IGR literature
can make a distinctive contribution to our understanding of British intergovernmental relations.

The two major objectives of this chapter are, therefore, to determine the
extent to which the IGR literature provides a basis for future research into
British intergovernmental relations and to assess the extent to which

specific explanations of the relationships between units of government are located within a broader interpretive framework.

From Federalism to Intergovernmental Relations

A number of commentators have noted the similarities between allegedly 'unitary' systems of government and 'federal' systems (Rose, 1976; Burkhead, 1974; Riker, 1969). In fact, the comparison of these two types of governmental system can be viewed as one of the classic topics of political science. Given the growing awareness of the plural nature of British government, it is appropriate to begin the discussion of the IGR literature by exploring in at least some detail the distinctive features of federal systems. However, the discussion will not focus on either normative or definitional questions, although there is an extensive literature on both topics (see Wright and Peddicord, 1975). The emphasis is placed on the models or theories of the relationship between the various units of government. More specifically, the development of the study of federalism into the more general study of intergovernmental relations will be explored.[1]

A useful starting point for examining the wealth of material on federalism is Birch's distinction between the institutional, sociological, process and bargaining approaches (Birch, 1966). The *institutional* approach is well illustrated by Wheare. His approach is to construct an 'ideal type' model of the features of federalism in a manner somewhat reminiscent of Weber on bureaucracy. The definition of federalism in terms of general and regional governments having coordinate and independent powers may not apply to all countries describing themselves as federal, but it does provide a benchmark against which to evaluate them (Wheare, 1946, p.11). This approach has been often criticized. It is claimed that the definition is too restrictive and that the approach is legalistic although, as Birch points out, it is not immediately apparent why this last point should be viewed as a criticism. Perhaps the major weakness of the approach has been that many new federations simply do not conform to the model (see, for example, Carnell, 1961). One is reduced to concluding that most so-called 'federal' systems are not really federal.

The *sociological* approach to federalism argues that it cannot be understood in legal or constitutional terms. As Livingston (1956, p.2) has pointed out, 'the essence of federalism lies not in the constitutional or institutional structure but in society itself'. Federalism is a reflection of social diversity. Thus

Federalism is ... not an absolute but a relative term; there is no identifiable point at which a society ceases to be unified and becomes diversified ... All communities fall somewhere in a spectrum which runs from what we may call a theoretically wholly integrated society at one extreme to a theoretically wholly diversified society at the other. (Ibid.)

The *process* approach views federalism as the process of federalizing. Birch quotes Friedrich to the effect that a federation is 'a union of groups, united by one or more common objectives, but retaining their distinctive group character for other purposes' (Birch, 1966, p.18). Thus the emergence of the European Community is an example of the federalizing process.

Finally, the *bargaining* approach to federalism emphasizes that it is 'a bargain between prospective national leaders and officials of constituent governments for the purpose of aggregating territory, the better to lay taxes and raise armies'. According to Riker (1964, p.11) such a bargain is a federal bargain when: '(1) two levels of government rule the same land and people, (2) each level has at least one area of action in which it is autonomous, and (3) there is some guarantee (even though merely a statement in the constitution) of the autonomy of each government in its own sphere'.

Birch's classification is useful for drawing attention to the sheer variety of approaches to the study of federalism. However, it is also important to place these four approaches in perspective and view them not as separate models but as representing a brief history of the development of federalism. Thus Livingston's spectrum of federalism is probably the first major attempt to move away from a static to a more flexible approach which recognizes the interdependence of the two levels of government. This shift reflects the growing recognition that 'dual federalism' had given way to 'cooperative federalism' – that the concurrent powers were in all probability a more significant feature of federalism than the separate powers.[2]

The need to incorporate this development into the definition of federalism is recognized even by those writers who do not belong to the behaviourist school of thought in these matters. Vile modifies Wheare's approach and emphasizes that interdependence is as important to understanding federalism as independence (Vile, 1961, pp.198–9). Similarly, in an earlier book, Birch pointed to the massive growth in concurrent powers and his definition of federalism emphasized the coordinate division of powers rather than their separation (Birch, 1955, p.306). But neither Vile nor Birch goes far enough for a number of other writers. Thus Friedrich's definition, noted above, could apply to any situation in which there is some kind of subdivision of powers. Sawyer talks of the 'federal situation'. He uses this phrase to refer to 'a situation where geographical distribution of the power to govern is desired or has been achieved in a way giving the several governmental units of the system some degree of security' (Sawyer, 1969, pp.2–3). In other words, federalism can merge imperceptibly into decentralization of any form. And Riker has gone so far as to ask, 'Does federalism exist and does it matter?' His answer to both parts of the question is a resounding 'No'. Federalism is only significant when states are being founded. It has little practical significance afterwards (Riker, 1969, pp.135–46).

The four approaches identified by Birch are not, therefore, simply separate models of federalism. They represent a brief history of the development of the concept. With the growing recognition of the importance of concurrent powers, approaches to federalism have laid increasing emphasis on the interdependence of the two levels of government. This theme directly corresponds to the concerns of the interorganizational analysis literature. However, it does not take us far forward. What models have been developed in the literature to describe and analyse this interdependence? In order to explore this question, it is necessary to go beyond Birch's fourfold classification, for three reasons. First, the differences between the process and bargaining approaches have become increasingly difficult to sustain. Second, his discussion of bargaining is limited almost exclusively to the work of Riker. Finally, the analysis is limited to state–centre relationships and does not give sufficient attention to the multiplicity of institutions and relationships within a federal system.

The process approach has been prominent in the study of the European Community, but it has not been the only one. Briefly, three broad approaches to the study of European integration have been identified (Hodges 1972). The *federalist* approach stresses the constitutional division of powers and the role of political institutions in creating a United States of Europe (see, for example, Hallstein, 1972). It corresponds to the institutional approach discussed above. The *transactionalist* approach stresses the importance of the underlying socioeconomic conditions and a 'sense of community' for integrating a particular region (see, for example, Deutsch *et al.*, 1957). Such a sense of community cannot emerge without some degree of interdependence, and such interdependence can only be established by transactions between the various parties. It corresponds to the sociological approach. Finally, the *neofunctionalist* approach stresses that integration is a process (see, inter alia, Haas, 1964; Lindberg, 1963; Lindberg and Scheingold, 1970). As a reaction against earlier approaches, the neofunctionalists are careful not to suggest either that there is an ideal typical system of government (federalism) or that integration is an 'assembly line process' which will necessarily occur if the underlying conditions are met. Rather, they emphasize the pluralist nature of modern society. It is argued that political elites will see supranational institutions as a means of meeting their pragmatic interests. They will negotiate and bargain across national boundaries and, as a result, there will be changes in their loyalties, expectations and political activity. The locus of decision making will shift from national to supranational institutions. The process of integration involves the gradual politicization of the issues considered. There is a 'spill-over' effect as actors discover that, to satisfy their pragmatic, technical interests, they have to broaden the agenda. More controversial issues come within the ambit of the supranational institutions. If the bargaining and negotiation on these issues is successful, national actors will entrust yet more issues to supra-national institutions. Such a brief account scarcely does justice to the various strands of neofunctionalist thought. Nor does it raise the real difficulties of this theory. But such problems are not of direct concern here (for a critical discussion, see Hodges, 1972; Wallace *et al.*, 1977). Of greater importance is the fact that the neofunctionalist theory is a combination of the process and bargaining approaches. And a great deal of the recent literature similarly draws no distinction between them. Rather, the emphasis falls on the continuously evolving nature of the bargaining relationship between states and the centre. The literature on European integration is just one of the more conspicuous examples of this combination of approaches.

The discussion of bargaining in the federal context also needs to be broadened. Riker's contribution may be of value, but his discussion of bargaining focuses on the historically unique federal bargain and, more specifically, on the structure of the party system which he views as crucial to the survival of a federation. But bargaining continues after the original federal compact has been struck. It is an ever-present, day-to-day feature of the relationships between the states and federal government. Thus May (1969, p.3) emphasizes that:

> despite the formal division of decision making, decisions taken by the central government and decisions taken by the unit governments affect the same people, and therefore affect each other. Because of this interdependence the two levels of government, although they cannot dictate one another's decisions, can and do seek to persuade, influence and bargain with one another.

It is necessary, therefore, to stress that the interdependence of states and centre generates extensive bargaining and negotiation.

Finally, it must be recognized that a major feature of federal systems is the sheer number and complexity of interactions between a variety of governmental institutions. A great many discussions of federalism, including that by Birch, focus on the state–centre relationship, but interactions between centre and locality, between states and between localities – in fact, between all the various units of government – are important. They are not only of interest in their own right but the complex of relationships affects the links between states and centre, a point clearly illustrated by the experience of the American federal government in its attempts to intervene in urban areas (see, for example, Martin, 1965).

The effect of incorporating the above three features into the discussion of federalism is to broaden the scope of the analysis considerably. In recognition of the fact that the subject has been extended beyond its traditional confines, the term 'intergovernmental relations' (IGR) has been coined. Although IGR has been described as a new field, this claim should be treated with a degree of caution. As with many such claims, there are great similarities with what went before. Nonetheless, the IGR literature does have some distinctive emphases. According to Anderson (1960, p.3), IGR designates 'an important body of activities or interactions occurring between governmental units of all types and levels within ... the federal system'.

This general definition has been elaborated by Wright (1974) who identifies five elements within the field. First, IGR recognizes the multiplicity of relationships between all types of government. Second, it emphasizes the interactions between individuals, especially public officials. Third, these relationships are continuous, day-to-day and informal. They are not fixed by agreements or rules and they are not spasmodic, although both the formal and informal basis of the links must be examined. Fourth, although the role of the politician has been recognized in federal relations, too little attention has been paid to the role of the administrator. IGR insists on the important role played by all public officials, be they politicians or administrators. The final distinctive feature of IGR is its policy component. Wright suggests that federalism translated questions of policy into questions of law. IGR emphasizes the political nature of the relationship and focuses on substantive policies, especially financial issues such as who raises what amounts and who shall spend it for whose benefit with what results. In summary, Wright (ibid., p.4) claims:

> The term IGR alerts one to the multiple, behavioral, continuous and dynamic exchanges occurring between various officials in the political system. It may be compared to a different, novel and visual filter or concept that can be laid on the American political landscape. It permits one to observe, classify and cumulate knowledge without obscuring other relevant data which prior political concepts have provided.

The usefulness of this 'visual filter' is not limited to the American political system. Recent work on the Federal Republic of Germany has emphasized the 'fragmented and complex' interrelationships between the *Länder* and the *Bund*. Coordinate and independent powers are of limited importance in German federalism. The horizontal division of powers between legislation and implementation is of greater significance. And yet 'there are no grounds for concluding that this horizontal division is less "federal" than the

American-style vertical division' (Johnson, 1973, pp.101, 132; see also Merkl, 1959; Mayntz and Scharpf, 1975).

Complexity and interdependence have become the key concepts in the analysis of federalism. However, there are problems with this development. Vile (1973, p.35) suggests that a state of 'complete indeterminacy' has been reached and that 'the slippery slope upon which W.S. Livingston embarked in the nineteen-fifties has reached its *reductio ad absurdum*. The time has come to reassess federal systems in terms of a definition which actually does help us to distinguish between different kinds of political system.'

Federalism has become virtually synonymous with decentralization. Discussion is no longer limited even to the more prominent federal institutions. The stage has probably been reached where the term 'federalism' has no distinct meaning. It can now be taken to refer to any division of powers between national and subnational and supranational institutions (Rhodes, 1978, pp.50–51, 54–5). This process of definition and redefinition has created the field of intergovernmental relations, but it too faces the problem of indeterminacy. Walker (1974, pp.17–31) points to the 'conflicting concepts' and the plethora of 'divergent interpretations'. Further, he suggests that the main concerns are defining the federal role, interpreting the partnership ideal and methods. The current preoccupations are fiscal arrangements and muddled intergovernmental management.[3] In other words, the emphasis has fallen on the operational aspects of IGR rather than on developing theory (ibid., p.18). As in the case of interorganizational analysis, it would appear that the literature on IGR provides a set of themes to be explored rather than a theory to be applied in a variety of contexts.

The suggestion that the literature on federalism and IGR has emphasized the themes of interdependence and complexity is scarcely novel. Fortunately, the IGR literature also contains models of the bargaining process in federal systems. It is necessary, therefore, to supplement the above general characterization of the literature with a discussion of some of these specific models.

Bargaining, Diplomacy and 'Topocrats'

Although May's (1969) study of federalism is primarily concerned with the effects of differences in size and wealth between units and with the financial relations between governments, these specific issues are analysed with a bargaining model of federal decision making. May contends that a federation is not two independent political systems but a single system containing within it a number of overlapping subsystems. He suggests that the earlier literature did not pay sufficient attention to the diversity of units and the bargaining between them because interest was concentrated on questions of legal form. But to understand decision making in a federal system attention has to be focused on the bargaining process and the interdependence of units of government. The characteristics of decision making in federal systems are summarized as follows:

> a) public policy decisions are taken at the two levels of government; neither level can dictate the decisions of the other;
> b) the decisions taken by the central government will be determined by three main factors: (1) the demands of the central government's electorate, which will largely determine the goals set; (2) the decisions taken by the unit governments, which, because they affect the same people on whom the impact of the central government's decisions fall, will act as a constraint on the central government's scope for effective action; and (3) the central government's power potential *vis-à-vis* the units as determined by (i) the provisions of the constitution and other rules of the game which at any time provide the framework within which bargaining takes place, and (ii) the central government's bargaining capabilities, which depend on such factors as the number of units in the federation, the structure of the federal system, and the role of particular personalities or groups;
> c) the decisions taken by each unit government, in a similar way, will depend on four main factors: (1) the demands of its electorate; (2) the decisions taken by the central government; (3) the decisions taken by other unit governments; and (4) the unit government's power potential *vis-à-vis* other units and the central government. (Ibid., pp.3–4)

This summary statement is elaborated in later chapters and May introduces a number of additional factors which influence bargaining capabilities. First, the civil service in a federation can exert influence in a variety of ways. Civil servants may take attitudes favourable to unit governments with them when they move to the central administration. The interchange of staff and the cooperation of staff in equivalent functions may foster the growth of national attitudes and standards (ibid., pp.29–30). Second, although 'the rules of the game and other environmental factors go a long way towards determining the pattern and outcome of bargaining', the way the government operates in a specific situation – strategic factors – is nonetheless important. A number of general strategies can be identified. A common strategy is to establish the legitimacy of one's demands by appeal to the constitution or, if this strategy is inadequate, to 'the intentions of the founding fathers', 'the national interest' or 'state's rights'. To give added weight to demands, there are a variety of methods for building up agreement, including formal and informal negotiations with parliamentary leaders, petitions and intergovernmental conferences. Alternatively, it is possible to resort to commissions or committees of inquiry. This method can either take the issue out of the bargaining process or delay any decision. Other strategies include the mobilization of electoral support, the use of sanctions, threat of secession, log-rolling and coalitions between unit governments. And in such bargaining the timing of one's intervention, the ability to release and withhold information and to make apparent concessions can have a decisive influence on the outcome (ibid., pp.31–5).

This bargaining model is used to analyse fiscal adjustment in a variety of federal systems. May (ibid., pp.164, 166) argues that grants do not 'necessarily imply a loss of "sovereignty" to units', and he suggests that 'the impact of grants on a unit depends not so much on the method of payment as on the strength of the bargaining powers of that unit in relation to the central government and the other units and the importance of unit governments as separate entities in the overall national political system'.

Such a brief summary scarcely does justice to May's work but enough has been said to show that this view of IGR has a marked affinity with the power-dependence model of interorganizational analysis (for further discussion see May 1970). Moreover, it has an obvious relevance to the study of central–local relations in Britain. Although a number of writers have recognized the bargaining relationship between the various units of British government, May's approach has the singular advantage that it presents an explicit model of this process.

Some of the disadvantages of May's model are obvious ones. His characterization of the bargaining process refers to a federal system. Accordingly, detailed adjustments have to be made for its application to Britain. The constitution as a source of rules of the game has to be modified to recognize the uncodified nature of the British constitution and the importance of *ultra vires* for local government. Secession, the Scottish National Party (SNP) notwithstanding, is not yet a viable strategy in the United Kingdom. Such details need not detain us. However, there are three other reservations about the model which require a more extended treatment. First, May's discussion of the basis of interdependence is limited. His emphasis falls on the fact that the two levels of government serve a common electorate and the demands of this electorate act as a constraint on both. But there are many bases to interdependence, a point emphasized in the interorganizational analysis literature. Second, his analysis concentrates on fiscal adjustment. He does not explore the consequences of this bargaining process for substantive policy. Finally, there is no analysis either of the causes of interdependence or of changes in the rules of the game. Fortunately, other studies enable us to fill some of these gaps.

In his analysis of federal–provincial relations in Canada, Simeon (1972, p.8) argues that 'neither sociological nor institutional factors can account for the actual performance of political systems or for their policy-making processes'. He specifies three sets of factors: broad social and cultural characteristics; institutional and constitutional factors; and the particular norms, attitudes, goals and perspectives of decision makers. The analytical framework is summarized as follows:

> there is a set of interdependent *actors*, or partisans; they operate within a certain *social and institutional environment*; they share some *goals* but differ on others ...; they have an *issue* or set of issues on which they must negotiate; none has hierarchical *control* over the others; they have varying *political resources*; they use these resources in certain *strategies and tactics*; they arrive at certain *outcomes*; and these outcomes have *consequences* for themselves, for other groups in the society, and for the system itself. (Ibid., pp.11–12)

Simeon stresses that this framework is dynamic, by which he means that the background factors (such as sociocultural characteristics), immediate factors (such as issues, goals and resources) and the consequences of actions interact with each other. Thus the consequences of a particular decision can affect the process and the background factors. An overwhelming proportion of the book is concerned with tracing the interactions between the several components of the framework. Three features of the argument warrant more detailed discussion: the context of interactions, political resources, and outcomes and consequences.

Simeon (ibid., p.20) is primarily concerned with the goals, perceptions and attitudes of individual decision makers, but he sees the social and institutional environments as the 'essential determinants' of these factors. This context is broken down into a number of constituent factors, including geography, regional economic disparities and different historical traditions, all of which are seen as contributing to the greater salience of regional and ethnic cleavages relative to class and economic cleavages. The institutional environment is also said to influence federal–provincial relations. Traditional institutions are said to be ineffective in resolving federal–provincial disputes and, as a result, direct intergovernmental negotiations have developed as the mechanisms for managing relations between governments. Similarly, the party system does not serve as a mechanism for intergovernmental adjustment. Another feature of the institutional environment is the centralized internal organization of government departments which focuses issues at the political level rather than diffusing them through the bureaucracy. Finally, the constitution sets parameters to the decision-making process. The important feature of Simeon's discussion is that the interactions between governments are not seen as the prime determinant of policy outcomes. There is an essential prior stage of analysis, namely the sociocultural context. The discussion of the interorganizational analysis literature concluded that, for the most part, it did not specify the context of interactions. Simeon's discussion is specific to Canada; nonetheless, he clearly makes the point that a focus on interactions is, of itself, inadequate. Any similar framework for the analysis of intergovernmental relations in Britain will obviously have to include some discussion of the broader context within which interactions take place.

Simeon's discussion of political resources similarly serves as a useful corrective to some of the major preoccupations of the interorganizational analysis literature. That literature tended to measure exchanges of resources such as manpower, information and money. For a political scientist, political resources are conspicuous only by their absence. Simeon not only recognizes the importance of such resources but also emphasizes that 'their distribution is highly variable and relative to both the issues and the time'. In a similar vein to Crozier, he points out that such resources are 'predominantly subjective', depending upon the beliefs and perceptions of the individual decision maker (Simeon, 1972, p.201). A number of types of political resource are discussed: legal authority, political support, skills and expertise, 'objective' information, size and wealth, procedures and rules of the game and factors specific to the negotiations. However, it is stressed that no fixed a priori classification of political resources will be adequate. Such resources are 'rooted in the social context, the issues, and the time, and, even more important, in the minds of the participants'. Resources are subtle, complex, continually shifting and double-edged (ibid., pp.223, 226). This emphasis is a valuable pointer to the distinctive nature of intergovernmental relations as compared with interorganizational relations.

Finally, in this brief synopsis, Simeon argues that the process of intergovernmental diplomacy has important effects on outcomes and important consequences for other actors in the political system. Thus, on the outcomes of particular issues, he comments:

> Because of the way federal–provincial negotiation brings in to the decision-making process certain interests and concerns which would not otherwise be involved, and because it gives provincial governments, as institutions, a major voice in national policy-making, the kinds of decisions made in the system and the interests brought to bear in policy-making are distinctive ... differences in some central characteristics of this adjustment process help to explain why the results in one case differ from that in others. (Ibid., p.277)

Furthermore, the 'most important determinant of the outcome, and of the relative influence of different actors, is the distribution of political resources (ibid., p.266). Similarly, federal–provincial diplomacy has consequences for other actors in the political system, including parliament, interest groups, the status of governments and ethnic conflict. Simeon (ibid., p.297) summarizes the position as follows:

> It is clear, then, that the process of federal–provincial negotiations has some important consequences for Canadian federalism – for the policies generated, for the participants themselves, for the way the process operates in other cases, for the constitutional and institutional arrangements of Canadian government, for different groups within the system, for responsiveness of the system to democratic values, for individual interest groups, and for political change itself. On the one hand the process is dependent on the wider environment; on the other hand it is an instrument through which the participants alter that environment.

To select particular elements from a framework is invariably misleading but in this case the act of selection serves to highlight its real contribution to understanding intergovernmental relations. The analysis of the context of interactions, the stress on political resources and the concern with outcomes and consequences were all identified as important omissions from the interorganizational analysis literature. Moreover, Simeon's analysis not only acts as a valuable corrective to that literature but also complements it with its analysis of perceptions, tactics and strategies. The description 'diplomacy' serves to highlight the parallels with, for example, Crozier's 'game'.

It would be misleading, however, to suggest that an appreciation of the 'game-like' quality of intergovernmental relations was restricted to only a few commentators. There are now a variety of case studies which draw attention to this feature of the relationships. Most important in recent studies has been the emphasis on bargaining not only between elected representatives but also between non-elected officials. Simeon's analysis reflects the distinctive features of Canadian federalism with its emphasis on bargaining between political actors. It is necessary to turn to other sources for an analysis and description of bargaining between officials. A useful summary statement is provided in Wright's (1978) review of IGR in the United States of America.

Wright distinguishes between three models of intergovernmental relations: the separated, the overlapping and the inclusive. In the separated model, the states and the national government are independent and the authority pattern is one of autonomy. In the inclusive model, the states are dependent on the national government and the authority pattern is hierarchical. In the overlapping model, the various units of government are interdependent and the authority pattern is one of bargaining. This latter model is seen as the 'most representative' of IGR practice and its chief characteristics are described as limited dispersed power, interdependence, limited areas of autonomy, bargaining–exchange relationships, and cooperation and competition. Bargaining is defined as 'negotiating the terms of sale, exchange or agreement' (ibid., pp.16–29). Much of the remainder of Wright's book is devoted to a description and analysis of this bargaining. The nature of this analysis will be illustrated by examining briefly his discussion of the actions and attitudes of local officials.

Without claiming that all officials follow all of the rules all the time, Wright provides illustrations of two categories of rules: pervasive and particularistic. Pervasive rules guide the behaviour of nearly all local officials. Particularistic rules are specific to one particular arena of local action, namely obtaining grants. Included amongst the pervasive rules are the following:

1. Maximize federal and state dollar revenues and minimize local taxes.
2. Maximize local flexibility and discretion while minimizing federal/state controls, regulations, guidelines, etc.
3. Accept the IGR Law of Gravity: 'The buck drops down to local officials'.
4. Maximize public participation and satisfaction while implementing an effective and efficient grant program ... .
5. Maximize respect and gain the confidence of other IGR participants by using the following sub-rules:
    a) demonstrate honorable and decent intentions;
    b) develop evidence of capable personnel and program performance; and
    c) package and 'sell' agency (or unit) accomplishments
6. Mobilize marginal resources ... .
7. Retain and enhance political/organizational 'clout' by:
    a) using favorable constituencies and contacts;
    b) neutralizing hostile interests;
    c) trying not to appear greedy; and
    d) husbanding power as if it were a finite currency ... .

The particularistic rules are subdivided into grant-seeking and grant-approval activities. Included amongst the grant-seeking rules are the following:

1. Know the regulations ...
2. Know the application deadlines ...
3. Know what the grantors want to hear ...
4. Know where the dollars are ...
5. An alternative rule to number 4 is: Know who knows where the dollars are.
6. Know the best matching ratios or formulas.

Finally, Wright identifies a number of intergovernmental games. These include: 'Liberty' or 'don't tell us how to spend *your* money'; 'Equality' or distribute the dollars evenly; 'Fraternity' or programme professionals stick together; 'We are all in the same mess' or appeals for intergovernmental cooperation and coordination; 'Turf protection' or defending the programme against all attacks and challenges; 'Project perfectionism' or defining grant requirements so strictly that only angels can qualify; and 'End Run' or bypass the states (ibid., pp.188–93). He concludes by describing IGR in the United States as 'a huge, complex building that is under continuous construction and reconstruction' (ibid., p.329).

Simply describing the current rules of the game, however, is insufficient. It is equally important to explore the origins and question of, and changes in, such rules. One important change in IGR in the United States in recent years, it is claimed, is the centralization of government and 'the transformation of the American polity into virtually a unitary system' (Beer, 1978, p.9; see also Reagan, 1972; Lowi, 1978). Wright's analysis clearly suggests that any such argument is an oversimplification. He points to the intensification of competition between governments in the 1960s and 1970s and especially the conflict between programme specialists and public interest groups (Wright, 1978, pp.61–3). This development has been analysed in some detail by Beer (1978, p.9) who argues that 'more important than any shifts of power or functions between levels of government has been the emergence of new arenas of mutual influence among levels of government. Within the field of intergovernmental relations a new and powerful system of representation has arisen.'

Of the new centres of influence which have arisen within government, two have been particularly important over the past decade: technocrats and 'topocrats'. The former are the professional programme specialists whose growing influence, Beer (ibid., p.18) suggests, has 'promoted the rise of a counter-vailing power in the form of the intergovernmental lobby'. This lobby encompasses the Public Interest Groups or the 'Big Seven': the Council of State Governments, the National Governors Conference, the National Conference of State Legislatures, the National Association of County Officials, the National League of Cities, the US Conference of Mayors and the International City Managers Association. Beer describes these bodies as 'topocrats', meaning that their authority is derived from place and thus they promote or defend the interests of a particular geographical area (see also Beer, 1973, 1976). The interests of technocrats are narrowly defined by their professional expertise. The interests of topocrats are not so constrained. They speak for a range of interests which are limited only by the geographic area of the governmental unit from which they are drawn. In other words, technocrats are sectional groups, whereas topocrats speak for the public interest of their area. This development has added a new system of representation to American federalism.

The analysis of intergovernmental relations has moved away from a focus on legal forms to a concern with the processes of interaction between various units of government. The studies discussed in this section have described these interactions as bargaining, as diplomacy and as a game. However, each of the models discussed has emphasized different features of the relationships. Some have focused on financial resources, whereas others have stressed the decisive influence of political resources. Some concentrate on the analysis of the process, whereas others stress the effects of this process on policy outcomes. Some describe and analyse the role of the politician, whereas others stress the role of the official. Finally, some examine the existing rules of the game, whereas others have explored changes in the rules and, in particular, the conflict between technocrats and topocrats and the ways in which this conflict has changed the system of representation in federal structures of government. But to what extent are these models and themes relevant to the analysis of British IGR? What are the strengths and weaknesses of the models?

Conclusions

Perhaps the clearest way to assess the contribution that the IGR literature could make to the analysis of British IGR is to demonstrate the similarities and the differences with the literature on interorganizational analysis.

The ways in which the two bodies of literature correspond are relatively obvious. The complexity of the environment of organizations is a theme common to both. In the interorganizational analysis literature, other organizations are a key component of the environment of any organization, and the environment and the organization permeate each other. The discussion of federalism demonstrated that the environment of any unit of government was similarly complex. Analysis could no longer be limited to the more prominent, traditional federal institutions. This shift of emphasis is consistent with the argument that the study of central–local relations in Britain cannot be limited to the links between central departments and local authorities. The complexity of the institutional environment must be recognized and analysis extended to include all public sector organizations.

An organization does not simply face a complex environment. It is also dependent upon elements in that environment. This essential interdependence of organization is a major theme of the interorganizational analysis literature. To modify Donne's phrase, 'no organization is an island'. The IGR literature similarly lays considerable emphasis on interdependence. The growing recognition of the interdependence of levels of government in federal systems led to the slippery slope of the 'spectrum of federalism'. However, the IGR literature seldom defines and explores the bases of interdependence. There have been few attempts to measure variations in the degree of dependence. Rather, there has been a preoccupation with describing and analysing the bargaining between levels of government. Nonetheless, the theme of interdependence is also relevant to the analysis of British central–local relations. Local authorities are not 'mere agents' of central government. They are political systems in their own right, with the capacity to resist central demands. Moreover, central government is dependent upon local authorities for information, for expertise and for the implementation of policy. Thus any discussion of the relationship must recognize that it can range from dependence to independence and that there are many bases to the relationship.

Given that any organization faces a complex environment composed of organizations upon which it is dependent, it has to find ways of managing that dependence. Both bodies of literature emphasize the bargaining which takes place between organizations. This process can be described in terms of strategies for managing uncertainty, or as a 'game', or simply as a bargaining model: whichever way, it is clear that the relationship is rarely one of control. There are 'rules of the game' known to the participants and within these rules 'strategies' are employed. And the success of participants in employing strategies depends upon their relative power. This power is not a function purely of the resources they possess, but also of the ability to translate the potential of these resources into desired results through the use of strategies. Moreover, no actor is ever powerless. The terms 'dependence' and 'interdependence' are employed to emphasize the reciprocal nature of relationships. Similarly, the emphasis on bargaining is a recognition of the fact that no actor is ever wholly controlled. And although the current literature on British central–local relations does not systematically describe the rules of the game and the strategies, it is clear that bargaining does take place.

The IGR and the interorganizational analysis bodies of literature have a number of common themes, therefore, and are capable of illuminating the 'forgotten dimensions' of British intergovernmental relations. Both stress the complex linkages between organizations, their interdependence and the importance of bargaining – all elements conspicuous mainly by their absence in both the conventional wisdom on, and the conventional critique of, British central–local relations. However, the existence of common themes does not mean that there are no significant differences between the two bodies of literature. For example, although both stress the rules of the game, strategies and bargaining, the interorganizational analysis literature rarely explores the consequences of this behaviour for policy and policy making. It tends to be concerned with variations in the patterns of interaction for their own sake. Important though this difference may be, it is not the most significant. Three aspects of the IGR literature are especially noteworthy.

First, there has been far more attention paid to the context of interactions. The interorganizational analysis literature emphasized the 'figure', or the interactions of organizations but it did not explore the 'ground', or the values and distribution of power supporting these interactions. As Simeon's analysis of Canadian federalism makes perfectly clear, contextual factors are the prime determinants of such interactions.

Second, various analyses of federal systems have emphasized the importance of political factors. This emphasis can take the form of an analysis of the effects of the party system on federalism; or the effects of a shared electorate on central government and units of government decision; or an analysis of the distribution of political resources between the unit governments. In each case, analysis is not limited to exchanges of personnel, equipment, clients, information or money.

Finally, a small number of studies have explored changes in the rules of the federal game. Much of the interorganizational analysis literature tends to take the rules of the game as 'given', thereby failing to recognize the ways in which the bargaining process can be skewed in favour of one set of participants. But the IGR literature, as in the case of Beer's (1978) analysis, has moved beyond bemoaning the trend towards centralization and explored the emergence of new arenas of influence.

Although it would appear that the IGR literature offers a valuable corrective to many of the weaknesses in the interorganizational analysis literature, it too has limitations, especially when applied to Britain. First, many of the models which have been developed are country-specific. Thus, Simeon's (1972) analysis of the context of interactions is specific to the Canadian system. It is not related to, for example, a theoretical characterization of advanced industrial society. Similarly, many of the discussions of the rules of the game treat the constitution of the particular federal system as a major source of such rules, often drawing no clear distinction between the formal rules and the behaviour of actors. Such limitations make it difficult to translate the details of the analysis into the British context.

Second, although there is an explicit awareness of the interdependence of the various units of government, the bases of that interdependence are rarely explored in any detail. Rather strikingly, there is a tendency to emphasize financial transactions between governments as the measure of interdependence. However, as the interorganizational analysis literature demonstrates, it is possible to identify a number of bases, not just the oft-cited financial basis. The consequence of this omission is that the IGR literature does not analyse the relative power of the various units of government by comparing their resources or by assessing the extent to which one resource can be substituted for another. Just as the interorganizational analysis literature tends to provide formal models of patterns of interaction without locating them in an analysis of the distribution of power, so the IGR literature tends to discuss broad trends in relative influence of units of government without specifying the bases of variations in their relationship.

Finally, and to return to the second major objective of this chapter, although the context of the relationships and changes in the rules of the game have been discussed in the IGR literature, the relationship between this level of analysis and the micro level of the games and strategies of actors has not been clearly articulated. Two criticisms should be noted. First, at the specific level, the effects of changes in the distribution of power on the 'game' are not fully explored. For example, topocrats may have emerged as a countervailing power to the technocrats, but to what extent do they still need to legitimize their own interests and actions by appeal to scientific–professional standards? Conversely, to what extent does the power of the technocrats depend upon their ability to find support for their programmes amongst a broader constituency than their professional community and bureaucratic actors? Second, at the general level, only a cursory attempt is made to explain the change in the distribution of power. The emergence of topocrats may be a reaction to the power of the technocrats, but why have the latter come to exercise such influence? As argued in Chapter 1, there have been a number of attempts to explain change in advanced industrial societies, but these macro theories, whether of post-industrial society or of corporatism, do not inform the analysis of changes in intergovernmental relations. However, although the literature on IGR may not have succeeded in reconciling the analysis of the context with the analysis of interactions, it has demonstrated that the link between ground and figure is an essential component of any attempted explanation of interactions and their consequences for policy making. The problem of the relationship between levels of analysis is by no means peculiar to the study of IGR and it will be discussed in more detail in Chapter 5.

At the outset, it was suggested that the IGR literature would not provide any ready-made model for the study of British IGR. However, it does suggest a number of themes which could be pursued in the British context. Recent work on the United Kingdom as a 'multinational state' emphasizes that the 'visual filter' of IGR can add to our understanding of British government.[4] The emphasis on bargaining, strategies and rules of the game appears potentially fruitful. Recognition of the variety of institutions involved in British IGR seems long overdue (but see Page, 1978; Madgwick and James, 1980; Birrell, 1978). An exploration of the relative importance of professional groups as against the national institutions of local government is particularly apposite given recent attempts to change the relationship between central departments and the national institutions. But these comments and suggestions for future avenues of exploration are in themselves inadequate. Future research needs to be guided by a framework of analysis and it is precisely such a framework that the IGR literature does not provide. It can suggest items any framework will have to encompass; it provides warnings about potential pitfalls for the unwary; however, the task of constructing a framework remains to be done.

Notes

1   An alternative starting point for the discussion of IGR is the concept of decentralization. However, the term is fraught with difficulty. Not only is it treated as a value in its own right which, it is claimed, promotes democracy, but it is also seen as a variable for comparing administrative structures. Even if the realms of normative political theory are foresworn, the problems do not cease because there are few indices capable of distinguishing between the various degrees of centralization and decentralization. There is a marked tendency to concentrate either on definitional questions or on describing particular forms of decentralization rather than comparing and explaining variations. This chapter concentrates on specific forms of decentralization in advanced industrial societies of which federalism is one of the most conspicuous examples. In so far as the concept of decentralization is employed it is treated as a variable. Units of government range along a continuum from centralized to decentralized: there is no one state of affairs which can be labelled 'decentralized'. The seminal review of the literature on decentralization is Fesler (1965). For an excellent discussion of the values served by decentralization, see Maass (1959). For attempts to construct indices of decentralization, see Sherwood (1967), Clark (1974), and Smith (1980).

2   The concept of 'cooperative federalism' has been often elaborated, especially in the American context. Thus we have Creative Federalism and the New Federalism. Both should be viewed as species of cooperative federalism, the major differences lying in their respective methods and views on how the partnership ought to work. As noted at the outset, this section will not discuss in any detail the workings of particular federal systems. The various species of American federalism are not discussed, therefore, because they are viewed as variants of the one theory: cooperative federalism. For a detailed discussion, see Reagan (1972) and Elazar *et al.* (1969).

3   A useful general survey of recent fiscal issues can be found in *The Annals* (1975), and Wright (1978, chs 4–8). On intergovernmental management, the seminal work on this topic is Sundquist (1969). He argues that 'the federal system is too important to be left to chance' (p.31). The maze of relationships and increase in the number of levels of government are said to require a coordinated approach in the form of a new regional coordinator or supradepartmental official (ibid., p.273). Management is the key to transforming a jumble into a system of relationships. This view has been sharply challenged in Wildavsky (1975). He defends the conflict and bargaining of the present system and points to the difficulties of planning and coordination in a pluralistic political system. See also Landau (1969); and Ostrom (1974).

4   An invaluable bibliography on this theme is Pollock and McAllister (1980). Useful discussions of Britain as as a multinational state can be found in Birch (1977) and Rose (1976).

5   A Framework for Analysis

Introduction

At the beginning of Chapter 1, it was argued that the subject of central–local relations seemed to be divorced from more general issues in the study of government. In addition, the existing theories or models of the relationship were seen to be inadequate, ignoring a number of important dimensions. However, it is possible both to provide a framework of analysis and to relate the study of central–local relations to broader issues by drawing upon a wider range of literature than is normally associated with the subject. Both the sociologists who explored interorganizational linkages and the political scientists who have explored intergovernmental relations have produced models or theories capable of illuminating the interactions between British governmental units. These bodies of literature are limited, however, in a variety of ways. In this chapter, the attempt is made to construct a framework of analysis which draws upon the interorganizational analysis and IGR literature but avoids some of their more obvious weaknesses. Most important, the framework does not focus solely upon the interactions between central and local government: the figure. Drawing upon corporatist theory, the analysis of the interactions is located within a broader context: the ground. More specifically, the changing role of government and its effects on the rules of the game will be explored.

Before turning to these particular tasks, however, a number of preliminary issues must be touched upon. The first issue concerns the distinctions between frameworks, analogies, models and theories. This area is a contentious one in the social sciences and there is limited agreement on the definition of the various terms (for a discussion of these problems and further references, see Ryan, 1970, ch.4). The framework presented here is a systematic inventory or classification of elements to be explored in the study of central–local relations. From this definition, it does not follow that the framework contains no explanatory statements. At various stages, explanations for variations in both the patterns of links and in the behaviour of various actors in central–local relations will be suggested. This lack of specificity is unavoidable, for two reasons. First, there is a paucity of research upon which to base detailed explanations and, second, 'Generating a theory involves a process of research' (Glaser and Strauss, 1967, p.6). The reader will not find a series of hypotheses for testing or refutation. 'Grand theory' (such as systems theory) with its hypotheses deduced from general axioms can become a futile exercise. Either attention becomes distorted onto trivial issues because they can be measured or the theory becomes the (mandatory) padding which prefaces the case studies but otherwise bears tangentially upon the substance of the research. The framework offered here is of a far more modest nature. Its rationale lies in its ability to focus attention on key features of central–local relations; to suggest, in as precise and systematic a way as current research permits, how the interactions between the two levels of government vary; and to provide an interpretation of the existing form(s) of such interactions.

Finally, it must be emphasized that the scope of the framework has been deliberately restricted. First, it does not purport to explain policy making at either the central or the local level. Intergovernmental relations are but one of many influences on policy. This chapter focuses on the intergovernmental aspects of policy making. In so doing, it is not claimed that such links are the most important influence on policy, only that they are important for some policies. Second, the exposition is cast in terms of central–local relations narrowly construed. As argued earlier, the network of intergovernmental relations is far broader than central–local relations. However, for ease of presentation, the narrower focus has been adopted. The framework could be extended to cover the range of public sector organizations and to compare the component parts of the system of intergovernmental relations.

Figure: the Analysis of Interactions

That aspect of the framework concerned with the analysis of interactions and the effects of interactions on local discretion contains five propositions:

1   Any organization is *dependent* upon other organizations for *resources*.
2   In order to achieve their *goals*, the organizations have to exchange resources.
3   Although decision making within the organization is constrained by other organizations, the *dominant coalition* retains some discretion. The *appreciative system* of the dominant coalition influences which relationships are seen as a problem and which resources will be sought.
4   The dominant coalition employs *strategies* within known *rules of the game* to regulate the *process of exchange*.

5   Variations in the degree of *discretion* are a product of the goals and the relative power potential of interacting organizations. This relative power potential is a product of the resources of each organization, of the rules of the game and of the process of exchange between organizations.

The remainder of this section discusses these propositions and their application to the study of central–local relations in more detail.

Dependence and Resources

Central to the analysis of the relationship between the organization and its environment is the concept of power–dependence. To repeat Thompson's (1967, p.30) definition, an organization is dependent upon another organization '(1) in proportion to the organisation needs for resources ... which that element can provide and (2) in inverse proportion to the ability of other elements to provide the same resource'. And dependence is the obverse of power. Thus a local authority is dependent upon a central department to the extent that it needs the resources controlled by the department and cannot obtain them elsewhere.

The power–dependence concept is employed in preference to the concept of power for a simple but nonetheless important reason. Many discussions of power treat it as a zero-sum phenomenon. In other words, a central department can only increase its power at the expense of a local authority. But it is possible that two interdependent organizations could both increase their power. As Talcott Parsons (1969, p.280) concludes: 'though under certain specific assumptions the zero-sum condition holds, these are not constitutive of power systems in general, but under different conditions systematic "extensions" of power spheres without sacrifice of the power of other units is just as important a case'. By employing the power–dependence concept, the intention is to focus attention on the reciprocal nature of power relationships. No matter how great the power of a central department over a local authority, it is still dependent to some degree on that local authority.

The advantages of this formulation of the relationship between an organization and its environment are threefold. First, the term 'environment' is no longer treated as a residual category covering everything 'outside' the organization. It refers solely to those other organizations with which a focal organization interacts. Second, complexity is given an explicit meaning. It refers to the number of other organizations and the scale refers to the number of other organizations and the scale of interaction. Finally, it identifies the bases of the power–dependence relationship between organizations; that is, resources.

The availability, distribution and substitutability of resources underpin the power–dependence relationships between organizations; these aspects are central to understanding the relative power of interacting organizations. The term 'resources' is defined broadly to encompass all those means for supplying the needs of public sector organizations. In the context of central–local relations there has been a considerable emphasis on the effect of financial resources on the relationship. This view of the resources available to both central departments and local authorities is too narrow. At a minimum it is possible to identify four other resources: constitutional and legal, hierarchical, political and informational. Even this listing is incomplete. Given the existing research and the subjective nature of resources, it is only possible to note some of the more obvious examples. Future research into central–local relations may well identify additional resources, such as task and technological resources and physical resources.[1] Moreover, the five resources discussed below may be capable of further subdivision: for example, constitutional–legal resources could be subdivided into generic and specific responsibilities.[2] Whatever the defects of the current list, it does have the advantage of drawing attention to the range of resources which can underpin the interactions of central departments and local authorities.

1 Constitutional–legal resources: the mandatory and discretionary powers allocated between local authorities and central departments by statute and constitutional convention.
2 Hierarchical resources: the authority to issue commands and to require compliance conferred by the position of an actor in an organizational hierarchy. Although the authority to obtain compliance will have a legal basis, hierarchical resources are treated as analytically distinct from constitutional–legal resources in order to emphasize the supervisory element in the relationship between centre and locality. This element can become routinized and elaborated to such an extent that the legal basis becomes a poor guide to the actual position. For example, the circulars issued by central departments may have no specific statutory basis but they may also be seen as legitimate interventions and as a means of central supervision.
3 Financial resources: the money raised by a public sector organization from services provided, from taxes levied (or precepted) and from borrowing.
4 Political resources: the access to decision making in other government units bestowed on elected representatives by political office, the legitimacy deriving from the fact of election and the right to build public support.
5 Informational resources: the information *and* expertise possessed by

actors. This resource can be organized in many ways but, in the context of central–local relations, the most notable examples are the professional groups in local government and the civil servants of central departments.

It should not be thought that the above resources will be employed in isolation from each other. In any particular interaction, a local authority or central department may well deploy a number of resources. Thus a professional group ostensibly providing technical information may also act to further its own values and interests. Such complexities do not invalidate the distinctions. Unless a range of resources is identified in the first instance, there is no way of exploring the bases of any interaction.

Finally, it is worth noting that the concept of power–dependence has the advantage of admitting that local authorities and central departments may be dependent upon each other to different degrees in different circumstances. Without denying that financial resources may be crucial in central–local relations, the framework recognizes the sheer variety of possible relationships. The resources required by central departments and local authorities are multifarious and this leads to complex patterns of power–dependence within the network of relationships. Local discretion (see below) can be viewed as a multidimensional concept and a local authority dependent along one dimension can have a high degree of discretion along another. Thus a financially dependent authority is not necessarily lacking in political or informational resources.

To this point, the discussion has focused on defining resources. It is also necessary to analyse resources in terms of the amount (or their availability and distribution), in terms of scope (or their substitutability) and in terms of means (or the strategies for managing relationships). A few examples will suffice by way of elaboration.

In the first instance, it is clear that there are differences between local authorities, and between central departments, in the availability and distribution of resources. For example, the Layfield Report demonstrates that local authorities differ markedly in their constitutional–legal and financial resources. Moreover, for individual services, the Report identifies the varying mixture of discretionary and mandatory powers and the differing degrees of precision with which powers are allocated between central and local government. In other words, central departments differ in the extent and precision of their controls over local authorities (Layfield Report, Annex 9 and Annex 12). Similarly, there are inequalities in the distribution of political resources. For example, not all local authorities are politically controlled and, in these circumstances, party channels of communication will be unavailable to councillors.

There may be inequalities in the distribution of resources but it does not necessarily follow that these inequalities are cumulative. The fact that a local authority or a central department lacks one resource does not mean it lacks others. One resource could be substituted for another. For example, a central department lacking the constitutional–legal resources to prevent (or encourage) a specific local initiative can attempt to get its way by withholding (or supplying) financial resources. Conversely, a local authority which has been refused financial resources can attempt to reverse this state of affairs by embarrassing the central department. Press and television reports on the adverse consequences of the centre's decision may lead to the decision being reconsidered.

At this juncture, the various resources have been defined and it has been argued that they are distributed unequally and that one resource can be substituted for another. The availability, distribution and substitutability of resources will affect the choice of means by a central department or a local authority for regulating its relationships. Before examining the various strategies in central–local relations, however, it is necessary to explore why a local authority or a central department 'needs' some resources and not others.

Goals

The second proposition states that the goals of a central department and of a local authority will determine which resources are needed. A local authority which wants to build council houses will have to raise the capital for such a development. This 'goal model' of organizations has been much criticized. It is argued that only individuals, not organizations, have goals – the problem of reification – and that formal statements of goals are useless guides to actual behaviour – the problem of formalism. However, these problems are not insurmountable. Organizational goals can be seen as the product of an internal political process of negotiation and bargaining between groups. Out of this process there will emerge a dominant coalition with an agreed set of temporary goals. Over time, however, goals are multiple, conflicting and changing. In this way, *formal* statements of the organization goals are replaced by an emphasis on identifying the *actual* goals of specific *groups* within the organization as they change over time (see pp.37–40 for a more detailed discussion and the appropriate references).

Goal setting is a constrained political process. The dominant coalition's discretion is limited not only by past decisions and its relations with other groups within the organization but also by the need to establish domain consensus, and by the goals and decisions of other organizations. Thus a central department may view a local authority's goals as 'illegitimate' and deny it needed resources. As a result, the local authority will have to negotiate its goals, or the claims it makes for itself in terms of the services it intends to provide and the population it intends to serve, with the central department and establish agreement or consensus about the scope of its activities and access to needed resources: domain consensus (see Thompson, 1967, p.26). There are some obvious examples of domain consensus, or lack of it, in central–local relations, including subsidized bus fares and rents for council houses.

Goals as defined above, therefore, are general stances or frameworks to guide decisions. Decisions are choices between specific, alternative courses of action. The concepts of goal and decision differ also in that only the former are statements about future or preferred domains. As John Friend (1977, p.40) has noted, decisions are acts which pass into history once carried out. Accordingly, decisions made within the context of broad, even vague, goals translate these goals into specific actions. In this process, decisions can elaborate and reformulate the original goal. Past decisions can certainly limit a local authority's or a central department's freedom to set new goals or even to elaborate existing ones. Thus a local authority and a central department must take account of each other's current goals and of both their own past decisions and those of the other organization. The dominant coalition is not writing on a clean slate. Options will have been foreclosed or slanted in certain directions. Past commitments and deployment of resources will limit today's ability to commit and deploy resources.

Dominant Coalitions and Appreciative Systems

Although goal setting is a constrained process, the response of the dominant coalitions to these constraints is not that of a parking meter to a 10 pence piece. The dominant coalitions will only perceive some relationships as problematic and negotiate with some departments over its goals. Such perceptions can differ markedly between decision makers even when they face what is ostensibly the same problem. They may disagree about the definition of the problem, its importance, the ways of solving it and the likely consequences of the various alternatives. The 'appreciative system' of the decision maker influences the goals pursued, perceptions of what is a problematic relationship and the definition of the resources required (see Vickers, 1965, ch.2; Young, 1977).

The concept of appreciative systems refers to that combination of factual and value judgements which describe the 'state of the world' or 'reality'. It is a record of past goals and decisions – the accumulated wisdom of a central or local department or its 'departmental philosophy' (Bridges, 1971, p.50) – and a general map for understanding and steering a course through the environment. Three components or dimensions of appreciative systems can be identified: interests, expectations and values or ideology. 'Interests' refers to the stakes of individuals in the organization, a stake commonly expressed in terms of demands for retaining or increasing control over the resources of the organization. 'Expectations' refers to the behaviour expected of an individual in a particular position within the organization by himself and by others. 'Values' refers to the most general evaluative standards used by the decision maker to interpret the environment and his relationship to it. In practice, of course, these components of the appreciative system are interwoven (for a more detailed discussion of these concepts, see the next section).

Although there are many difficulties in exploring the various facets of the appreciative systems of government actors (for a constructive review of the difficulties, see Young and Mills, 1980), the concept is important for understanding central–local relations. For example, it may be possible to explain why so many local authorities *accept* central intervention in terms of the expectations of local decision makers; that is, they do not expect action on their part to have any effect on a central department and, as a result, they simply implement the central department's policy.

The relationship between central departments and local authorities is not solely determined, therefore, by the resources of the various participants. It is also affected by the goals and perceptions or appreciative systems of the participants. Nor are these the only influences. The control of needed resources by a central department will only make it relatively more powerful than a local authority if those resources are deployed effectively. In other words, the discussion of resources has been a discussion of the relative power *potential* of central departments and local authorities. It is necessary to explore the process of exchange between centre and locality in order to extend the analysis beyond a discussion of potential power.

The Process of Exchange, Rules of the Game and Strategies

The preceding pages have drawn upon the (admittedly diffuse) literature on the sociology of organizations. In examining the process of exchange between central departments and local authorities, this particular literature is less helpful than that on intergovernmental relations. Whereas the former tends to emphasize the bases of interactions, the latter more commonly focuses on describing and analysing the process of interaction. Thus a number of studies have emphasized the bargaining or diplomatic relationship between levels of government (see pp.63–71). To avoid the specific or narrow connotations of the terms 'bargaining' and 'diplomacy', the term 'process of exchange' is used to cover the variety of forms which interactions between central and local government can take. Accordingly, bargaining can be viewed as that specific form of exchange involving concessions by one participant for resources controlled by the other.

It has been argued that the degree of discretion of participants in central–local relations is a product of the goals and decisions of each level of government and of their relative power in terms of resources. However, this relative power remains only potential power unless the resources are effectively deployed. Such effective deployment is affected by both the rules of the game and the process of exchange between the two levels of government. Rules of the game are the less formal but no less important rules which 'largely define the institutions of society ... they set the approximate limits within which discretionary behaviour may take place' (Truman, 1951, pp.343–4). Thus 'There emerges complicity among ... groups based on the sharing of mutual experience and complementary interests and on adherence to the same collective norms' (Crozier and Thoenig, 1976, p.551).

There is one obvious reason for emphasizing that rules of the game exist in British central–local relations: the fact that they have never been studied. And the lack of research means that it is difficult to identify examples of such rules and their effect on discretionary behaviour. However, two examples can be tentatively offered. First, it can be argued that there is a rule asserting the value of local democracy or local self-government. In fact, Mackenzie (1961, p.5) has argued that 'local self government is now part of the English constitution'. The rule is considerably vaguer than such explicit legal rules as *ultra vires*, but it is not without importance. It requires that the rights and duties of local authorities be respected and any derogation of these rights and duties will be met with an outcry. Thus Crosland has suggested that ministers believe the ringing phrases about local democracy and, at one and the same time, hate it when local authorities pursue policies diametrically opposed to those of the government of the day (Boyle *et al.*, 1971, p.171). Such an ambivalent or schizophrenic response is one way of recognizing the existence of the rule.

The second possible example can be labelled the rule of consultation. Thus, for a given policy initiative, local authorities have a right to be consulted, by central government before the policy becomes law. Quite clearly, local authorities are not always consulted, but it is not uncommon in these circumstances for protests to be made to the responsible minister. Breaches of a rule are often the clearest indicator of its existence.

A number of other possible rules could be identified, but the exercise becomes increasingly speculative. It is perhaps more important to stress both that such rules do exist and that there is considerable scope for research designed to identify them and to describe their application, adjustment and decline.

The key characteristic of the process of exchange between central and local government is the strategies of the participants. The term 'strategies' refers to the means employed by either a central department or a local authority for imposing upon the other level of government its preferences concerning the timing of, the conditions for, and the extent of the exchange of resources. Unfortunately, there is no existing classification of strategies which can be applied to the relationship between central and local government. There are, of course, a number of studies which identify strategies employed either in other governmental systems or between private sector organizations (see p.47). These include such obvious strategies as forming a coalition, cooptation and confrontation, as well as the less obvious, such as the use of supra-organization and appeals to legitimacy. It is also possible to identify examples of strategies being used in central–local relations. Thus central government, through its control of constitutional–legal resources, is able to determine precisely its relations with local authorities. Such a move can be described as a strategy of 'authoritative allocation' (Benson, 1975, pp.244–5) and the reorganization of local government provides a clear example. The search for money from the European Community by local authorities is an example of the use of a supra-organization (Hull and Rhodes, 1977 pp.49–52). Finally, appeals to legitimacy, or claims that central government broke the rules of the game, can be found in the reactions of local authorities to the reorganization of local government.

Neither central nor local government is wholly free of constraints in this choice of strategies. The amount of resources available to a local authority will affect its choice of strategies. A local authority with considerable resources may well have more scope to choose amongst the available strategies than one with limited resources. Similarly, the more limited the opportunities for substituting one resource for another, the less the scope for choosing amongst available strategies. And both of these statements presuppose that the dominant coalition of the local authority perceives that the relationship is a problem and decides that it can do something to influence the central department involved. Finally, it is possible that the variety of strategies employed will be affected by the nature of the problem. If there is little agreement between a central department and a local authority, relations could be both dynamic and conflictual, with both sides employing a variety of strategies and expending a considerable amount of time and energy managing the relationship.

In brief, it is plausible to suggest that strategies are employed in central–local relations and that the existing literature can be used to provide a checklist of possible strategies. It is not possible, however, to document in any detail the process of exchange between central and local government.

Although strategies are the key feature of the process of exchange, they are not the sole feature. At least two others can be identified: personalities and the number of units. 'Personalities' is an elusive concept but it cannot be omitted from the analysis of central–local relations. Exchange is a question not just of available strategies but also of the details of their deployment. The timing of interventions and the ability to anticipate the moves of the other side will be influenced by the experience, skills and commitment of individuals. Individual appreciation of tactics can vary greatly. Accordingly, 'personalities' has been included in the analysis to stress that individual abilities influence the process of exchange between central and local government (see pp.64 and 66).

It can also be argued that the relationship will be affected by the number of units involved. Thus, irrespective of resources, strategies or personalities, the larger the number of participants, the more complex the process of exchange, the greater the constraints on participants and the more difficult it will be for any participant to attain his desired outcome.

To this point it has been argued that the discretion of each level of government is influenced by the goals, decisions and relative power potential of the other. In turn, their relative power potential is a product of the resources, the rules of the game and the process of exchange. Finally, the process of exchange is influenced by the resources of the participants, strategies, personalities and the number of units. In brief, each level of government is constrained by the other and, consequently, discretion has to be negotiated. It now remains to consider the concept of discretion in more detail.

Discretion

Studying the outcomes of the relationship between central and local government is important if anything is to be concluded about the relative power of the participants. The analysis of the bases, amount and scope of power–dependence tells us about the relative power potential of the participants. The analysis of the means for regulating power–dependence relations only tells us about the relative power of participants if we can infer something about the results of employing the resources. It is preferable, however, to explore directly whether differences in the bases or the means bring about different results (Dahl, 1969, pp.83–4).

It is possible to identify a number of different types of outcome. For example, one could explore changes in the structure of interactions: that is, changes in their size, frequency, density, compactness and diversity. However, this section focuses on the effects of variations in central–local relationships on policy making or, more specifically, on changes in the degree of discretion in policy making.

The concept of discretion has already been distinguished from the broader concept of local autonomy. It has also been limited to the interactions between public sector organizations. The concept can now be defined more precisely as 'the room for decisional manoeuvre possessed by a decision-maker' (Jowell, 1973, p.179) in the context of interactions between public sector organizations. A local official or a civil servant has discretion, therefore, 'whenever the effective limits on his power leave him free to make a choice among possible courses of action or inaction' (Davis, 1969, p.4). In this definition, discretion is a matter of degree and even a local authority subjected to the closest supervision by a central department will have some degree of discretion. Nor should it be thought that the limits on decision makers are solely legal in origin. As the preceding analysis should have made clear, there are a range of constraints. Thus a local authority is subject to *ultra vires* and this limits its discretion. But even where its actions are *intra vires*, discretion will be limited by financial, hierarchical, political and informational constraints. Moreover, constraints can be self-imposed. The dominant coalition of the local authority may not realize it has room for manoeuvre or it may decide not to take advantage of whatever discretion it has.

There are further problems with the dependent variable of discretion in policy making. The term 'policy making' is an elusive one. It is possible to identify various stages in the policy-making process. For example, Herbert Simon (1960, p.2) distinguishes between the intelligence, design and choice stages, and to this one could add, at a minimum, the stages of implementation and review. There is, however, no agreed characterization of the stages of the policy process (for an alternative conception, see Agger *et al.*, 1964, p.40). Once the various stages have been distinguished, there is the problem that, in practice, they tend to merge. The process of implementing a policy may elaborate and even reformulate the original policy design. It can be difficult to identify where design ends and implementation begins (see Social Science Research Council, 1979, App.II. pp.11–26 for a detailed discussion). Finally, it is difficult to draw firm distinctions between a policy, a decision and a goal. Often no distinctions are drawn and there is a marked tendency to use the terms interchangeably. For Ira Sharkansky (1970, p.1) policies are simply 'actions taken by governments'. Raymond Bauer reserves the term 'policy' for decisions 'which have the widest ramifications and the longest time perspective' and notes that the description of a particular course of action as a policy 'is somewhat dependent on the perspective of the individual who views the event' (Bauer and Gergen, 1968, p.2). Moreover, many discussions of the policy process and of policies treat these terms as synonyms for goal setting and goals. In fact, many discussions of policy making adopt a 'goal model' of public sector organizations (see, for example, Quade, 1976, pp.20, 33–4, 83–101).

In the absence of any agreed convention on the definition of policy and the stages of the policy process, each study adopts the definition best suited to its purposes. A distinction has already been drawn between goals and decisions (see p.83 above). For the purpose of this study, goals and policies can be treated as synonyms. Thus policies can be viewed as the claims a local authority or a central department makes for itself in terms of the services it intends to provide and the population it intends to serve. Decisions are choices between specific, alternative courses of actions.

It should now be clear that discretion in policy making is a complex dependent variable. It involves the exploration of variations in the degree of discretion at the various stages (however delineated) of the policy-making and decision-making processes. Attention cannot be limited to the initiation of major policies. For example, it is relevant to explore the degree of discretion of local authority in the (ostensibly) routine decision making associated with the implementation of a policy. A central department may severely limit the discretion of local authorities at the intelligence and choice stages of policy making, but local authorities may have considerably more discretion at the design, implementation and review stages. Nor should it be assumed that a local authority or a central department has discretion in decision making simply because it seems to be a more detailed, or less controversial, process than that associated with setting goals and policies.

Although the literature on central–local relations provides examples of discretion (or the lack of it) at various stages of the policy-making and decision-making processes, these variations have not been systematically related to variations in the attributes of participants. Local authorities have considerable discretion in the implementation of some major policies, but it is not clear why this is the case. Is it because they have a monopoly of the relevant expertise? There are also examples of the central control of local decisions, but it is not always clear why such control should be exercised – tree inspection, for instance (Expenditure Committee, 1977, p.1085) – or even if it is exercised effectively. Unfortunately, therefore, the discussion has to remain at a general level.

Existing research may not suggest detailed explanations of how variations in central–local relations affect policy making, but it is possible to identify a number of questions which could be profitably explored in order to clarify the relationship. To begin with, many discussions of central–local relations adopt a 'top-down' model of policy making: that is, goals are set up by a central department and implemented by a local authority. The above discussion suggests that it is equally important to explore the reverse situation – the redefinition of a policy or goal in the process of implementation – if we are to perceive the full scope or limits of local discretion.

Second, it would appear to be important to explore in some detail the concept of 'policy' or 'goal'. It is possible that central–local relations are composed of a series of discrete policy areas each with its own distinctive characteristics. For example, the education policy area might have completely different characteristics from those of housing and, as a result, there may be marked differences in the degree of discretion available to the participants in the two areas. In such circumstances, it would not be possible to proceed on the assumption that central policies had similar characteristics and to focus on variations in relationships and degrees of discretion. Rather, one would have to systematically compare both different policy areas and their respective relationships.

It is inadequate, of course, simply to describe the differences between the policy areas. It is also necessary to explore why these differences occur. For example, the differences between the education and housing policy areas may well stem from the greater professionalization of the former. Because of the prominence of the professional in education, the link between centre and locality may be a functional one: that is, between official counterparts in the two levels of government. If such a professional policy community exists, it may not be relevant to explore variations in discretion between the two levels of government. Rather, the variations to be explored would be those between policy communities and between the professionals and the 'rest', irrespective of the level of government.

And this discussion of variations in the degrees of discretion of the two levels of government emphasizes that the topic is not being explored solely because such variations are intrinsically interesting. The problem of central–local relations cannot be exclusively defined in terms of central control of local expenditure. It is more accurately described, to reintroduce Bell's terms, as the problem of the accountability of bureaucracy in post-industrial society (see pp.8–11). In other words, the decisive power in modern society lies with bureaucracies and their managers, with political control becoming less and less effective. No-one regulates central–local relations except the participants. Thus, in French central–local relations, Crozier and Thoenig (1976, p.556) argue that the participants are primarily concerned to defend their interests and privileges in a closed and secret game. In exploring discretion in British central–local relations, it is equally important to relate the analysis of interactions to the broader context of the power of bureaucracies. Are the participants in the policy communities accountable or, as in France, is the system closed, with any constraints being self-imposed? An analysis of the 'ground' of central–local relations is essential for any attempt to explain the patterns of interaction.

Ground: the Distribution of Power, Rules, Interests and Values

The framework for the analysis of interactions has been described as a power–dependence framework and, like many other approaches to interorganizational analysis, it focuses on power as resources. As argued earlier, such a focus begs certain key questions about the rules of the game, the distribution of resources and the interests and values sustaining the rules and the distribution of resources. Although the framework includes all these concepts, it does not explain the origin of the rules, it takes the distribution of resources as given and it treats values and interests as intraorganizational phenomena. It does not, therefore, explain changes in patterns of interaction. In order to provide such an explanation, it is necessary to link, explicitly, the micro-level analysis of interactions to a macro-level analysis of the changing role of government. Recent developments in the theory of corporatism, allied to the earlier discussion of organizational power (see pp.48–50), suggest the form of such linkages.

There are two problems in applying the theory of corporatism to the study of central–local relations. First, the theory comes in a great many versions and much of the discussion is at a level of generality which does not suggest any immediate points of contact with the study of central–local relations. Second, in so far as the theory has been used to analyse governmental policy, it has been concerned with economic policy, industrial policy and industrial relations. When, as in Winkler's (1976; 1977) case, the theory is applied to British government and encompasses administrative changes, there are a number of fundamental weaknesses in the analysis (see p.8). This section raises a series of questions about central–local relations derived from the corporatism thesis. It does not present yet another revision of corporatist theory. Rather, the object is to specify in some detail the ways in which the power–dependence framework needs to be extended if it is to provide an explanation of changes in central–local relations.

For this purpose, Schmitter's (1979, p.13) 'ideal-type' definition of corporatism is particularly useful:

> Corporatism can be defined as a system of interest representation in which the constituent units are organized into a limited number of singular, compulsory, non-competitive, hierarchically ordered and functionally differentiated categories, recognised or licensed (if not created) by the state and granted a deliberate representational monopoly within their respective categories in exchange for observing certain controls on their selection of leaders and articulation of demands and supports.

Schmitter is not suggesting that any governmental system possesses all these characteristics. He is concerned to establish the extent to which a system is developing these characteristics. And a number of the weaknesses found in other variants of corporatism are avoided by the emphasis on institutional and empirical characteristics in this definition. He does not limit corporatism to a particular ideology or set of values. He does not suggest 'that corporatist associations will be the only constituent units of the polity – completely displacing territorial entities' (ibid., p.44). His distinction between 'societal' and 'state' corporatism avoids the problem of limiting corporatism to the situation in which the various interests are created by and are dependent upon the state. In addition, Schmitter's definition of pluralism is virtually the antithesis of that for corporatism. Thus, in a pluralistic system, there is an unspecified number of competitive, voluntary interests; they are not hierarchically ordered; they are not licensed by the state; and they have no monopoly of representation (ibid., p.15). It is the comparison of corporatism and pluralism which makes Schmitter's approach particularly useful.[3] Some variant of pluralism is commonly employed in the analysis of British government and politics. In assessing the extent to which British government is developing the institutional and empirical characteristics of corporatism, one is assessing, at one and the same time, the extent to which the rules of the game and the distribution of resources are changing.

Finally, in common with most corporatist theorists, Schmitter (ibid., p.24) relates corporatism to its social context:

> corporatization of interest representation is related to certain basic imperatives or needs of capitalism to reproduce the conditions for its existence and continually to accumulate further resources. Differences in the specific nature of these imperatives or needs at different stages in the institutional development and international context of capitalism, especially as they affect the pattern of conflicting class interests, account for the difference in origins between the societal and state forms of corporatism. (See also Schmitter and Lehmbruch, 1979, pp.63–94)

To this 'macro-hypothesis', he adds a number of specific imperatives, such as concentration of ownership, competition between national economies and expansion of the role of public policy. In brief, Schmitter's theory of societal corporatism retains the virtues identified earlier – the focus of the interdependence of organizations, the power of the state and the broad socioeconomic context – but it avoids the problems arising from stressing a particular ideology and the directive role of the state.

The next step is to apply the theory of societal corporatism to the study of central–local relations. The various points are in the form of questions because the objective is *not* to argue that Britain is a corporate state but to compare the pluralistic, power–dependence framework, with its emphasis on intergovernmental bargaining to the corporatist model and identify the ways in which the rules of the game and the distribution of resources might be changing.

Pressure Group or Network?

The literature on central–local relations has tended to focus on the activities of either individual local authorities or local authority associations. But this ostensibly unexceptional focus requires some important assumptions. It implies that the pattern of interactions between central and local government involves an unspecified number of units, and that the behaviour of a unit can be explained solely in terms of its characteristics, such as membership or internal organization. Although individual local authorities can act as 'institutionalised pressure groups' (Scarrow, 1971), it is possible that the above assumptions handicap any attempt to explain the behaviour of the various units of government. For example, only a limited number of units may be able to participate. Most important, the behaviour of any one unit may depend on this pattern of interactions with other units. The size, frequency, diversity and density of interactions with all other units, especially if there is any continuity in these characteristics, can affect interactions with any one unit. In other words, any unit of government is a member of a network and its behaviour is a product of its characteristics and the characteristics of the network. Such an argument may seem remarkably banal to anyone familiar with the literature on interorganizational analysis. However, a focus on the networks within which individual units of government are embedded is an essential first step if other aspects of the corporatist thesis are to be explored.

Function or Community?

A common feature of definitions of corporatism is the emphasis on functionally differentiated interest representation or 'corporations'. The form of such functional differentiation in central–local relations is not, however, self-evident. The overwhelming bulk of the literature on corporatism focuses on economic and industrial policy and, in particular, on the two corporations based respectively on capital and labour. Such a focus is unduly restrictive when discussing corporatist trends in central–local relations. A different and wider range of interests needs to be considered. In this context, the distinctive features of a 'corporation' are shared interests and decision making removed from the informal democratic, institutional framework. Functional differentiation is not limited, therefore, to any particular interest. Two forms of differentiation need to be considered: policy communities and a national community of local government.

Interactions of the networks could be structured by policy area or function and, consequently, it may be possible to identify 'policy communities' or 'personal relationships between major political and administrative actors – sometimes in conflict, often in agreement, but always in touch and operating within a shared framework. Community is the cohesive and orienting bond underlying any particular issue' (Heclo and Wildavsky, 1974, p.xv; see also Hogwood, 1979, pp.18–42). In other words, local authority departments providing a particular service have regular contacts and a shared framework with the corresponding central department or section thereof. In all probability such policy communities will not be limited to the relevant departments of government at the various levels of government. They will also be composed of the affected professional associations and other interest groups. As a result, a comparison of the roles of units of government may be of less importance than a comparison of 'public' and 'private' actors *within* a policy community.

An interest in a particular policy area is not, however, the only shared interest of local governments. Each type of local authority has some shared interests and all types of local authority have an interest in the preservation of local government. Accordingly, it is relevant to ask if there is a 'national community' of local government based on the local authority associations and their various joint bodies: collectively referred to here as public interest groups (see p.70).

The available evidence suggests that the networks are structured as policy communities (Layfield Report, 1976, pp.82–3). However, rather than prejudging the issue, the emphasis should be placed on comparing interactions *within* each policy community between the constituent units; interactions *between* policy communities; and interactions independent of, or *across*, the policy communities. The objective is to assess the relevance of the atomistic, pluralist model of interactions rather than stipulate the form of networks.

Fragmentation or Structure?

Pluralist theory tends to assume not only that there are multiple participants in any issue but also that each participant is competing with the others. If the pattern of interactions is in the form of policy communities, such assumptions seem unwise. For example, it has been argued that the local authority associations are key actors in central–local relations. It has also been suggested that large local authorities have more influence over central departments than small local authorities (Griffith, 1966, pp.33, 528). However, such generalizations ignore the possibility that a local authority association or a large local authority may be peripheral to policy communities which are composed of a limited number of organizations. The importance of any particular unit of government could vary from policy community to policy community and the relative power potential of a unit of government may be a product not of its own characteristics but of network characteristics.

Corporatist theory also challenges the pluralist assumption of extensive competition while accepting the growing importance of some groups for policy making. It suggests that, in place of fragmentation, there is an underlying structure of interactions based on policy communities. And it cannot be assumed that there is extensive competition within or between policy communities. Agreement can be negotiated within and between policy communities or it can be imposed by central departments. In fact, a broad consensus on policy objectives or goals can be a distinctive feature of policy communities (see below).

Nor can it be assumed that the participants in policy communities are local governments or central government. It may be more accurate to talk of the relevant functionally specialized section of these organizations. Thus a local education department may have closer links with the relevant central department than with other departments in the same local authority. The basis of fragmentation is functional specialization and not type of government organizations. The distinction between 'public' and 'private' collapses and the emphasis is switched to the interdependence of a variety of organizations.[4] The contribution of corporatist theory is to raise afresh questions about the ways in which this variety is structured. And policy communities are not the only possible structural form. Two counter trends can be identified: (1), the introduction of corporate planning and management in local government can be seen as a means of countering the functional links between centre and locality; (2) it is also possible to identify two conditions under which public interest groups can play a prominent role. First, where issues span policy communities (such as finance) the public interest groups could act as 'clearing houses' or 'sub-parliaments' for individual local authorities or, in the case of the local authority associations, for other public interest groups (see Mackenzie, 1976, p.354). Second, the local authority associations could be of central importance when the interactions are limited to public interest groups; provided the contents of such interactions are complementary to the immediate interests of the affected group and do not directly affect its pre-existing links with either central departments or local authorities.

Rather than viewing central–local relations as a complex bargaining game involving many organizations, corporatist theory raises the question of whether interactions are based on policy communities or a national community. But the analysis of the structure of networks has been general and omits a number of key issues. Some of the detailed features of these network structures are discussed below.

Open or Closed?

The foregoing discussion assumes, for the most part, that the most significant interactions are interactions at the national level. Thus policy communities have been discussed as if their members were the national professional associations, national interest groups, central departments and public interest groups. However, any such community will be composed of organizations which, constitutionally, are accountable to their members and in some cases to elected representatives. Interactions are not limited to the national level.

It could be argued that each participating organization has close contacts with its membership and that this contact takes the form of briefing and debriefing national representatives. There are, of course, many forms of reporting back: for example, annual conferences, 'house' journals and regional committees. In such an 'open' organization, the more varied the interests of the membership, the greater the constraints on the leadership. However, the inability of members to hold leaders to account has often been documented (Michels, 1962). Given the available evidence on this topic in the study of central–local relations, it is perhaps more plausible to argue that, for example, the policy communities are 'closed': that is, contact between leaders and membership is limited (Isaac-Henry, 1978). And at least two reasons for this development can be identified: first, the bureaucratization of the internal structures of organizations as they grow in size; second, the pressure upon an organization from other participants in the policy community to commit itself to an agreement without continual reference back. As a consequence, the organizations with a policy community are hierarchically ordered or closed.

In the study of central–local relations, many of the organizations differ from the interest groups which are the focus of corporatist theory because they are controlled by elected representatives. As a result, the terms 'open' and 'closed' can have a distinct, second meaning besides that of links with organizational members. They also refer to the political accountability of officials to elected members (and, of course, to the accountability of elected members to the electorate). To avoid any confusion, the accountability of officials and of elected members is discussed separately below.

Representation or Intermediation?

The term 'interest group' suggests that the prime function of such a group is to represent its members, articulating their demands and protecting their interests. However, an organization, whether it be a professional association, a public interest group or a trade union, may have its own interests distinct from those of its members, may not know or articulate members' demands and may attempt to control members. In such circumstances, the term 'intermediation' (literally, 'coming between') seems more appropriate (Schmitter, 1979, p.93). Thus a closed policy community comes between local and central government: that is, the policy community or network has its own interests and advances its own proposals. Over time, each network has evolved its own approach to problems: established routines of contact, shared perceptions and values, and the stock of tried knowledge and polices are brought to bear on new problems. This shared 'appreciative system' of the network could differ markedly from that of members.[5] And, because the network or policy community contains participants from central departments it can appear to members that their organization is representing the interests of the central department rather than their interest.

Not only can policy communities appear to be separated from member interests but also they can have a monopoly of representation. This access can be granted by central departments or conceded by them, but the effect on the membership is the same: the channel for articulating their demands is not carrying out this function, and it is the only channel. The links between leaders and members cannot be reduced to a question of frequency and form of contact. Analysis must also include the content of interactions and explore the origins of a particular proposal, the interest(s) it is designed to further and its consequences. In a different context, Heclo and Wildavsky (1974, p.xvi) have argued that the consequences of community are delay, ambiguity, contradiction and self-abortion, while 'the citizens who are to be served and problems that must be met may slowly recede from view until they appear as if viewed from the small end of a telescope, distant, blurry and easily blinked away'.

The extent to which local government has been or is being absorbed into Whitehall's 'village community' is not only pertinent in the era of the Consultative Council on Local Government Finance but also raises the question of whether the much-vaunted increase in central control is control by statute and circular, or indirect, social control of a more pervasive nature. If the premises of decisions are shared premises, removing the myriad of detailed controls will change little.

Sectional or Public Interest?

At various junctures, reference has been made to the interests of policy communities. The concept of interests had a number of distinctive features when used in connection with public sector organizations. Many such organizations are perhaps best described as hybrid pressure groups because, in addition to their pressure group, bargaining activities on behalf of their members' or the policy communities' sectional interests, they are also part of the structure of government. Thus one of their distinguishing features in pluralist theory is their integrative function or the need to accommodate a range of interests: to act both as broker and as arbiter of demands in the public interest. Accordingly, public sector organizations both represent their sectional interest and promote the public interest as they perceive it, subject to the check of political accountability.

Some support for this distinction can be found in a few studies of the local authority associations. Cross (1954) suggests: 'The broadness of [the Association of Municipal Corporations – AMC's] interest tends to make its wholly common interest less intense. It speaks for County Boroughs on the one hand and on the other for a large section of the population living largely under county government. Perhaps this generality of interests adds to its responsibility.' And the ability of the AMC to speak for a large section of the population rather than its own sectional interest is legitimated by its representative character: 'it is representation having its roots in the elective principle, with a line of accountability, and having its ultimate source of authority in practically speaking the whole of the adult population of England and Wales' (Cross, 1954; see also Isaac-Henry, 1980).

In contrast to the pluralist view, corporatist theory does not define the role of government as that of broker. Rather, the emphasis falls on the extension in the scope of government intervention, the necessity of the state's regulatory and integrative tasks to sustain the condition of capital accumulation, and the process, the autonomy of the state to meet its own needs for growth and power (see pp.5–7). A detailed discussion of this conception of the role of government is less important at this particular point than the consequences which follow from the extension of government power. At least three consequences can be identified.

First, with the extension of its tasks, government increasingly resorts to delegated and mediated enforcement. Thus local government is bypassed by the allocation of functions to quangos: that is, central government favours indirect, concealed forms of administration. In addition, potential dissent is forestalled by the cooption of the affected parties. In other words, the legitimacy previously accorded to local authorities by the fact of their elected, representative nature no longer guarantees access to decision making and, increasingly, they have to take second place to the functionally differentiated, closed policy communities.

Second, public sector organizations are vulnerable to central intervention. It may be, as Shonfield has argued, that corporatism has developed more slowly in the United Kingdom because of 'the traditional British view of the

proper relationship between public and private owner [in which] the two ...
are thought of as utterly distinct from one another'. But such attitudes offer
little protection to local government (Shonfield, 1965, p.99). As Sharpe
(1979, pp.42–3) has argued:

> Given the massive growth of government over the last half century or so, the
> reduction in the number of organisations with whom a central government has to
> deal is an important objective whether these organisations are 'private' pressure
> groups or 'public' local authorities. In this sense, all central governments have a
> very strong interest in the aggregation of groups and interests within the State
> *and a particularly strong desire to aggregate the units of local government.*
> (Emphasis added)

Finally, but closely related to the first two points, the political accountability of public sector organizations has declined. As noted earlier, the
policy communities can be closed in the sense of not being accountable to
the electorate. Not only are functions allocated to non-elected bodies but the
sectional interests of policy communities dominate any attempts at defining
a broader public interest. The responsibility for decisions now lies with the
policy communities, but they are not subject to the constraints of parliamentary accountability. The legitimacy of policy no longer resides in its approval by elected representatives but in its scientific, rational basis.

Technocrat or Topocrat?

In theory at least the official at either the central or local level is accountable
to the politician for his actions. It has been accepted that the official can
play a major role in policy initiation but nonetheless his proposals must gain
political approval and remain subject to political veto. With the growth in
importance of policy communities, however, such checks are of decreasing
relevance. Thus Heclo and Wildavsky (1974, p.2) reject the distinction
between minister and civil servant, preferring to describe both as 'political
administrators' bound together by 'kinship' and 'culture'. In other words,
the participants within a policy community have a common 'appreciative
system' which serves both to bind them together and to protect them from
other policy communities and from the various mechanisms of political
control. In Bell's (1976, pp.128–9) terms, political conflict is now predominantly between the professional or political technocrat and the populace,
and the locus of this conflict is large-scale organization.

However, the rise of the technocrat has not necessarily been unchallenged.
Beer (1978) has argued that the rise of the technocrat has promoted a new
system of representation in the topocrats (see pp.70–71). To return to an
earlier theme, therefore, it is necessary to ask whether there is a national

community of public interest groups acting as a countervailing power to the policy communities. In applying these concepts to British central–local relations, care has to be exercised in the use of the terms 'professional' and 'technocrat'. They are not synonyms. Although the term 'professional' tends to imply sectional interests, it is worth emphasizing that in British local government professional groups are centrally involved in the development of services and enjoy quasi-official status. They are not confined necessarily to a particular policy area. They can provide information and expertise to public interest groups and central departments. To employ a somewhat florid metaphor, they are one of the tentacles of leviathan. Of all the professional associations, it is not clear how many play a role spanning a number of policy areas. It is important, therefore, to determine the extent to which the roles of the professional associations are a product of differing definitions of the scope of their knowledge and interests. Are they limited to a particular policy community (technocrats) or do they span a number of such communities (topocrats)?

Finally, the rise of the technocrats raises a number of issues about the basis of legitimacy of policy decisions. Habermas (1971, p.105) has argued:

> the development of the social system seems to be determined by the logic of scientific–technical progress. The immanent law of this progress seems to produce objective exigencies, which must be obeyed by any politics oriented toward functional needs. When this semblance has taken root effectively, then propaganda can refer to the role of the technology and science in order to explain and legitimate why in modern societies the process of democratic decision-making about practical problems loses its function and 'must' be replaced by plebiscitary decisions about alternative sets of leaders of administrative personnel ... it can also become a background ideology that penetrates into the consciousness of the depoliticised mass of the population, where it can take on legitimating power.

The notion of 'best professional practice' provides a persuasive, acceptable rationale for policy decisions. But to what extent is the power of the professional limited by 'the cantankerousness of politics'? Certainly, there have been examples where professional advice has been effectively challenged, with high-rise building and motorway construction providing the more spectacular examples of recent years. The power of policy communities may not lie, however, in their ability to influence the outcomes of particular issues.

Issues or Agenda?

It is virtually axiomatic in pluralist theory that power resides in the ability to determine the outcome of particular issues. As argued in the discussion of organizational power (see p.48), power can also reside in the rules of the game which may favour one or more of the participants. With the development of societal corporatism and the growing importance of policy communities, there are a number of changes in the rules of the bargaining game.

First, recognition by the government, extending to the licensing of participants, and the compulsory nature of participation become features of the game. Obviously, political necessity can dictate that a particular group or organization be accorded recognition but, and this is the key point, participation itself ceases to be voluntary. Whether because of the pressures of the situation, licensing, cooption, legislation or professional accreditation, it is not possible to withdraw from the game. For example, it is difficult to see how the local authority associations could have refused to participate in the Consultative Council on Local Government Finance.

Second, if each policy community has a distinct appreciative system, it has, in fact, an agenda of 'relevant' issues and problems. Only some matters will be deemed appropriate ones for decision and, to the extent that domain consensus has been negotiated between policy communities, the issue scope of the policy community will be highly restrictive. It is perhaps too easily assumed that organizations are continually negotiating with each other. It is equally plausible to suggest that they are primarily concerned to avoid each other. Such conflict avoidance presupposes a restricted domain and a limited agenda of issues simply because an extensive domain and a broad issue scope increases the possibility of contact with other organizations.[6] But irrespective of whether an organization avoids conflict or negotiation, it is clear that power resides in the ability to control the agenda and that such controls stem as much from the expectations, interests and values of the participants as from deliberate manipulation.

Finally, with the increasing scope of government intervention and the interpenetration of the public and private sectors, there is a growing acceptance of the necessity of such intervention in the interests of national economic management. It is, therefore, no longer necessary to justify state intervention itself. It is only necessary to demonstrate that this particular intervention is required in the interests of economic management. The issue at stake concerns only the form of the intervention. To the extent that local authorities accept the legitimacy of such arguments by central government, they have considerably limited their own room for manoeuvre and conceded considerable scope for policy initiatives to central departments. The point emerged clearly in the evidence given by the Society of Local Authority Chief Executives (SOLACE) to the Expenditure Committee. Sir Stanley Holmes, President of SOLACE, commented:

accepting that the overall control is essential in the interests of the national economy, and accepting that, I suppose, Parliament cannot bring itself in relation to many services to allow them to drop below a minimum level, having said that, one would have thought there was a case for greater liberation, greater freedom of decision, inside the broad framework.

However, later in their evidence, the Chairman of the Expenditure Committee pointed out that this acceptance of central government's responsibility for fixing the total monies allocated to local government implied that they also accepted 'how the money is rationed out, which means how the rate support grant formula is fixed'. It may be desirable for local government 'to make decisions on the functions and the duties which Parliament has given them' once 'the financial resources for local government have been fixed' but, and this is the crucial point, any such decisions only represent discretion at the margin: 'the broad framework' could perhaps be best described as a strait-jacket' (Expenditure Committee, 1977, pp.737, 741, 744).

Resources or Control?

In pluralist theory, the resources of the participants are of key importance in explaining their relative power potential. However, corporatist theory suggests that the relative power of central and local departments cannot be explained solely by reference to their respective resources. Power also lies in the rules of the game. At various points, it has also been suggested that legitimating ideologies or values are similarly important to understanding the relative power of participants in central–local relations. Three aspects of power as the 'mobilization of bias' have been identified: the appreciative systems of policy communities, the scientific–rational ethos and the inevitability of state intervention. Without repeating earlier discussions, a focus on power as mobilization of bias suggests that control can reside *not* in the distribution of resources but in the prior acceptance that someone has the right to take that decision. Appeals to the scientific ethos, to best professional practice and to the imperatives of the economic management all serve to justify decisions whether or not those decisions are in the interests of affected parties. However, it cannot be assumed that the various aspects of values discussed above are complementary, compatible or unchallenged. Belief in the value of local democracy still prevails. The values of policy communities may conflict with those of a national community. There is little or no evidence on this aspect of power in central–local relations. Corporatist theory does suggest, however, that the ever-growing state intervention is leading to ever-burgeoning state control. Central government increasingly selects the leaders and regulates the demands of groups. It could be argued that one of the major functions of the Consultative Council on Local Government Finance is precisely such social control. The basis of such control may lie in central government organized monopoly of legitimate violence (Schmitter, 1979, p.21) or it may lie in the consensus on goals and procedures between central and local government in which the latter accepts that the control of local expenditure is an essential prerequisite of effective national economic management. Whatever explanation is preferred, corporatist theory highlights the importance of studying the ways in which legitimating ideologies are a source of power for some participants.

The discussion and comparisons of pluralist and corporatist theory were designed to identify the ways in which the power–dependence framework needed to be extended. Building upon the earlier discussion of organizational power, it has been argued that corporatist theory is an extremely useful tool for exploring changes in the rules of the game and in the distribution of resources. Although the institutional and empirical characteristics of corporatism cannot be found in Britain, nonetheless the sharp, even exaggerated, contrast it provides with pluralist theory highlights the changes that could take place in central–local relations. In summary form, the major trends predicted by corporatist theory include the emergence of closed or hierarchical, non-competitive, compulsory, functionally differentiated policy communities with their own interests, expectations and values or legitimating ideologies. They have a concomitant ability to control the policy agenda and resist attempts to hold them to account by either members of constituent organizations. They have a monopoly of representation in the policy area and in exchange they are subject to controls in the selection of leaders and they are expected to regulate both their own demands and those of members of constituent organizations. Accordingly, the influence of individual local authorities and of public interest groups is severely constrained. Territorial politics are bypassed. The research task is clearly one of exploring the extent to which these characteristics are a feature of British central–local relations. To repeat a point made at the outset, the purpose of this section is not to argue that Britain is a corporatist state but to provide benchmarks against which to assess changes in central–local relationships. In the final section of this chapter, the pressures for change and the implications of these pressures both for the power–dependence framework and for future research will be assessed.

Concluding Discussion: the Rationality of Ambiguous Confusion

The sharpness of the contrasts between pluralist and corporatist theories, and the marked changes that the latter indicates for central–local relations, do not thereby render its various predictions implausible. As Schmitter (1979, p.15) points out, there is considerable common ground between the two theories:

> (1) the growing importance of formal associational units of representation; (2) the persistence and expansion of functionally differentiated and potentially conflicting interests; (3) the burgeoning role of permanent administrative staffs, of specialised information, of technical expertise and, consequently, of entrenched oligarchy; (4) the decline in the importance of territorial and partisan representation; and (5) the secular trend toward expansion in the scope of public policy and (6) interpenetration of private and public decision arenas.

And drawing upon Shonfield's work, Schmitter also suggests that the role of government in fostering full employment, promoting economic growth, controlling inflation, regulating business cycles, regulating working conditions, resolving industrial disputes and protecting business men and organizations from the adverse consequences of economic risk all serve to foster corporatist trends (ibid., pp.28–9). That such trends can be identified in British government and are closely related to the economic context seem unexceptional conclusions. Of greater importance is the precise form of the relationships between the economic context and the role(s) of government. Or, to rephrase the issue for the study of central–local relations, 'To what extent is the changing economic context of British government changing the relationship between central and local government?'

It is possible to identify some of the predicted changes in at least incipient form. The functional nature of the links between centre and locality has been noted on a number of occasions (see, for example, Sharpe, 1979, pp.45–7). Conversely, the creation of the Consultative Council on Local Government Finance and the increase in the size of the local authority associations (see Isaac-Henry, 1980) can be viewed as a strengthening of the role of public interest groups and of the national community. More recently, the role of officials in, and the secrecy surrounding, the RSG negotiations has been described (see Harris and Shipp, 1977; Taylor, 1979). And, of course, the theme of the Layfield Report was the lack of accountability in the relationships between central and local government (Layfield Report, 1976, chs 4 and 5). In other words, central–local relations could be said to display corporatist features. Within particular policy areas, the links between central and local government are rational in that actors at the two levels of government have common interests in the development of that policy area. However, the links between such policy communities are ambiguous and, when the system is viewed as a whole, as in the case of public expenditure decisions, the pattern of relationships is confused. There is competition not only between the various policy communities but also between the policy communities and both public interest groups (especially the local authority associations) and those central and local departments charged with responsibilities spanning policy areas. And paralleling Crozier's analysis of French central–local relations, the participants may have a vested interest in a system of confused and ambiguous relationships (see, for example, Hepworth, 1977, p.16). But to what extent is this system stable and what are the pressures for change?

The Layfield Report predicted a growth in central accountability if positive steps were not taken to strengthen local accountability (Layfield Report, 1976, p.74). Equally, corporatist theory would predict an intensification of corporatist features with ever-growing state intervention to manage the economy. When I completed this book in March 1980, the Conservative government's proposals to reform the grant system also suggested that central government was attempting to strengthen its ability to control local expenditure (SOLACE, 1980). Assuming that the system of ambiguous confusion is transitional, two questions are of paramount importance. First, to what extent is the emergence of corporatist features in central–local relations a function of changes in the British economy? Second, what are the consequences of these changes for the power–dependence framework?

Unfortunately, current knowledge about central–local relations does not permit specific answers to the questions. There is an abundance of generalizations about the role of the state in capitalist society, but few studies documenting the interrelationship between economic change, state intervention and the consequences for particular policy areas and institutional arrangements. Unsatisfactory though the conclusion may be, it is only possible to urge that future studies of central–local relations should not focus on particular issues but explore the evolution of particular policy areas over a substantial period of time and attempt to determine the relationship between, and relative importance of, exogenous and endogenous change. Similarly, it is not possible to specify in detail the consequences of corporatist trends for the power–dependence framework. However, it is possible to identify, in general terms, two important consequences. The power–dependence framework focuses on the resources and strategies, ignoring changes in the rules of the game and the distribution of resources. Corporatist theory, as argued in the previous section, points to important changes in the rules of the game and stresses the importance of legitimating ideologies in constraining the arenas within which resources can be deployed. In other words, by exploring the changing role of government, corporatist theory permits an analysis of other facets of power besides power as resources.

It was argued at the beginning of this chapter that the intention was to develop a systematic inventory or classification of elements to be explored in the study of central–local questions. Although the framework includes a number of suggestions which attempt to explain variations in the patterns of interactions and in behaviour of actors, of its very nature it poses more questions than it answers. Accordingly, it is perhaps time to draw together the various questions and indicate which areas of research are of prime importance.

First, the framework directs attention to the question of why the relationship between central and local government varies through its focus on the bases of the power–dependence relationship. It asks whether financial resources are the crucial determinant in the relationship. Can the other resources compensate for financial weakness? How significant are the other resources in central–local relations? For example, although it is clear that there is contact between national and local politicians, we do not know how extensive it is or how important it is for policy decisions involving both levels of government. The same questions can be posed for each of the resources.

Second, the framework poses the question of how the relationship varies. The agent and the partnership models answered the question virtually by definition. The framework admits that the relationship can vary from a high degree of discretion to a high degree of dependence and directs attention to the conditions underpinning these variations. It points to the variety of channels of communication between the two levels of government and raises questions about the relative importance and efficiency of these various channels. It also suggests that any satisfactory exploration of the way in which the relationship varies must analyse the various stages of policy making, the characteristics of different policy areas and the differences between relationships involving policy and goals and those involving decisions.

Third, it raises a series of questions about the way central departments and local authorities manage their relationships with each other. To what extent do participants recognize and work within agreed rules of the game? To what extent do public interest groups comprise a national local government community and provide individual local authorities with an effective central negotiating and bargaining capability? To what extent do participants employ strategies to manage their relationships? To what extent do participants compete for discretion in designing and implementing policies? In addition, within these general areas, a number of specific questions are raised. For example, on the rules of the game, attention is focused on identifying the rules and describing how they are applied in specific situations. A similar range of questions can be raised about the use of strategies.

Finally, the framework focuses on changes in the role of government and raises a series of questions about changes in the rules of the game and in legitimating ideologies. It also stresses the importance of a historical perspective relating changes in central–local relations to changes in the economic context of government.

Given the defects of the literature on central–local relations discussed earlier, it can be argued that the framework offers the opportunity to repair some of the more glaring omissions. The questions raised are in those areas not currently explored by the literature. Moreover, these questions are not a wholly idiosyncratic list of 'interesting' issues. The framework poses a series of related questions only some of which are specific to the study of central–local relations. Herein lies the rationale of the exercise and, it is hoped, the claimed utility of the framework will be demonstrated by future research.

A major objective of this book has been to provide a framework for the analysis of central–local relations, but it was not the only objective. It has also attempted to show that the subject can illuminate facets of British government of more general concern to social scientists. More specifically, it has been argued that the study of central–local relations is a fruitful locus for the analysis of corporatism, of the power of the profession in government and for exploring the problems of accountability created by the interdependence of a multitude of complex governmental bureaucracies. Without repeating the earlier discussions of these topics, it is worth emphasizing that these are not peculiar or unique features of central–local relationships but a widespread phenomenon in British government. Future research into central–local relations need not adopt a traditional legal–institutional approach and ignore these issues. In fact, to omit the power of professionals and the accountability of bureaucracies from the study of central–local relations would be to ignore two of its most important features. Bare-footed empiricism in whatever form will contribute little to our understanding of intergovernmental relations. The vocabulary on intergovernmental relations in Britain needs to be expanded and this book presents one attempt to develop a different vocabulary. Independently of any merits of the framework offered here, the need to ground the study of intergovernmental relations in a macro perspective remains paramount.

Notes

1 Task and technological resources refer to the technology essential to tasks (such as computers) and task refers to the workflow activities of an organization. Dependence arising from the need for task and technological resources can be found in local government: for example, refuse collection and refuse disposal. However, examples in the area of central–local relations are difficult to identify. Physical resources refer to the land and buildings controlled by a local authority. Again, it is difficult to identify examples

of the way the control of such resources affects central–local relations. Both these resources seem relevant to county–district relations.

2   John Friend has suggested that a central department may treat local authorities as a class of similar organizations, justifying its actions by referring to its general responsibility to a wider constituency than individual local authorities. On the other hand, a local authority may resist being treated as part of a broad class of organizations and seek one-to-one links with the central department, justifying its actions by referring to its specific knowledge of, and responsibilities for, the local area. Letter to the author, dated 4 September 1978. Quoted with permission.

3   Other authors who make similar comparisons, many of whom also draw on Schmitter's work, include Crouch (1977; 1979), Beer (1980), McFarland (1979), Richardson and Jordan (1979).

4   In contrast to Marxist theories of the state, corporatist theory recognizes the variety of governmental institutions. See p.12, note 1.

5   Although it is unusual usage, the term 'members' also encompasses individual local authority departments. Thus the local department may participate in a policy community, but it does not articulate or even share the interests, expectations and values of either fellow local departments or the elected council.

6   I am grateful to Renata Mayntz for drawing my attention to the importance of conflict avoidance. Personal commmunication.

PART II
FROM INSTITUTIONS, TO
POLICY, TO INDIVIDUALS

6 'Power-Dependence' Theories of Central–Local Relations: a Critical Assessment

Introduction

The publication in 1979 of the report of the Social Science Research Council's Panel on Central–Local Government Relationships initiated a major research programme. This research was to be guided by the 'Rhodes framework' (as it came to be known). The purpose of this chapter is to revisit the framework and assess its strengths and weaknesses after three years of experience in its application and development.[1]

I assume a passing familiarity with the initial formulation[2] and concentrate, therefore, upon critical assessments of the framework and future theoretical developments. To anticipate the major conclusions, it will be argued that the framework failed to distinguish clearly between levels of analysis, focused on relationships rather than policy content and paid insufficient attention to the context of intergovernmental relations (IGR). The bulk of the chapter will elaborate and illustrate these arguments.[3]

It was always my hope that the framework would be viewed as a starting point which invited critical assessment and stimulated further theoretical inquiry. In my discussion of the several critiques, I have tried to identify common themes which will serve this positive purpose of identifying theoretical developments rather than to defend my approach in all its details. There are five broad sections: the historical dimension to intergovernmental relations in the United Kingdom; the power of central government; the micro-level analysis of the interactions between central and local actors; the meso-level analysis of the patterning of interactions and the policy process; and the macro-level analysis of the causes of change in the policy process.

Initially, and for the purposes of exposition, it is important to distinguish the various levels of explanation, but equally it will be important to discuss the relationships between them.

A Critical Appraisal

The Historical Dimension

Bulpitt has argued that 'a major problem has still to be resolved, namely: "What do we mean by the term central–local relations"?' He continues:

> for the Panel, and ultimately it would appear for Rhodes, central–local relations is defined first in terms of intergovernmental relations, and then redefined more narrowly as the relations between central departments and local authorities.
> This approach has two obvious, and in my view unfortunate, consequences. First, as Rhodes admits, the broad issue of local autonomy cannot be tackled and the narrower concept of 'local discretion' has to be substituted... Secondly, there is no way such a narrow scenario can be used to provide answers to the broad general questions in which the Panel constantly expresses an interest. (Bulpitt, 1980)

In place of the framework, Bulpitt (1983, p.1) argues for a focus on 'territorial politics' or:

> that arena of political activity concerned with the relations between the central political institutions in the capital city and those interests, communities, political organisations and governmental bodies outside the central institutional complex, but within the accepted boundaries of the state, which possess, or are commonly *perceived* to possess, a significant geographical or local–regional character.

A number of important consequences follow from this definition. First, it avoids the narrow scope of a focus on central–local relations. Second, it is a central perspective focusing on the resources, intentions and operations of the central authorities. Finally, a focus on territorial politics also requires an analysis of territorial development: that is, a historical perspective.

Thus Bulpitt argues that the centre has not sought extensive control of local authorities Rather, it prefers to concentrate on 'high politics' – for example, economic management – and to leave 'low politics' – for example, marginal expenditure increases for specific services – to local government and other devolved and deconcentrated units of government. In order to understand central–local relations, therefore, it is necessary to understand the changing role of government, but the framework does not admit of this kind of historical analysis (see also Jones, 1979, p.41).

If the framework betrays 'the social democrat's distaste for history', then Bulpitt's alternative displays the cavalier antecedents of the High Tory: the framework emphasized the importance of the peripheral regions and the dangers of a focus on central departments and local authorities (Rhodes, 1986). It is capable of answering broad questions, for example on corporatism and the power of the professional. It may not focus on Bulpitt's preferred general questions, although even here it would seem to offer some insights on the strategies of the centre (ibid., ch.7).

Moreover, Bulpitt's formulation is not without its weaknesses. As he recognizes, the literature on centre–periphery relations from which the focus on territorial politics is derived is inordinately diffuse. The various approaches encompass theories of territorial dependency or internal colonialism; the study of cultural or ethnic nationalism; and studies of the interactions between administrative and political elites (Tarrow, 1977, pp.18–35). In addition to the usual proliferation of definitions, it is not clear whether the phenomenon is common to all countries or just some, and there is a tendency to assume a single centre when there may be a multiplicity. In Bulpitt's own formulation, the distinction between 'high' and 'low' politics has a tautological flavour: that is, because the policy or function is local government's responsibility, it must be 'low' politics. Certainly, it is inordinately difficult to distinguish empirically between 'high' and 'low' politics. The centre's interest in such 'low' matters as public health or education is long-standing (Finer, 1957; Chester, 1981). Finally, there is a potentially misleading implication in Bulpitt's analysis that local government is but one of a series of equally important institutions which raise questions of interest about territorial politics. In the UK context (if not comparatively), local government is among the most important of such institutions and cannot be equated with the territorial structures of, for example, the nationalized industries. Obviously, it is important to recognize the range of territorial interests and it is incorrect to assume that territorial politics begins and ends with local government. But that is a far cry from relegating local government to the status of just another territorial structure.

However, Bulpitt's critique does raise a number of pertinent issues, in particular his emphasis on the centre's management strategies and on locating central–local relations (narrowly defined) in their historical context. The problem with Bulpitt's suggestions is that they are presented as an alternative to the framework when in fact they are complementary (Rose 1982). The stress on territorial politics tells us little, for example, about relationships on specific issues such as secondary reorganization, whereas a focus on specific issues – on resources and bargaining – tells us little about trends in the relationship. Bargaining between central departments and local authorities must be seen in a broader, *historical* context which encompasses the range of interests and organizations beyond the centre.

The Power of Central Government

The best and most sustained critique of the framework's treatment of central government is provided by Page (1982): 'the problems of the framework arise from the characterisation of the relationship as one of "bargaining" ... it fails to incorporate the recognition that fundamental inequalities can exist in a relationship of interdependence ... interdependence does not mean equality or even near equality'. Page accepts that the framework recognizes the inequality in their relationship, but argues that the discussion is 'highly ambiguous'. Thus, although it is accepted that the centre has the ability to define what is bargainable and what is not, the conclusion that the relationship varies from 'agent' to 'bargaining' is 'unsatisfactory'. Page (ibid. p.322) suggests that both bargaining and agency are the result of the same relationship of constitutional superiority:

> The relationship between central and local government is not so much a variety of 'different' types of relationship, but rather one relationship between a constitutional superior and subordinate in which the centre has a differential disposition and ability across different services and activities to set parameters varying in their tightness and consequently varying in the discretion they permit local government actors.

He suggests that the problem stems from the assumption in the framework that, when levels of government are embedded in complex networks, *the scope for unilateral influence upon the policy process is limited* (ibid., p.336). This assumption may be implicit but it is present and, as a result, the discussion of 'persistent asymmetry' is indeed ambiguous. In sum, although the framework recognized that bargaining was not necessarily between equals, it did not give sufficient weight to the centre's monopoly of legislative resources and its consequent ability to structure relationships with local government.

Page suggests how the framework could be modified. Drawing upon the work of Keohane and Nye (1977), he argues that relationships of interdependence are 'almost always asymmetrical' and, as a result, it is possible to talk of 'unilateral leadership'. This leadership can exercise influence in three ways: by example, by persuasion and inducements, and, most important in this context, by 'hegemonic leadership' (or structuring the rules). Such hegemonic or structural power exists when one state is powerful enough to maintain the essential rules governing interstate relations, and willing to do so. In addition to its role in maintaining a regime, such a state can abrogate existing rules, prevent the adoption of new rules that it opposes or play the dominant role in constructing new rules. (Keohane and Nye, 1977, p.44)

Structural power or changing the rules rather than adapting its own policies to existing rules is a highly apposite, shorthand description of changes in the grant system (Rhodes, 1986).

This formulation still leaves a number of unresolved problems. If the basis of structural power lies in the centre's monopoly of constitutional resources and consequent ability to change the rules, it is still necessary to explain why and how that power is exercised differentially between policy areas; the existence of compliance in the absence of central legislation; and changes in the predisposition to exercise that power over time. It is also important to specify the conditions under which bargaining takes place. Later sections of this chapter will discuss variations between policy areas and over time. At this juncture, however, it is important to enter a caveat to Page's thesis.

In attempting to correct the emphasis on bargaining, Page lays far too much stress on unilateral action. That central government can take such action is not disputed, but the unintended consequences of such action can be severe. Compliance may give way to recalcitrance. Goals in one policy area may be attained at the expense of other policy areas. The Local Government, Planning and Land Act 1980 is currently the favourite example of those proponents of the unilateral action thesis. It is a double-edged example. Rhodes (1984) has pointed out that the cuts in expenditure were service-specific and were more severe on capital than current expenditure; that total public expenditure was *not* reduced between 1979 and 1983 and that local government's current expenditure grew by some 9 per cent in real terms over the same period; that conflict between centre and locality has led to an increase in litigation; that local authorities have adopted risk avoidance strategies such as 'creative accountancy'; that Labour-controlled local authorities have not reduced expenditure but increased rates to offset grant losses; that local government cuts have increased expenditure for other government services, such as social security and national health services; and that the cuts have created problems neither intended nor desired by central government, such as the decline of the construction industry and an intensified housing shortage.

Unilateral action is not cost-free. As the costs become visible, the government can either intensify the attempt to direct local authorities or it can recognize its dependence on local authorities and employ different strategies to gain compliance. In short, there is a tension between inter-dependence and the exercise of executive authority and analysis must focus on the interaction between the two. Neither bargaining nor control is the appropriate focus even when the relationship is asymmetric.

This caveat also directs attention to the broader question of the British political tradition. Some considerable time ago, Griffith (1966, pp.506–7) pointed out:

> The two sides are not equal. The Departments are stronger and make far more of the important decisions. They promote the new laws, including those which confer new powers on local authorities. Governments are, at the political top, single party machines having party policies which they will implement. No discussion of the relationship between central departments and the local authorities is real which fails to recognise that the Government will seek to ensure that its policies are carried into effect.

Central–local relations operate in a political system characterized by a strong executive tradition and can be no more divorced from the effects of the larger system than any other facet of British government. Accordingly, Page's analysis needs to be extended beyond a discussion of executive authority to encompass other features of the British political tradition, including party politics, non-executant central departments and elite fragmentation.

The Micro Level of Analysis

Of all aspects of the framework it is the analysis of the resources of, and bargaining between, central departments and local authorities which has attracted most critical attention. And few criticisms of the framework have proved as unproductive as the several attempts to refine and redefine specific concepts. There would seem to be little point in further practice at philological gymnastics and, accordingly, only two topics will be considered: resources and the internal political process.

Resources   Resources were defined as the means for supplying the needs of public sector organizations. Their highly subjective nature and variability both over time and between issues was noted but, as Gyford and James (1983, p.27) suggests:

> It may be useful to make explicit a distinction which Rhodes leaves as implicit: this is the distinction between resources as prizes and resources as weapons. The resources which are bargained *for* may not necessarily be the same as the resources which are bargained *with*: after all, at the gaming table there is a distinction between the chips and the cards.

They argue for the utility of this distinction without insisting either that some resources are always the price – for instance, money, authority – or that the prize of one round of bargaining cannot be the weapon in another round: that is, no resource can be classed as a basis of influence for all issues over time. It is this failure to emphasize the variable, transmutable quality of resources which is perhaps the major weakness of the initial formulation of the concept.

The internal political process　In Chapter 5 (see p.89) I commented on implementation that: 'many discussions of central–local relations adopt a 'top-down' model of policy making ... it is equally important to explore the reverse situation – the redefinition of a policy or goal in the process of implementation'. This same theme was emphasized by the SSRC Panel on Central–Local Government Relationships and was subsequently developed in the research carried out by the School for Advanced Urban Studies (SAUS). While recognizing that 'exchange theory', as they characterize the framework, provided a useful starting point they also consider that it needs to be extended to include the various forms of negotiation, such as persuasion, bargaining and 'power games'. They call for a theory of bargaining tactics *and* a theory able to capture the interactions, tactics and subprocesses of negotiation that surround the act of bargaining itself. The framework may recognize the importance of negotiative behaviour but, equally, it does not analyse it (Barrett and Fudge, 1981; Barrett and Hill, 1982). The problem with a focus on negotiative behaviour, however, is that it is 'context-less'; it ignores the hard realities of politics and power, ignoring the structural limits to negotiation (Fudge and Barrett, 1981, p.263). SAUS are aware of this problem and argue for a complementary analysis of actors' interests and 'assumptive worlds' (ibid., 1981, pp.264–70). Thus a focus on the distribution of resources between actors and on the socialization of actors into certain ideologies should link the analysis of negotiative behaviour to the macro-level power–interest structure of society.

For the purposes of this chapter it is sufficient to establish the need to develop the analysis of the internal political process. However, there is one other important point. The framework has been characterized as concerned with the micro level of analysis. The above discussion suggests that this description is best reserved for the analysis of bargaining tactics and negotiative behaviour with interorganizational dependence (and resource exchange) as part of the meso-level context within which such behaviour occurs. SAUS's analysis of implementation has established the potential fruitfulness of an exploration of negotiative behaviour. It is now necessary to situate their analysis in a broader context.

The Meso Level of Analysis

Rhodes distinguished initially between the 'figure', or the pattern of interactions, and the 'ground', or the distribution of power which sustains the pattern of interactions. Corporatist theory was used to analyse the ground and this section assesses its utility for that task. And at the outset it is necessary to distinguish between corporatism as a classification of a form of state and corporatism as a theory of the state. The former, referred to here as the meso level of analysis, has the more limited scope of providing a model of government–interest group relations whereas the latter, discussed in the next section as the macro level of analysis, is a theory of power, explaining changes in the structure of British government.

Most reviews of the framework do not critically discuss the 'ground' and this lack of response to the corporatist component is significant. To raise questions about the role of central government is appropriate but it raises the further question of how the role of government has changed. The discussion of the 'ground' was an *explicit* attempt to explore this changing role. Many critics, although objecting to my discussion of the role of the centre, neither discussed the analysis of its changing role nor offered an alternative account. Such an approach stunts theoretical development. Further refinements of the power–dependence model are not of cardinal importance. This and the next section will argue that the major theoretical effort should concern the changing role of government, that is, the focus must be on the 'ground'.

One of the major exceptions to this general comment is Dunleavy's (1984) critique of intergovernmental theory. He argues that the framework is premised on substantive neopluralist theory. It is said to concentrate on explaining overall tendencies towards governmental fragmentation and decentralization. Thus governments confronted by the limits to rational policy making have increasingly resorted to professionalized policy systems. Problems are factorized and policy emerges from the interactions of administrative networks. However, the framework remains limited because it cannot explore either variations across policy areas or substantive social conflicts and it is normatively loaded, assuming 'end of ideology' views (ibid., pp.58–60). This critique requires some qualifications.

First, the organizational and technological imperatives which are said to explain the fragmentation of, and the interdependence between components of government may not provide a full explanation, but they are an essential component of any explanation of fragmentation and interdependence. Second, the 'normative loading' of the theory does not involve the acceptance of 'end of ideology' views *per se*: such a comment is a reflex response to neopluralist formulations. The theory does assert the centrality of mechanisms for the mutual accommodation of interests in advanced industrial societies but this claim is distinctly more modest than the deterministic 'convergence of interests' asserted by the logic of industrialization thesis. Third, it is not self-evident that the biases of intergovernmental theory are more disabling than the biases of alternative substantive theories. It would be preferable to specify more precisely the problems to be addressed and to focus on the relative strengths and weaknesses of the various substantive theories for analysing those problems.

Finally, it is not clear whether the problems Dunleavy identifies in intergovernmental theory are inherent to it or are the defects of particular expositions and applications. Certainly the failure to analyse specific policy areas has been noted by other critics. Hampton (1981) has emphasized the need to 'recognise the political connotations' of the analysis of central–local relations and focus on 'key questions affecting the social distribution of resources'. In a similar vein, Hill (1982, pp.111–12) argues that the framework occupies the mainstream of writing on interorganizational policy making but that 'the policy thrust of such studies has been, it seems, underemphasised'. In other words, the framework lacks policy content *but* this defect is not an inherent one: intergovernmental theory can be developed to encompass and explain policy outcomes.

Whatever the qualifications, the broad thrust of Dunleavy's critique is welcome. The emphasis on policy content and its distributional consequences, coupled with his concern for explicit substantive theory, are necessary correctives to the framework's overemphasis of organizational relationships *and* his comments offer the prospect of theoretical development.

It is doubtful whether the corporatist theory offers equal opportunities for theoretical development. In this section, the main concern is to explore the extent to which corporatism has identified a distinctive change in the pattern of interest group–government relations. For Schmitter, a corporatist system of interest intermediation has a number of distinctive features including aggregation, licensing of groups, a monopoly of representation and the regulation of members by group leaders (Schmitter, 1979, p.13). However, these characteristics are rarely found in unsullied form, a state of affairs which has prompted adjectival and definitional proliferation: for example, neocorporatism, liberal corporatism, bargained corporatism. Nor is it self-evident that the pattern of government–interest group relations identified by corporatist theory differs greatly from that contained in neopluralist accounts. Jordan (1981, p.113) has asked, rhetorically, 'Isn't it merely pluralism in a new environment?' At times, corporatism is merely equated with the institutionalization of government–interest group relations. Both empirically and theoretically, corporatism fails to provide a distinct model of government–interest group relations (Schmitter, 1980; Richardson and Jordan, 1979; for critiques, see Jordan, 1981; Cox, 1981; Marsh and Grant, 1977).

A total rejection of a corporatist theory would be premature, however. Rhodes has argued that 'policy communities' are a distinctive feature of policy making in central–local relations (Rhodes, 1986, ch.2). Relationships within these policy communities are asymmetric: the government has the capacity to constitute policy communities by controlling, for example, membership, access, the agenda and the timing of consultation. Such deliberate attempts to aggregate interests are a distinct, if not unique, emphasis in corporatist literature. Strategies of incorporation do not amount to a corporatist *system* of intermediation but, as a strategy, it is distinct from consultation or clientelism: it is a means of establishing such forms of group–government relations. It is also a prominent feature of developments in central–local relations, visible in the attempts to strengthen the associations and in the creation of the Consultative Council on Local Government Finance. To dismiss the corporatist literature as 'pluralism in a new environment' is to devalue the incidence and impact of strategies of incorporation. Corporatism has served to highlight, therefore, developments in group–government relations but without offering a distinct or unique account of these developments.

These remarks relegate the concept of corporatism to strategies of incorporation in group–government relations and rescue little from the critics. They also raise in acute form the need for an adequate metaphor of central policy processes. The choice of metaphors is embarrassingly wide. It will be argued below that the concept of 'policy communities' avoids the connotations of, for example, hierarchy and discipline associated with corporatism and yet recognizes the limited number of actors in any policy area. It does not stipulate a set of rigid characteristics rarely approximated in reality but it does recognize the changing pattern of group–government relations and orders the complex interactions of central and local actors.

The Macro Level of Analysis

It could be argued that corporatist theory presents a relatively clear statement of 'a form of state', but it indisputably presents an ambiguous 'theory of the state'. The criticism that corporatist theory offers no distinct theory of the state and is associated with a wide range of different theories is widely documented. However, its proponents have attempted to relate changes in government–interest group relations to a macro theory of socioeconomic change. An equivalent attempt is required in order to explain the changing role of government and the consequent effects on central–local relations.

The major weaknesses of the initial formulation of the 'ground' were the failure to distinguish the meso and macro levels of analysis within corporatist theory and the failure to specify the theory of the state employed at the macro level. Given the extensive use that was made of Schmitter's formulation, the macro-level explanation relied heavily on an autonomous view of the state with its monopoly of legitimate violence, with asides on the functional imperatives of capitalism: a distinctly uneasy alliance (Jessop, 1979, pp.187–8). Such implicit theorizing is intrinsically undesirable and could be described as 'unhelpful' (other critical accounts of corporatism as a theory of the state include Panitch, 1980; Westergaard, 1977)! Once this general point is established, a detailed discussion is unnecessary. The more important task is to provide an alternative conceptualization of the changing role of government: a task undertaken in the next section.

The following conclusions draw together in summary form the major defects of the framework.

- The frameworks fails to distinguish clearly between the micro, meso and macro levels of analysis and, consequently, does not adequately explore the relationship between these levels.
- At the micro level, the framework does not present an adequate account of intraorganizational political processes and of the ways in which they are related to interorganizational processes.
- The conception of 'resources' conflated resources as prizes with resources as weapons and underemphasized their subjective, volatile, transmutable nature.
- The use of corporatist theory to analyse the 'ground' failed to distinguish between corporatism as a form of state – the meso level – and corporatism as a theory of the state – the macro level.
- At the meso level, corporatism provides a rigid metaphor of government–interest group interactions which is rarely encountered in British politics.
- The conception of the role of central government does not reflect the centre's hegemonic or structural power.
- At the macro level, the explanation of the changing role of government was implicit and ambiguous.
- The framework lacked a historical dimension.
- The framework failed both to explore and to explain variations between policy areas.

This list of criticisms is extensive and the amount of theoretical reconstruction required is substantial.

Towards a Theoretical Reconstruction

The first step in rebuilding intergovernmental theory is to confront the question of whether the game is worth the candle. Are there any alternative approaches which offer more substantial research payoffs? The past decade has seen a burgeoning neo-Marxist literature on both the state and urban polices, although few such studies have been concerned with intergovernmental relations (Dunleavy, 1980a, pp.126–31). There is one notable exception to this comment: Peter Saunders' 'dual-state' thesis. This section critically reviews his approach before sketching a revised neopluralist approach.

The Dual State

At its simplest, this thesis argues that there are three significant dimensions along which national and local political processes differ: economic function, mode of interest mediation and affinitive ideology (the major sources are Cawson, 1982; Cawson and Saunders, 1983; Saunders, 1980; 1981; 1982). The state has two major economic functions, social investment and social consumption. Social investment refers to those aspects of state provision which constitute constant capital for the private sector (for example, physical infrastructure) and it functions primarily in the interests of capital. Social consumption refers to those aspects of state provision which are consumed individually by the population as a whole or by sections of it (health care and public housing, for example) and it functions primarily in the interests of sections of the population other than capital, although it may well benefit the latter. There is a tension between these two economic functions because increases in social consumption via increased taxation may adversely affect private sector profitability – referred to as a 'rationality problem'. There are three decision-making strategies that the state can employ to confront this problem: bureaucratic intervention, pluralist competition or corporatism. Saunders (1982, p.60) argues that 'there has developed a bifurcation of British politics, for while social consumption policies are still by and large resolved in the competitive arena of democratic politics, social investment has been insulated by means of the corporate bias'.

However, this development creates tensions between rational planning and democratic accountability manifested, for example, in overload in the demand for services which impairs the government's ability to manage the economy. Allied to this rationality problem there is also a legitimation crisis as state intervention and a belief in the needs and rights of citizens under-mine both private property and the market principle. Saunders (ibid., p.61) relates the foregoing distinctions to the levels of the state apparatus. Thus

> local government in Britain is typically concerned with the provision of social consumption through competitive modes of political mediation and organised around the principle of citizenship rights and social need. Central and regional levels of government, on the other hand, are typically the agencies through which social investment and fiscal policies are developed within a relatively exclusive corporate sector of politics organised around the principle of private property rights and the need to maintain private sector profitability.

There are, however, many problems with this ideal-typical schema. First, the distinction between the economic functions of the state poses intractable classification problems. State expenditures do not fit neatly into one or other category. As Clegg (1982, p.5) notes: 'the variety of interest involved, the special case of commuting, the fact that means of transport in urban areas are generally an indivisible form of support for both production and con-sumption activities create intractable problems for analysis'.

And as Dunleavy (1984, p.5) points out, education can be classified as a means of legitimation, as social investment in human capital or as a type of collective consumption and, as a result, state expenditures will be socially contingent, varying from society to society and over time. Nor is the prob-lem simply one of *a priori* classification. It also 'undermines the causal sequence of the dual state model by suggesting that institutional allocations are logically and causally prior to the differentiation of state activities into social investment or consumption categories'.

Second, functions cannot be unequivocally allocated to the different lev-els of the state apparatus. The functions of local government encompass both social investment and consumption. For example, Goodwin (1982) concluded from his study of Sheffield that the local authority actively sus-tained capital accumulation. Similarly, Martlew's (1983) review of central–local financial relationships stresses the interdependence and shared interest of central and local spending departments (Sharpe, 1984).

Third, corporatist modes of political mediation are not specific to the central–regional level. As Houlihan (1983) has argued, the existence of corporatist structures at the local level weakens the dual state thesis; and the work of Flynn (1983) and King (1983) clearly demonstrates the existence of such structures.

Fourth, the range of decision-making strategies considered is unnecessar-ily restrictive, omitting policy systems dominated by professions. Dunleavy (1984, p.77) has argued that we need to focus on the role of professions in originating, disseminating and implementing new ideas and suggests that professionalized policy systems should be seen as a fourth decision-making strategy. And if the professions are accorded importance, it raises the further problem that policy initiation in local government is *not* a response to local political inputs (pluralism) but is heavily influenced 'by professionally promoted "fashions" which are nationally produced' (ibid., p.77).

Finally, the dual state thesis is fundamentally a functionalist theory; that is, policy making is 'explained' in terms of a set of predetermined functions of the state in capitalist society. As Saunders (1980, pp.184–5) recognizes, this raises a number of problems. Thus all state interventions must presumably serve the functions of either legitimation, investment or consumption, or some combination of these three and, *pace* his earlier critiques of neo-Marxist theory, Saunders' current formulation denies that the state has distinct interests and acts to promote its own needs for growth and power. Such an 'autonomous' conception of the role of government may have its weaknesses, but the scope for such action should surely be a matter for empirical investigation, not definition, as should the range of functions performed by the state.

The 'dual-state' thesis has been discussed in some detail because it is virtually the only neo-Marxist influenced theory which has directly addressed the topic of central–local relations, But, even in the most developed form to date, theories of the local state seem flawed. There are, however, a number of important points which emerge from this account of the dual-state thesis.

First, the implicit macro-level theorizing in the initial formulation of the framework needs to be replaced by an explicit consideration of the role of government: the power–dependence model must be explicitly 'contextualized'. Second, Saunders' emphasis on the conflicting functions of the state and the importance of these tensions as a source of change is potentially fruitful. Without denying that one function is to maintain the existing socioeconomic structure, it is as important to stress the *range* of functions – regulatory, productive, allocative, legitimation, maintenance and growth – and determine empirically which are exercised in any given policy area. Third, Saunders' argument that, in performing its varied functions and managing the conflicts between them, government can deploy a range of strategies is useful. Although his typology is unduly restrictive, it provides a useful starting point for an analysis of the varied nature of state interventions. Fourth, Saunders' schema emphasizes the relationship between government services and classes and interests and does not focus on institutions or governmental process *per se*. As argued earlier, it is particularly important to extend analysis to such distributional questions. Finally, the interrelationships in Saunders' model between governmental functions, interest mediation and ideology are a valuable corrective to the institutional focus so common in the study of central–local relations. It is these general points which have to be incorporated into a reformulated neopluralist approach.

Reconstructing Intergovernmental Theory

In the course of criticizing the framework, two points of theoretical departure were noted: the meso level or the analysis of policy communities, and the macro level or the analysis of the changing role of government. This section omits the micro level of negotiative behaviour and sketches an approach to the analysis of the meso and macro levels (for a full discussion, see Rhodes, 1986, ch.2).[4]

'National Government Environment' refers to central governmental institutions and their socioeconomic environment as they affect subnational units of government (Stewart, 1983, pp.65–8). In the United Kingdom, three features of this environment have been important: economic decline, fragmentation and executive authority.

As far as economic decline is concerned, up to 1974, there was a remarkable consensus on the management of the British economy. Government intervention to promote economic growth was to provide the wherewithal for redistributive social policies and the continued expansion of the welfare state. Such Keynesian macroeconomic management policies may have suffered setbacks, particularly from recurrent balance of payments crises, but 'stop–go' policies rarely dented the consensus. The 'rate of growth' may have been relatively small compared to our major competitors but, for much of the period, there was growth. And the underlying economic trends were obscured by the rush to modernize British industry and institutions in the 1960s: the heyday of planning. The escalation of world commodity prices in the 1970s starkly revealed the weakness of the British economy. Whilst arguments reign over the causes of decline, particularly about the effects of the public expenditure as a proportion of GDP, few would dispute that the problem was compounded of high inflation, high unemployment, declining productive capacity and a lack of international competitiveness. Local government expenditure had grown throughout the 1950s and 1960s as a proportion of total public expenditure – it was the prime vehicle for the provision of welfare services – and, as a result, reduction of that expenditure became a prime objective of both Labour and Conservative governments.

It is not being implied necessarily that the expenditure on particular services was reduced. The term encompasses actual reductions in expenditure and, crucially, changes in the expectations of, and aspirations to, incremental service expansion (Stewart, 1980). This associated 'ideology of retrenchment' – the belief on the part of local politicians and officers that the size, and especially the rate of growth, of local expenditure should be curtailed in deference to central government's responsibility for, and its stated views on, the management of the economy – has become a pervasive component of local government's 'responsibility ethic' (Bramley and Stewart, 1981, p.60). This ethic has been articulated most cogently by the Treasury with support from both the 'topocratic' professions and the national community of local government.

Related to the country's fluctuating economic fortunes has been the periodic reassertion of structural power by the centre, manifested in changes to the rules of the game and in the strategies deployed to effect control of local services and expenditure. Since 1979, in particular, the 'conventional' nature of the rules has been highlighted by their abrogation. But most notably, throughout the post-war period, the centre has exercised its ability to choose between a wide range of strategies of intervention.

The government's structural power resides not only in its constitutional superiority. Majority party control of Parliament, coupled with the non-executant or 'hands-off' role of central departments, provide both the means and the incentive to the exercise of executive authority. That authority is exercised in and through a multiplicity of policy communities and the phrase 'fragmented elitism' captures both the force of that authority and the nature of its dispersion.

In terms of fragmentation, functional differentiation in British government has produced a set of professional–bureaucratic complexes, or policy communities, each of which has personnel sharing an ideology, expertise and a career structure, and spans the boundaries of government institutions, national and subnational. In sharp contrast to the usual view of Britain as a unitary state centred on a supremely authoritative body, the Cabinet, able to command both Parliament and the civil service, the centre is fragmented and executive authority is dispersed. The phrase 'central government' is convenient shorthand but potentially misleading because it accords the centre a unity it does not possess. But fragmentation and dispersion should not be treated as equivalent to decentralisation. Fragmentation refers to fragmentation at the centre. Dispersion refers to the distribution of authority between policy communities and not its redistribution away from central departments. Fragmentation *and* centralization coexist at the centre. Thus, with the extension of functional differentiation, there has been an extension of national policy programmes, the emergence of centrally defined services and standards and the movement of decision-making power from small to larger (that is, central) jurisdictions.

Key actors in this development have been the professions. The obvious example is the role of the medical profession in the National Health Service, but the list of examples is extensive (Dunleavy, 1980b; Haywood and

Alaszewski, 1980). Quite obviously, professional influence varies between policy communities and from issue to issue within a given policy community. Equally, there is the key distinction between the 'technocratic' or professional programme specialists and 'topocratic' professions or associations of chief executives (Beer, 1973; 1976; 1978). The emerging role of the latter constituted an important challenge to the more widely appreciated influence of the 'technocrats'. However, irrespective of such variations, the institutionalization of professional influence has to be seen as a key process in British policy making of the post-war period.

The consequences of functional differentiation and fragmentation are not specific to the professions or to central government. There have also been marked effects on local political elites: the channels for articulating local government interests have changed. With the increase in the complexity of the policy process and in its own dependence on other actors for the implementation of policy, the centre has sought to restrict the number of interests to be consulted for any given policy by aggregating them. Consequently, there has been a movement of access to the process of decision making from local political elites to the national community of local government which forms an intermediate tier of representation.

If the centre acted to aggregate local government interests, it insulated itself from other territorial pressures. Paralleling the function-specific policy communities for England, the centre created and sustained territorial policy communities in Scotland, Wales and Northern Ireland. The Welsh Office was created in 1964 and, along with the Scottish Office, it gradually accumulated functions throughout the period. There were also distinct arrangements for the relationship with local government, with the territorial office becoming, in this respect, the 'centre' of centre–local relations. Aggregation and insulation were opposite sides of the same coin: both were strategies for managing IGR within the constituent nations of the United Kingdom.

As policy making becomes increasingly differentiated, the 'logic' of the process generates imperatives to coordinate. This logic has been cogently explained by Hanf (1978, pp.1–2):

> Territorial and functional differentiation has produced decision systems in which the problem solving capacity of governments is disaggregated into a collection of sub-systems with limited tasks, competencies and resources, where the relatively independent participants possess different bits of information, represent different interests and pursue separate, potentially conflicting courses of action. At the same time, however, governments are more and more confronted with tasks where both the problems and their solution tend to cut across the boundaries of separate authorities and functional jurisdictions.
>
> A major test confronting political systems in any advanced industrial country is therefore that of securing co-ordinated policy actions through networks of

separate but interdependent organisations where the collective capabilities of a number of participants are essential for effective problem solving.

With this emphasis on fragmentation, there is the danger that British government will appear wholly directionless and uncoordinated. But implicit in the notion that fragmentation is a 'problem' is the presumption that someone at the centre wants coordination. To explore this presumption it is necessary to examine the changing scope of executive authority. As Birch (1964, p.243) has noted: 'Another and most important tradition of British political behaviour is the tradition that the government of the day should be given all the powers it needs to carry out its policy.' In short, leaders know best and this facet of the British political tradition, coupled with the centre's monopoly of legal (legislative) resources, underpins the structural power of central government. Three facets of executive authority are relevant for the analysis of intergovernmental relations.

First, with the ever-increasing functional differentiation of British government, the tradition of 'leaders know best' has *not* been supplanted. Rather, the exercise of executive authority has become constrained and its effectiveness reduced. As a result, there is a tension between executive authority on the one hand and the interdependence of centre and locality on the other. If authority is unilaterally exercised, the governments have to confront unintended consequences. If compliance is sought, governments have to confront 'slippage' or the adaptation of policies in the process of implementation. And yet it is precisely such slippage which provides the incentive for unilateral action.

Second, the source of executive authority neither resides in prime ministers nor is exclusive to political leaders. Ministers responsible for domestic departments operate in spheres distinct from the prime minister – to a substantial degree, they are 'sovereign' in their own 'turf' – and coordination is achieved and conflicts resolved in and by the Cabinet and its multifarious committees. However, coordination at the political level is supplemented by bureaucratic mechanisms. The most important mechanism is the Treasury. Its guardianship role in the coordination of public expenditure is crucial. Other means of bureaucratic coordination include interdepartmental official committees, the Cabinet office and the official committees which 'shadow' ministerial cabinet committees. Fragmentation of British policy making has generated a concern about the 'central capability' of government and called forth a variety of coordinating mechanisms and networks of varying effectiveness.

Finally, the increasing awareness of the limits of executive authority has had a number of partisan consequences: most notably, the resurgence of ideological politics (Plant, 1983). In brief, the post-war consensus on the welfare state and the mixed economy managed by Keynesian techniques has foundered on the end of economic growth, fears about the deleterious effects of an enlarged and increasing public sector on the private sector, and disenchantment with the ability of governments to realize their stated policies. The response of the Conservative Party has been to reject all planning and corporatist solutions and to assert the virtues of social market liberalism: the belief that economic recovery depends upon restricting the role of the state and expanding the scope for market forces in the allocation of public goods. But the limited state required decisive state action for its realization and the tradition of leaders knowing best received its clearest expression for many years in the Conservative government of 1979–83. The ideological debate about the role of the state in British society has occupied centre-stage in British politics and the Conservative resolution of the problems of state intervention has fed and reinforced the desire for decisive government action.

Policy Networks

It has been argued that territorial and functional differentiation takes the form of service-specific professional–bureaucratic complexes. These policy networks can be more formally defined as 'a cluster or complex of organisations connected to each other by resource dependencies and distinguished from other clusters or complexes by breaks in the structure of resource dependencies (Benson, 1982, p.148). Obviously, such networks can be diffuse or tightly integrated. In the context of British government, they often (but not invariably) take the form of policy communities with the following characteristics:

1   *functional interests*: that is, the organizational networks are based on the service interests (that is, departments) in central and local government;
2   *extensive membership*: encompassing a variety of 'private' interest groups – most notably the 'technocratic' professions and trade unions – and quasi government and quasi non-governmental organizations as well as public interest groups;
3   *vertical interdependence*: that is, a non-executant role of central departments which are dependent, therefore, on other organizations and groups for the implementation of policies for which, nonetheless, they have service delivery responsibilities; and
4   *compartmentalized horizontal structure*: extensive internal organizational span focused on the 'lead' central department coupled with rigid horizontal articulation of policy making; that is, the network is insulated from, and often in conflict with, other policy communities.

Policy communities are relatively stable with continuity of membership. Decisions are taken within the communities and this process is substantially closed, commonly to other communities and invariably to the general public (including Parliament). Policy communities are, therefore, *integrated* networks.

Space precludes a general discussion of policy communities (see chapter 7 below) but it is important to be more precise about the relevance of the concept to the analysis of IGR. The national local authority associations and the local government professions are participants in the function specific policy communities (for example, education, fire) but, in addition, there is a policy community for local government. This national community of local government has a number of highly distinctive features:

1 *shared general interests* of local government, most notably in grant negotiations, the structure and functions of local government and local government pay negotiations;
2 *exclusive membership*, limited to the Department of the Environment (DoE) and the representatives of elected units of government;
3 *limited vertical interdependence*; that is, there are extensive exchanges of finance and manpower as well as considerable formal and informal contact between national organizations which have *no* executive service delivery responsibilities; and
4 *externalized horizontal structure*; limited internal organization span, coupled with flexible horizontal articulation; that is, the community itself is focused on the associations, joint bodies, topocratic professional societies and the DoE but penetrates a wide range of functional policy communities.

Along with the policy communities based on local authority services, it forms part of the national local government system or 'the set of organisations and actors which together define the national role and state of opinion in local government as a whole' (Dunleavy, 1981, p.105). The national local government system is a key means by which local government can convey a wide variety of different views to Whitehall and it also provides a framework within which any individual local authority can situate their own problems, concerns and strategies. Local authority actors (both councillors and officers) do not decide policies for their area in isolation; instead, they often look to the national local government system for guidance about what standard of service to provide, for ideas to imitate or to avoid, for ways of tackling common problems, and for justifications or philosophies of particular strategies. Some councils are innovators across a wide field of policy, but they are rather exceptional. Most councils most of the time follow national trends in the local government world, or national trends in their kind of authority facing their kind of general problem under their kind of political control. Each of them will innovate from time to time in one issue area or another, adding their own small contribution to the national picture. But most of the time local decisions are made within nationally defined parameters of what counts as good policy, rather than helping to redefine those parameters. Individual local authorities are influenced by and exert influence through the national local government system (and its constituent networks).

For local authorities in the constituent nations of the United Kingdom, the picture differs in its detail. The relationships between, for example, the Scottish Office and 'its' local authorities constitute a separate network but its roots lie in shared territory cross-cut by functional allegiances. Moreover, the scale of the network exercises an influence on its form. There are far fewer local authorities and regular interaction does not require the rather elaborate procedural and institutional arrangements that exist in England. Most important, the networks of each constituent nation (except England) have a secretary of state representing and defending their interest in the Cabinet. Such direct political linkages contrast sharply with the professional–bureaucratic links so characteristic of English IGR.

This section has identified the way in which the framework of analysis needs to be reconstructed and it has introduced some unusual terminology. The most important terms are summarized in Figure 6.1. It now remains to relate this reformulation to the earlier discussion and to identify the ways in which the revised framework explains changes in IGR.

The metaphors of policy networks and policy communities have a number of advantages. First, they suggest that there will be multiple networks at the centre and direct attention to the comparison of policy areas, the degree of integration within networks and the extent of articulation between networks. In short, they provide the policy focus lacking in the original framework. Second, the metaphors counter the affliction common in the study of public administration of a preoccupation with specific institutions; the relationships *between* organizations are accorded prime importance. In short, the focus on policy is integrally related to the analysis of organizational linkages to explain variations in both the policy process and policy outcomes (see below). Third, a focus on networks admits the possibility that subnational actors may be key national actors and avoids the all-too-easy adoption of a 'top-down' view of IGR. In other words, networks are a key feature of the context of negotiative behaviour. Fourth, the definition of networks as complexes of resources-dependent organizations relates the micro and meso levels of analysis. The concepts of resources, exchange, strategies, rules of the game and appreciative systems, which were so central to the original

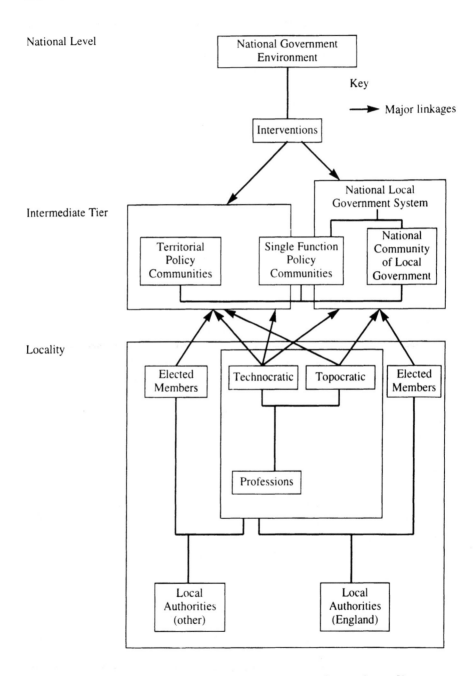

Figure 6.1   The structure of IGR in Britain: a schematic outline

power–dependence framework, remain relevant for the analysis of relationships within policy networks. Policy communities will have distinctive structures of dependencies. Variations in the distribution of resources and the pattern of exchanges will be central to the explanation of variations in the behaviour of actors.

Finally, the concept is also relevant to the analysis of the distribution of resources. The major public services have client groups which are a source of demand for the maintenance and growth of that service. Such support and demand is an important resource for policy communities in their struggle either against cuts in public expenditure or for additional money. But citizens consume services differentially: their interests vary not only between services but also within services: for example, subsidies for council housing and tax expenditure in the form of mortgage relief. Public services generate social conflicts. Moreover, 'powerful (national) ideological structures ... socially created and sustained by dominant classes, groups or institutions ... make available to individuals in different social locations particular perceptions of their interests *vis-à-vis* state policies and the interest of other social groups' (Dunleavy, 1980, p.74).

The national local government system is one such national, ideological structure and the networks of resource exchange that constitute the policy communities can be viewed as the dominant groups and institutions sustaining that structure. Policy communities are, therefore, a key mechanism in the distribution of resources between interests.

If the concept of policy communities contextualizes the analysis of negotiative behaviour and facilitates the analysis of the distribution of resources, it does not explain the changing salience of policy areas. Such an explanation lies in the relationship between policy communities and the national government environment.

The critical discussion of the dual state thesis concluded that any reformulation of the framework needed to contextualize organizational relationships and focus on the conflicting functions and the range of strategies of agreement. In contrast to many Marxist interpretations of the 'state', this discussion of the national government environment presents a picture of fragmented elitism which refuses to see government either as a unity or as a whole, serving the interest of a particular class, or even as acting necessarily in the interest of one fraction of capital (or of the working class) in the long-term interest of capital. In contrast to conventional pluralist accounts, it also refuses to see government as the arbiter or referee between competing group claims acting in the public interest. Rather, without denying that government can and does act to sustain the existing socioeconomic structure, it quite clearly implies that government has a range of functions – regulatory, productive, allocative, legitimation and so on – numbered amongst which are the interest of the individual policy communities with their own needs for maintenance, growth and power. In short, the 'state' is not primarily a tool of the capitalist class or a neutral referee but 'an independent entity with organisational needs of its own, thus serving as a broker between the capitalist class and other classes and meeting its own needs for growth and power in the process' (Perrow, 1979, p.215). The consequences of this conception of government for policy making are that values and interest institutionalized in policy communities are a crucial constraint on policy initiatives.

The interrelationship between the processes within the national government environment are many and varied. The contradictions between them are crucial to understanding changes both in central strategies of intervention and in the fortunes of the policy communities. For example, during the early 1970s, central strategies of intervention[5] emphasized bargaining for local compliance. With the intensification of economic decline, the centre sought to strengthen the national community as an ally against the policy communities and pursued strategies of incorporation. The institutionalization of professional interests in policy communities was, however, a source of substantial inertia and, as British economic decline coincided with world recession, the resurgence of ideological politics led to the adoption of directive strategies. But the unilateral exercise of executive authority had to confront central dependence on local authorities. With an independent source of tax revenue, a significant minority of local authorities confronted central direction, ignoring spending targets and severely constraining central policy on local expenditure. Thus the key contradictions arise from the conflict between central structural power and interdependence; and between the institutionalization of professions and economic decline. In the early 1980s, the government's ability to acquire new formal powers of control has not proved to be a stable substitute for strategies directed at securing the compliance of policy communities, the national community of local government and individual local authorities.

These brief remarks should have made the point that the analysis of the relationship between policy communities and the national government environment encompasses both the functions and the strategies of the centre. At this juncture it is sufficient to note that the revised framework can generate explanations of changes in IGR.

Conclusions: What has been Achieved?

Given the degree of reconstruction, it would be as well to comment on what, if anything, has been achieved. At the time the framework was produced, the *theoretical* literature on IGR was distinctly limited. It was an early contribution to a now extensive literature which helped to establish IGR as an object of theoretical study in the United Kingdom. On the debit side, the framework also skewed the research agenda. It played down the importance of the context of IGR, of policy content and of the interests and conflicts generated by the distribution of public services.

The bulk of the chapter has sketched how these defects might be overcome, but the specific suggestions should not obscure an important shift in the conception of the object of study. The phrase 'central–local relations' suggests a bias towards the analysis of *institutional* relationships. Such analysis does not always provide an adequate account of policy systems. To focus on policy communities is to assert the primacy of policy networks and policy content over the relationships between particular types of institutions. The phrase 'central–local relations' is, therefore, an inappropriate definition of the subject. 'Intergovernmental theory', with its emphasis on fragmentation, professionalization and policy networks, is more appropriate. In the almost classic fashion of governmental policy making, problems are not solved but superseded. Understanding policy making in British government will only grow by a process of problem succession and the reflections in this chapter are intended as a contribution to the process.

Notes

1 I would like to thank Bill Jenkins (Kent), Rob Flynn (Salford), Ed Page (Hull), David Marsh (Essex), Mike Goldsmith (Salford) and Brian Hardy (Loughborough) for their comments on an earlier draft.
2 The full statement of the framework is contained in Chapter 5 above. Summary statements can be found in Social Science Research Council (1979, pp.13–15 and Appendix 1). Hereafter, all references to the framework are from Chapter 5.
3 Criticisms of the framework are taken primarily from published sources. On occasion, reference will be made to research reports submitted to the Social Science Research Council (SSRC) and to conference papers. Such sources have been kept to a minimum because it is relatively difficult to obtain copies of them.
4 The origins of this reformulation lie in research on the local authority associations (Rhodes, 1986). My prime concern was to explain changing patterns of government, national community and policy community relationships. The project focused, therefore, on the characteristics of, and trends in, government intervention in these relationships: an appreciably narrower remit than theories of the local state but nonetheless an analysis of the *context* of relationships. The remit is also appreciably narrower than a theory of intergovernmental relations. The research focused on central government and the national or central representative organizations of local government. The analysis of trends in a specific context is, of course, only one step towards the construction of a macro theory. If this section does not formulate a comprehensive theory of intergovernmental relations, nonetheless it should aid those who make the attempt.

5   The term 'intervention' follows the usage in Stewart (1983, pp.60–62): that is, actions by the centre which impinge on the activities of local authorities but which do not necessarily achieve the purposes of the centre.

7 New Directions in the Study of Policy Networks[1]

Introduction

This chapter has four objectives. First, it summarizes recent theoretical discussions in Britain of the concepts of policy communities and policy networks. Second, it presents a typology of policy networks based upon both these recent theoretical discussions and a series of case studies of policy networks 'in action' in British government. Third, it addresses a series of crucial questions about the utility of the policy networks' approach. Finally, it identifies some new directions for future research.

The chapter draws upon three major sources of empirical and theoretical work: the Economic and Social Research Council (ESRC) research initiative into the relationship between central and local government in Britain, referred to here as the intergovernmental relations initiative (IGR) (Goldsmith and Rhodes, 1986); the ESRC research initiative into the relations between government and industry (GIR) (Wilks, 1989); and the Nuffield Foundation's workshop on the comparison of policy networks in British government (Marsh and Rhodes, 1992).

The IGR Initiative

The IGR initiative was strongly influenced by the organization theory literature and its application to intergovernmental relations. Indeed, Chapter 5 above (see also SSRC, 1979) explicitly sets out to apply intergovernmental theory to British central–local relations. This literature tends to be state-centred rather than society-centred and concentrates more upon the political structures within which relations between governments and interests occur, rather than upon the interpersonal relations between those people who occupy key positions within the network.

Rhodes (1990, p.19) views policy making in central–local relations as based upon an exchange relationship, it is a 'game in which both central and

137

local participants manoeuvre for advantage deploying their constitutional–legal, organisational, financial, political and informational resources to maximise their influence over outcomes'. This exchange relationship occurs within a policy network. So for Rhodes the policy network is a meso-level concept. It offers a model of interest group intermediation; that is, a model of the relationship between interests and government (see also Schmitter and Lehmbruch, 1979; Marsh, 1983, pp.1–3). Following Benson (1982, p.148) Rhodes defines a policy network as 'a cluster or complex of organisations connected to each other by resource dependencies and distinguished from other clusters or complexes by breaks in the structure of resources dependencies'.

Rhodes (1986, ch.2) elaborates this definition, distinguishing between five types of networks ranging along a continuum from highly integrated policy communities to loosely integrated issue networks. These networks are further distinguished according to their membership composition, the extent of interdependence between their members and the distribution of resources between members.

Policy communities are networks characterized by stability of relationships, continuity of a highly restrictive membership, vertical interdependence based on shared service delivery responsibilities, and insulation from other networks and invariably from the general public (including Parliament). They have a high degree of vertical interdependence and limited horizontal articulation. They are highly integrated. These policy communities are based on the major functional interests in and of government, such as education and fire (Richardson and Jordan, 1979; Rhodes, 1986, ch.8). If by contrast they encompass the major territorial interests, for example in Scotland, Wales and Northern Ireland (Rhodes, 1986, ch.7), they are better viewed as *territorial communities*.

Professional networks are characterized by the pre-eminence of one class of participants in policy making – the profession. The most cited example of a professionalized policy network is the National Health Service (see Rhodes, 1988, and citations). The water service provides a further example wherein the constraints on water engineers seem particularly weak (see Cunningham, 1992). In short, professionalized networks express the interests of a particular profession and manifest a substantial degree of vertical independence while insulating themselves from other networks.

Intergovernmental networks are the networks based on the representative organizations of local authorities. Their distinctive characteristics are topocratic membership (and the explicit exclusion of all public sector unions); an extensive constellation of interests encompassing all the services (an associated expertise) and clients of local authorities; limited vertical interdependence because they have no service delivery responsibilities, but extensive horizontal articulation or ability to penetrate a range of their networks.

Producer networks are distinguished by the prominent role of economic interest (both the public and the private sector) in policy making, their fluctuating membership, the dependence of the centre on industrial organizations for delivering the desired goods and for expertise, and the limited interdependence amongst the economic interests.

The distinctive features of an *issue network* are its large number of participants and their limited degree of interdependence. Stability and continuity are at a premium and the structure tends to be atomistic (Heclo, 1978). The Rhodes model is presented in Table 7.1. This attempt to express the Rhodes model in tabular form immediately reveals some of its problems. It is presented as a continuum but, while it is easy to see why the policy

Table 7.1 Policy communities and policy networks: the Rhodes model

Type of network	Characteristics of networks
Policy community/Territorial community	Stability, highly restricted membership, vertical interdependence, limited horizontal articulation.
Professional network	Stability, highly restricted membership. Vertical interdependence, limited horizontal articulation, serves interest of profession.
Intergovernmental network	Limited membership, limited vertical interdependence, extensive horizontal articulation.
Producer network	Fluctuating membership, limited vertical interdependence, serves interest of producer.
Issue network	Unstable, large number of members, limited vertical interdependence.

community and the issue network are at the ends of the continuum, the locations of the other types of network on the continuum are less obvious. Indeed, the Rhodes model appears to conflate two separate dimensions. Clearly, policy networks differ according to their integration, stability and exclusiveness and the distinction between policy communities, policy networks and issue networks which Rhodes adopts is common in the literature. However, networks also differ according to which interest dominates them; as Rhodes implies, they may be dominated by professional interests, economic interests or government (see Saward, 1992). However, Rhodes' model suggest that there could be no such thing as a professional- or producer-dominated *policy community*. By implication, policy communities are either dominated by the government or they serve the interest of all the members of the community, given that over time they develop common interests. In addition, Rhodes' scheme implies that, by definition, a producer network is necessarily less integrated and cohesive than a professional network, yet this issue is best regarded as an empirical question. For this reason I revise the distinction between policy communities and issue networks (see below) by leaving open the question of the interests served by the policy community or network.

The GIR Initiative

The GIR initiative took a more broadly society-centred approach and emphasized interpersonal rather than structural relations. Indeed, despite the fact that the GIR initiative was designed to build upon the model produced in the IGR studies, the model developed by Wilks and Wright owes more to the work of Heclo and Wildavsky (1974) than it does to Rhodes and the IGR initiative. Heclo and Wildavsky concentrated upon 'personal relationships between political and administrative actors – sometimes in conflict, often in agreement, but always in touch and operating within a shared framework' (p.xv). Here the stress was upon the Treasury as a village community; the emphasis was upon disaggregation and interpersonal relations.

In fact there are three major ways in which the Wilks and Wright model differs from Rhodes' model. First, the GIR initiative emphasizes the disaggregated nature of policy networks in the industrial policy sector and, indeed, suggests that such disaggregation exists in all policy sectors. So industry is 'neither monolithic nor homogeneous', government is 'fragmented, differentiated and fissiparous' and the key to understanding government–industry relations is to disaggregate to subsectoral policy networks. Second, there is an emphasis upon interpersonal relations as a key aspect of the policy network or community. In particular, Grant *et al.* (1988, p.11) emphasize that policy communities do not 'conform to ... administratively imposed boundaries', communities are not simply, or, mainly, reflected in stable political structures but are also the product of continuing personal interaction.

Such an emphasis upon disaggregation and personal relationships does distinguish the GIR approach from the IGR initiative, but the claims of each approach can be assessed by empirical investigation. It is a matter for empirical investigation whether the policy networks and policy communities model can only be used at the subsectoral level. In addition, we can also assess the extent to which interpersonal relations, rather than structural relations, are the most crucial element within each policy network. We return to both these questions below. However, the major difference between the two models presents more problems because Wilks and Wright distinguish between policy networks and communities in a way which is at odds with the rest of the literature.

Wilks and Wright distinguish between the 'policy universe', the 'policy community' and the 'policy network'. The 'policy universe' consists of 'the large population of actors and potential actors [who] share a common interest in industrial policy, and may contribute to the policy process on a regular basis'. The term 'policy community' is reserved for a more disaggregated system involving those actors, and potential actors, who share an interest in a particular industry and who interact with one another 'exchanging resources in order to balance and optimise their mutual relationships'. The 'policy network' to Wilks and Wright becomes 'a linking process, the outcome of those exchanges, within a policy community or between a number of policy communities' (Wilks and Wright, 1987, p.299).

The relationship between these different concepts is illustrated in Table 7.2 (from Wilks and Wright, 1987, p.300). Wilks and Wright argue that their new conceptualization has advantages over that offered by Rhodes and others which essentially distinguishes between networks and communities according to the closeness of the relationships involved. In particular, they argue that their model allows them to recognize that not all the same policy issues in the same policy subsector are handled in the same network; and members of a policy network may be drawn from different policy communities within the same policy area, or even from different policy areas. We would not dispute either of these points but, as Jordan has argued, the traditional view of policy networks and policy communities can cope with such qualifications. More importantly, Jordan (1990, p.335) is surely also right to suggest that 'the main argument against the Wilks/Wright terminological usage is that they have been pre-empted. The terms they use already have an accepted currency and it is simply too confusing to use the terms differently unless the alternative terminology has clear advantages.' For this reason I reject the Wilks and Wright redefinition of the concepts.

Table 7.2   Policy community and policy network: the Wilks and Wright model

Policy level		Policy actors
Policy area	Industry, education, transport, health etc.	Policy universe
Policy sector	Chemicals, telecommunications, foundries etc.	Policy community
Policy subsector (focus)	Basic chemicals, pharmaceuticals, agrochemical	Policy network
Policy issues (examples)	Health and safety	Drug licensing
	Research & development	Company profits
	Company profits	'Limited list'
	'Overcapacity'	

A Typology of Policy Networks

The typology in Table 7.3 is developed from the Rhodes model; it distinguishes between policy communities and issue networks and builds upon the findings of the case studies reported in Marsh and Rhodes (1992). The two types of interest group intermediation are seen as the end points of a continuum. The term 'policy network' is used as the generic term encompassing all types. The typology is the product of UK field work. It is comparative between policy areas, but it was never designed to be comparative across countries. Nor does it seek to provide an encyclopaedia of all possible forms of interest intermediation. Our objective is to scrutinize critically the utility of one concept; policy networks.

A policy community is viewed as having the following characteristics: a limited number of participants with some groups consciously excluded; a dominant economic or professional interest; frequent interaction between all members of the community on all matters related to the policy issues; consistency in values, membership and policy outcomes over time; consensus, with the ideology, values and broad policy preferences shared by all participants; exchange relationships, with all members of the policy community having some resources; bargaining between members with resources; and the hierarchical distribution of resources within the participating organizations so that leaders can guarantee the compliance of their members. There is a balance of power, not necessarily one in which all members benefit equally but one in which all members see themselves as involved in

Table 7.3   Types of policy network: the characteristics of policy communities and issue networks

Dimension	Policy community	Issue network
Membership		
No. of participants	Limited number, some groups consciously excluded	Large
Type of interest	Economic and/or professional interests dominate	Encompasses range of affected interests
Integration		
Frequency of interaction	Frequent, high-quality, interaction of all groups on all matters related to policy issue	Contacts fluctuate in frequency and intensity
Continuity	Membership, values and outcomes persistent over time	Access fluctuates significantly
Consensus	All participants share basic values and accept the legitimacy of the outcome	A measure of agreement exists, but conflict is ever-present
Resources		
Distribution of resources within network	All participants have resources; basic relationship is an exchange relationship	Some participants may have resources, but they are limited; basic relationship is consultative
Distribution of resources within participating organizations	Hierarchical; leaders can deliver members	Varied and variable distribution and capacity to regulate members
Power	There is a balance of power among members; although one group may dominate, it must be a positive-sum game if community is to persist	Unequal powers, reflecting unequal resources and unequal access; it is a zero-sum game

Source: Adapted from Marsh and Rhodes (1992, p.251).

a positive-sum game. Of course, these characteristics form an ideal type and actual relationships between government and interests in any policy areas should be compared with it.

The issue network involves primarily policy consultation not shared decision making because there is no shared understanding either among interests or between the interests and the bureaucracy. It is characterized by competition between a large number of participants and a range of interests; fluctuating interaction and access for the various members; the absence of consensus and the presence of conflict; consultation rather than bargaining; and an unequal power relationship in which many participants have limited resources and restricted access.

It is important to stress the diagnostic role of this typology (cf. Grant *et al.*, 1988). Inevitably, no policy area will conform exactly to either list of characteristics; hence the need to retain the term 'policy networks' as a generic description. It is equally important to focus on trends in a given policy area: to explore the extent to which it is becoming more or less integrated or an interest is becoming more or less dominant.

Advocates of corporatist theory were criticized for eroding the concept's distinctiveness with adjectival proliferation (Jordan, 1981). However, the policy networks approach is based on the assumption that any adequate characterization of the policy process must recognize variety and, therefore, it encourages adjectival proliferation. There will be many intermediate cases. Thus a policy network might restrict access to a privileged few with only some of the actors interacting frequently and the membership of the network changing regularly. Power and resources might be distributed unequally within the network, with some groups losing consistently. Moreover, policy networks can vary along several dimensions. A policy community can be tightly integrated because of continuity and consensus or because there is a powerful dominant interest. Consequently, to talk, for example, of a professionalized policy community makes it clear that a dominant profession is the basis of integration. In short, the typology specifies the key characteristics of policy networks, thereby providing a set of diagnostic criteria and setting the outer limits of the analysis.

Key Issues

This typology of policy networks may help to clarify the concepts involved, but it leaves a number of key questions unanswered:

● Is the concept of policy network a useful tool for understanding policy making in Britain?

- Are the types of policy network mutually exclusive and exhaustive?
- How and why do networks change?
- How important are interpersonal relations?
- Does the existence of the network affect policy outcomes?
- Which interests are dominant in the networks?
- What are the normative implications of policy networks for representative democracy?
- What is the relationship between the meso-level concept of policy networks and macro-level theories of the state?

The rest of this section discusses these questions in more detail, drawing upon the case studies in Marsh and Rhodes (1992) of agriculture, civil nuclear power, youth employment; smoking, heart disease and health services; sea defences; information technology; and exchange rate policy. This selection of policy areas cannot be described as representative, but it does cover a wide range, from broad policy areas like health or agriculture to narrower ones such as sea defences or smoking. There is one obvious bias in the selection of cases: the majority focus of 'heroic' or political policy areas, with only the sea defences case study being 'humdrum' or technical.

Is the Concept Useful?

All authors are able to identify the existence of policy networks which had at some time affected policy outcomes. Two of the case studies found policy communities: agriculture and civil nuclear power.

Smith (1992) argues that from 1945 until the early 1980s there was a tight agricultural policy community in which two actors, the Ministry of Agriculture, Fisheries and Food (MAFF) and the National Farmers Union (NFU) had a common set of beliefs. They believed that the state should intervene in agriculture, provide price support and increase production. This view was accepted within government, even by the Treasury which, given its role in controlling public expenditure, might have been expected to object. Indeed, the issue to be faced within the agricultural community was not whether prices and production should be increased but rather by how much. The policy community was underpinned by a set of institutional structures. In particular, the 1947 Agriculture Act established an annual review which surveyed the state of agriculture and determined agricultural prices for the following year. It gave farmers a statutory right to bargain and excluded other groups from the process.

In contrast, Saward (1992) suggests that a professional policy community existed in the early years of nuclear power policy. The research scientists in the Atomic Energy Authority (AEA) were at the heart of nuclear decision making from the creation of the AEA in 1954 until the early 1970s. The AEA was joined in the policy community by the supply industry, the Central Electricity Generating Board (CEGB) and its predecessors, and the relevant government department, initially the Ministry of Supply, then the Ministry for Technology. The AEA was formally responsible to the relevant department, but there was little accountability, in large part because of the degree of secrecy (there were clear links between the civil and military wings of the nuclear programme) and the level of technical expertise involved. In effect, the AEA and its scientists were the sole advisers to successive governments and were the dominant force in a highly integrated community.

In both cases, the policy community manifested a high degree of continuity, but was not permanent. Smith (1992) shows how the agricultural policy community came under increasing stress in the 1980s and Saward (1992) argues that the professional policy community associated with the nuclear power programme was replaced by a looser producer network in the mid-1970s. Policy communities may be characterized by continuity, but they do change and this change needs to be explained (see below).

Other authors identify a variety of policy networks rather than policy communities. For example, Cunningham (1992) argues that in the sea defences case there was a tight and stable professionalized policy network; that is, a network near to the policy community end of our continuum. Here the role of the engineers was central to the setting of the agenda for decision making. They controlled the policy agenda and established that the key question was not whether a threatened area should have its defences upgraded but how the area should be protected and to what standard. Other interests were consulted – the landowners in the area, the District and Parish Councils and the Nature Conservancy Council – but their influence was insignificant when compared to the influence of the engineering profession in setting the agenda for decision making. However, the influence of the professionals, who invariably favour a high level of protection, is clearly constrained by the financial implications of such decisions. As a result, by contrast with the case of agriculture, the policy preferences of the professionals in this network have not been consistently implemented.

Cunningham's (1992) network and those networks identified by Read (1992) in relation to smoking policy, and Wistow (1992) in the health services are relatively stable and integrated. In contrast, Marsh (1992) suggests that the network in the youth employment field has a lower degree of integration and has been subject to major changes. He charts the reduction in the size of the policy network to its present domination by the Department of Employment, the Training Agency and employers. The educational and trade union role in the network has been systematically reduced, particularly since 1988.

None of the case studies identifies an issue network, although a number of authors use the concept (see below). There are policy issues on which there is broad access to policy making. For example, Marsh and Chambers (1981) describe the range of groups participating in the abortion issue. Similarly, Rhodes (1988, pp.343–64) documents how government attempts to create a network on the inner cities failed because of the diversity of interests, inadequate resources and the inability to identify a distinctive turf for the network (for further examples, see Marsh, 1983). Policy networks exist in most areas of policy making and access to the policy process is limited to the privileged few. An issue network, as opposed to a policy community, will exist only if there is no threat to the interest of either an economic or producer group or a professional group. Issue networks exist but they are the exception rather than the rule, at the periphery rather than the core of the policy agenda.

Parenthetically, it is worth emphasizing that issue networks remain networks, with the implication that relationships are ordered. Heclo (1978) emphasizes both increases in the number of participants and the shift away from 'iron triangles'. But. as Jordan (1981, p.121) argues, there is ambiguity in Heclo's analysis: although he is describing a process of atomization and fragmentation, 'Heclo also hints at order in the chaos. There is a fragmentation but there remains the "logic" of policy making which acts as a drive towards more stable, regulated, predictable relations' (see also King, 1978, p.377). Consequently, issue networks are viewed here as a type of network, albeit a loosely integrated one with multiple participants, and not as the antithesis of networks.

The policy network concept can be used at *both* the sectoral and the subsectoral level; it does not need to be reserved for subsectoral analysis as suggested by Wilks and Wright (1987). Wistow's (1992) analysis of health policy and Smith's (1992) study of agriculture both demonstrate that the concepts are useful at the sectoral level. In contrast, other authors use the concept at the subsectoral level: for example, Marsh (1992) on youth unemployment, Saward (1992) on nuclear power, Read (1992) on smoking and Mills (1992) on diet and health while Cunningham (1992) identifies the existence of a network at a disaggregated level. It might be argued that using the concept in this way undermines its utility by stretching its meaning. However, each author identifies a network, or more rarely a community, using a standard definition. More or less tightly integrated networks exist at every level.

How do networks at the sectoral level affect subsectoral networks? Mills' (1992) analysis of the diet and health issue suggests that policy making in that area was constrained by the assumptions and goals of agricultural policy. The assumption in the agricultural policy community was that more food should be produced. The incipient diet and health policy network initially believed that more food would lead to better health. Mills (1992) shows that it has been difficult to challenge these assumptions effectively. The link between dietary policy and food policy, and the consequent treatment of dietary policy as a subsector of agriculture policy, has significantly affected policy outcomes. The articulation between sectoral and subsectoral levels needs further analysis.

Are the Types of Networks Mutually Exclusive and Exhaustive?

The case studies suggest two qualifications to the typology of networks. First, the types are not mutually exclusive: a producer network and an issue network can coexist within the same policy area. Second, the typology is not exhaustive because policy networks can have two tiers, a core and a periphery. In other words, *within a policy network*, there is a clear distinction between members with resources and influences and those without.

In his study of the smoking issue, Read (1992) emphasizes the close links between the tobacco industry and government over the last 250 years. However, in the last 30 years there has been a growing threat to the industry, in large part because of the increased evidence of the links between smoking and cancer and heart disease. The opposition to the industry has been associated with the growing role of the medical profession, particularly the British Medical Association (BMA), and the activities of Action on Smoking and Health (ASH). Their activities acted as a catalyst to changes both with the policy network and in the strategy adopted by the industry. However, neither ASH nor the BMA are in the policy network. They are not involved in negotiations concerning cigarette advertising or sponsorship. They are not consulted on key issues which are decided within the network. Read (1992) argues that these groups are part of a broader issue network within which the smoking and anti-smoking lobbies compete, not so much to influence government, but to change public opinion and, in particular, the decision of smokers and potential smokers.

A similar distinction is also invoked in a less developed form by Saward (1992), Smith (1992) and Marsh (1992). In essence, the issue network is conceptualized as the 'outsider' against which the policy network defines itself. The issue network includes the excluded groups who have an interest in the issue but have little or no access to government. At the same time, members of the policy network may become involved in the issue network if they feel their interest threatened by activity in that network. So the tobacco industry helped create a lobby group, FOREST (Freedom Organisation for the Right to Enjoy Smoking Tobacco), in 1979 specifically to compete with ASH to influence elite, public and consumer opinion. The existence of

FOREST allows the industry to retain this position in the policy network, a privileged position which in large part ensures its interests are protected, while its surrogate competes with ASH and the BMA in the issue network.

Read (1992) also identifies different levels within the 'smoking' policy network. He argues that the producer group, together with the key central departments – the Treasury and the Department of Trade and Industry – are at the core of the network. Other interests, notably the advertising industry and the Sports and Arts establishments which accept tobacco sponsorship, share economic interests with the producer groups. They are involved in the network, but at the periphery of the network, not its core. Smith (1992) distinguishes between the inner and outer circle of the agricultural policy community. The inner circle involves groups intimately involved in policy making on a day-to-day basis (MAFF and the NFU). The outer circle includes groups with access to the ministry only when an issue specifically affects them. The NFU is involved at all stages of the detailed bargaining over prices in the Annual Review while the Country Landowners' Association and the food processors only have an occasional meeting with MAFF to express their views on the Review.

These distinctions do not add a great deal to the analysis of networks. In essence, all that they imply is either that members of a policy network have unequal resources, or that some interests are outside the network but, on occasions, are consulted, or that the boundaries of any network are permeable. It is important to recognize that the members of a policy network have unequal resources and limited influence over policy and that networks are only *relatively* closed to a range of interests. However, the foregoing distinctions serve primarily to obscure network boundaries. Pross (1986, p.99) refers to the 'attentive publics' of policy networks, a more apposite phrase because it draws attention to the range of possible actors but does not treat them as members of the network.

How and Why do Networks Change?

All the case studies highlight change within their networks and attempt to explain those changes, most commonly by references to changes in the environment of the networks. Four broad categories of exogenous or network–environment changes are identified in the case studies: economic, ideological, knowledge and institutional.

Almost all the case studies recognize that economic changes are a source of instability in networks, although only Marsh (1992) and Saward (1992) emphasize its importance. Saward argues that the major reason for the shift from a professionalized community to a producer network in the nuclear power policy area was the adoption of a more commercial ethos by key actors and organizations in the network which owed a great deal to the deepening economic recession in the early 1970s. The fact that a policy network developed in the youth employment field is evidence of the importance of economic factors. The growth in unemployment, and in particular in youth unemployment, led to major changes in the importance and resources of the Manpower Services Commission (MSC) and to the development of a policy network involving the Department of Employment, MSC, CBI, TUC and educational interests. Other authors attribute an indirect effect to the economy; it is mediated through government policy, as in the case of health.

Although this section has focused on the effects in the economic cycle, the effects of other kinds of market change cannot be ignored. For example, when technical innovation is allied with particular economic interests within a market, there can be marked effects on network relationships, as occurred with the Pressurized Water Reactor.

If economic factors are the catalyst of change, the form of the response is greatly influenced by the ideology of the governing party. Party is the blade for prising apart the mollusc's shell of Whitehall and the policy networks. The Conservative Party and the ideology of the New Right were a wellspring of policy initiatives during the 1980s, giving the policy agenda a distinctive twist and mounting a serious and continuous challenge to the established routines of the policy networks. The '3Es' of economy, efficiency and effectiveness were foisted on the NHS. Government-imposed financial restraints constrained the water engineers and their priorities. The trade unions were deemed the enemy within, the educational professions were 'handbagged' and both were excluded from gestation and development of youth training and vocational education. Add such distinctive policies as privatization and contracting out and the impact of party ideology becomes all too clear. Many a policy initiative may have faltered in the process of implementation, but the impact of party on setting the policy agenda and the process of policy innovation is considerable.

The third broad factor which affects network stability is knowledge. Any change in the information or knowledge about a particular issue can have an important affect on the network. The major source of stress within the smoking network has been the development and dissemination of knowledge about the linkage between smoking and ill-health. Similarly, knowledge about the relationship between diet and health has introduced significant stress into the diet and health network. Saward (1992) makes a related point when he argues that changes in the nature of the technology itself can result in changes in the network, especially if new interests are associated with a new technology. So, in the nuclear power field, the rise of the importance of the producers, and particularly of the General Electrical Company, in the network was a reflection of the adoption of the more cost-effective Pressurized Water Reactor. Similarly, it is in the interests of doctors to promote technical change within the NHS because it is one way of sustaining the pressure for more resources.

Finally, the European Community (EC) institutions have become significant actors in several policy areas and catalysts for change. As Peterson (1992) shows, the Commission played a key role in developing collaborative research and development (R & D) schemes and, once information technology (IT) and communication R & D had been established, in redirecting it to incorporate wider concerns (such as environmental R & D). As Wallace (1984) has argued, transnational policy networks are beginning to emerge. Grant *et al.* (1988) document the European chemical industries policy network. Coates (1984) describes the 'boring' implementation processes of the foods standards policy community: it is a routinized European policy network. Intergovernmental bargaining and national interests may continue to characterize EC policy making. The Commission's power of initiative may remain constrained by *realpolitik*. Nonetheless, supranational institutions can change both policy and relationships and must be included amongst the factors both constraining and providing opportunities for national policy networks, as well as fostering the emergence of transnational policy networks.

As Stones (1992) argues, there is a danger with these examples that change may be seen as independent of the policy network: that is, as a *deus ex machina*. However, just as economic change is mediated through party ideology, so technical change is not a functional imperative but is mediated by economic and professional interests. In other words, the policy networks are part of the process of change. Stones is correct to emphasize that the analysis of change cannot be reduced to a simple environmental stimulus–policy network response model. Actors in the network shape and construct their 'world', choosing whether or not, and how, to respond. Thus, in the National Health Service (NHS), such 'impersonal' or 'objective' forces as sociodemographic changes have to be interpreted. They can be seen variously as indicators of need, grounds for increasing resources or evidence for redistributing resources between the acute sector and the Cinderella services (for example, those for the elderly) – always assuming that such data was seen as relevant to current policy concerns.

There is also a danger of adopting too rigid a view of networks so that such phrases as 'relatively closed' become synonymous with 'totally impervious to outside forces'. No network is ever wholly closed. One of the strengths of the network approach is that it recognizes that the government is not an undifferentiated whole. It is a department or a section of a department, which is involved in a policy network or policy community, not the government as a whole. As such, general government policy constrains departmental responses but it does not determine them. Each department attempts to maximize its autonomy within that overall constraint. Similarly, interest groups which oppose the network have been a major source of political instability for networks. Saward (1992) points to the growth of the environmental and anti-nuclear groups in the attentive publics which began to challenge the nuclear power network at inquiries, forcing adaptations in that network. Smith (1992) also suggests that the growth of consumer and environmental groups has had some influence on the process of change within the agricultural policy community. Read (1992) argues that the activities of ASH and the BMA have meant that the tobacco industry has had to rely on other interests (such as the advertising industry and the Sports and Arts establishment) for support within the network.

It also had to compete ideologically with ASH and the BMA. Sir Geoffrey Vickers (1965) argues that policy making should be understood not as 'goal seeking' but as regulating changes in relationships by setting and resetting norms and standards. On this view, policy networks do not necessarily seek to frustrate any and all change but to contain, constrain, redirect and ride out such change, thereby materially affecting its speed and direction. Policy networks may be conservative with a small 'c', but it is a dynamic conservatism and they cannot be ascribed a passive role in process of change.

There are also problems with such phrases as 'exogenous sources of change' and 'environmental change'. The environment of a policy network includes, for example, other parts of the government such as the departments and their associated policy networks as well as such broad factors as economic change. The environment is not 'given'; it is both constituted and constitutive and the analysis of the 'appreciative system' of actors (Vickers, 1965) in the policy networks is central to understanding this interactive process.

Change in policy networks can also be endogenous. Consensus within networks is the product not of 'one-off' negotiations but of a continuing process of renegotiation which can be characterized as coalition building. The prospect of elite dissension is, therefore, an ever-present one. It is possible to adopt an excessively rational approach to policy change. Chance and opportunism play a part, as do political crises, whether in the guise of salmonella or of Chernobyl.

However, these several comments do not begin to provide an explanation of policy change, First, focusing on policy networks will never provide an adequate account of policy change because such networks are but one component of any such explanation. Second, there is no agreed definition of, or criterion for, measuring the degree of change policy networks. When is a change a radical change? Is it defined by the perceptions of participants? In short, the concept of policy networks does not provide an explanation of policy change. The case studies do not repair the omission, but identify a key research priority: the role of networks in policy innovation.

If the case studies do not explain the process of policy innovation, they do tell us something about the process of change in policy networks. First, the bulk of the case studies show that policy networks exist to routinize relations; they promote continuity and stability. Indeed, the bulk of the literature sees policy networks as a major source of policy inertia, not innovation. Second, those networks with a dominant economic or professional interest are the most resistant to change, as in the case of the tobacco industry or, more spectacularly, the capacity of doctors to resist major political interventions. Third, the degree of change is contingent upon the salience of the issue. The more peripheral issues are to the government's programme and electoral fortunes, and the more limited is the range of interests affected, the greater is the capacity of the network to run its own affairs. The case study of sea defences illustrates the benefits of routinization, whereas the diet and health case study illustrates the instability generated by the growing politicization of an issue. Finally, the policy networks changed incrementally, most commonly along one dimension only. The exception is the case study of nuclear power; this network changes along several dimensions simultaneously. The other networks tended to respond incrementally, often by coopting rival interests and values.

Interpersonal or Institutional Linkages?

Wilks and Wright (1987) stress the importance of interpersonal relations as the cement of the policy network (but see also Wright, 1989, on the context of such relationships). In general, the case studies play down, although they do not neglect, interpersonal links. Only Cunningham (1992), Stones (1992) and, to a lesser extent, Read (1992) and Saward (1992) emphasize such links. The emphasis in most of the case studies is upon the institutional links between the interests involved in the network. For example, doctors are involved in such a large number of advisory committees and other positions at the Department of Health that their interests can be described as institutionalized in government. Such linkages are strengthened, of course, by interpersonal links. As Read (1992) demonstrates, the tobacco industry's institutional links are reinforced by personal contact, particularly with the Arts and Sports establishments.

The institutional and interpersonal links in any network are best regarded as both constraints and resources which can have an effect upon any exchange within the network. For example, tobacco tax is an important source of revenue. The government is conscious of its dependence on this revenue, but it also uses the threat of increased revenue in negotiations with the industry. Similarly, any interpersonal network of relations may also act as a constraint or a resource. The question of which aspect of the network is most important is an empirical one.

Do Networks Affect Outcomes?

All the case studies suggest that networks affect policy outcomes. The existence of a policy network, or more particularly a policy community, constrains the policy agenda and shapes the policy outcomes. Policy communities, in particular, are associated with policy continuity. Agriculture may represent the archetypal case in which there was policy continuity for almost 50 years, but continuity has also been the hallmark of policy in the smoking, nuclear power, diet and health services and sea defences networks. What is more, there is ample evidence from the case studies that the existence of a policy network or policy community is a key cause of that continuity.

Of course, there has been policy change, both in the shape of the policy networks and in the policy outcomes, but the existence of a policy network or community acts as a major constraint upon the degree of policy change. Certainly, the analyses of Smith (1992), Wistow (1992), Mills (1992) and Read (1992) indicate that the policy networks have been successful in resisting policy changes. Thus Mills shows the way in which the MAFF-dominated policy network reduced the stress which had been introduced into the food policy area by the recommendations of two government-appointed committees, the National Advisory Committee on Nutrition Education and the Committee on the Medical Aspects of Food Policy. Policy changes in health and dietary education and regulations on nutritional and fat-content labelling were minimized. In brief, policy networks foster incremental outcomes, thereby favouring the status quo or the existing balance of interests in the network.

Which Interests are Dominant?

This question is, of course, crucial. The policy networks literature draws its inspiration, in part, from the literature on subgovernments (see Jordan, 1990; Ripley and Franklin, 1980; Rhodes, 1990). The approach offered a critique of the pluralist model of decision making and power distribution. As McFarland (1987, p.135) puts it, the subgovernment 'is a coalition of interest groups, public administrators and members of Congress serving on the relevant committees that control the administration of public policy for the benefit of those within the sub-government. Such policies usually benefit established economic interests.'

The emphasis, then, was upon the existence of close, closed and continuing relations between interest groups and government which negotiated policy between them to their mutual advantage. As such, it clearly implied an elitist power structure. The model was starkly captured by the image of the 'iron triangle', with the interest group, the bureaucracy and the Congress linked by common interests in a positive sum game, although, as Ripley and Franklin (1980) make clear, the pattern of relationships varies from policy area to policy area.

The metaphor of 'the iron triangle' does not fit Britain where, for example, parliamentary select committees play no role remotely equivalent to congressional committees in the policy process. However, the policy networks metaphor does suggest that policy in Britain is the product of an elitist power structure, albeit one fragmented between functional areas. All the case studies identify policy networks which were, to a greater or lesser extent, exclusive. In each area a limited number of groups enjoyed privileged access to policy making, shaping both the policy agenda and policy outcomes. There is little evidence that a plurality of groups are involved in policy making in the areas under consideration.

Second, there are two key resources which give groups privileged access to decision making; economic position and knowledge. The case studies consistently show that producer groups and professional groups are the groups which, together with the government, dominate the policy networks. Other groups rarely enjoy any significant role in the policy network but, rather, form the attentive public attempting to undermine the position of the producer or professional group.

Third, although trade unions might be regarded as a producer group, they play little part within any of the networks under discussion. Indeed, in almost all the policy areas examined their role is similar: they are drawn into consultations with the government when the dominant non-governmental interest in the network thinks that their contribution would support that dominant interest's view. The study of the youth employment policy network presents a partial exception. The TUC played an important role in the MSC between 1974 and 1988, but it was always a subsidiary role. In fact, as Marsh (1992) shows, the presence of the TUC on the MSC helped to legitimate a policy to which large sections of the union movement objected. What is more, in 1988 the government, in effect, excluded the TUC from the policy network.

Finally, it could be argued that, although the case studies indicate that access and influence are concentrated within networks, the government still holds the ring both against the producer and professional interest in the network and between networks. However, while none of the authors sees the government as simply the creature of a particular interest, there is little evidence that it is operating in the general or public interest. Government is fragmented and, in many cases, individual departments and a powerful interest have developed a *common* interest and policy, and the network fosters the mutual interests of its members against outsiders. The pattern of policy making is essentially elitist. It may be that different professional or producer groups and different sections of government departments, or different government agencies, dominate in different policy areas. One would not expect the BMA to play a key role on sea drainage policy or the NFU to play a key role in relation to the abortion issue. There is clear structural inequality in the access of interests to, and their influence over, government policy making.

What are the Normative Implications?

The costs of institutionalized interest group politics have been cogently and forcefully identified by Lowi (1969, pp.85–97, 287–97). To paraphrase his argument, policy networks destroy political responsibility by shutting out the public, create privileged oligarchies, and are conservative in their impact because, for example, the rules of the game and access favour established interests. In Lowi's terms, interest group liberalism 'corrupts' democratic government; it confounds public expectations about democratic government; it renders government impotent; it frustrates government attempts to foster justice; and it erodes the formal mechanisms of representative democracy. Lowi objects vehemently to the belief that a system of group competition is self-correcting and that groups are good. He prefers to see them as a necessary evil to be curbed by legal means. He indicts pluralist theory for failing 'to grapple with the problem of oligopoly or imperfect competition as it expresses itself in the political system' (ibid., p.295; for additional citations, see McFarland, 1987).

The case studies presented here are conspicuously silent on the accountability of networks. They describe a system of *private* government subject only to the most tenuous forms of accountability. The legitimacy of networks is not political but resides in the claims to superior expertise and/or to increased effectiveness of service provision. It is no accident that the growth of policy networks coincides with the growth of public sector professions. The relationship is a true symbiosis. Professional expertise and effective service delivery legitimize the oligarchy of the policy network, whilst membership for the network enhances professional control over both the service and, most important, the accreditation of its providers. The mystique of scientists and doctors serves not only to reinforce their role in the nuclear and health networks respectively but also to strengthen the networks' claim to make policy free from the 'irritating' constraint of political, especially electoral, legitimacy.

This interpretation of the normative implications of policy networks is essentially pessimistic. Other authors (such as Heclo, 1978; see below) emphasize access to networks and competition between interests. Optimism and pessimism to one side, policy networks raise the thorny and perennial problems of the relationship between parliamentary and functional representation and between political responsibility and private government by interest groups. Such normative questions do not disappear just because the literature on policy networks ignores them.

What is the Relationship to Theories of the State?

The concept of policy network is perhaps most closely associated with pluralism in one or other of its multiple guises. Neopluralist accounts of policy networks explore the impact of professional influence, the logic of technical rationality, the privileged position of a selected number of interest groups and the complex interdependencies within decentralized governmental structures. The problem of government is to steer disaggregated structures of interdependent organizations. The limits to rational policy making, the factoring and professionalization of policy systems, and the emergence of policy from network interaction are said to be recurrent features of advanced industrial societies. Oligopoly has replaced competition in the political marketplace. Like the original literature on 'iron triangles', this neopluralist approach is a direct attack on naive pluralism. (For a more detailed summary and citations, see Dunleavy and O'Leary, 1987 ch.6; Kaufman *et al.*, 1986; Rhodes, 1988.)

In more recent years, American pluralists have hit back. They have played down the significance of subgovernments and pointed to a dramatic growth in the number of interest groups lobbying national government in the 1970s and emphasized the autonomy of the American executive institutions (see McFarland, 1987, pp.135–6). There has been a renewed emphasis upon two basic tenets of pluralism: the potential independence of government from the pressures of particular interest, and the existence of actual and potential countervailing power alliances which prevent the dominance of economic interests. Heclo's (1978) work represents another strand in this revised defence of pluralism from attack by the proponents of the subgovernment model. He asserts that 'fairly open networks' have replaced 'the closed circles of control' (ibid., p.88). In fact, Heclo argues that 'issue networks' are much more common than subgovernment; that closed networks are the exception rather than the rule.

In the British context Richardson and Jordan (1979, p.74) see the policy making map as 'a series of vertical compartments or segments – each segment inhabited by a different set of organised groups and generally impenetrable by "unrecognised groups" or by the general public'. Richardson and Jordan see the existence of such relatively closed policy communities as entirely consistent with pluralism. There is a variety of policy networks in which selected interests enjoy privileged access, but the networks do open up the policy process to a range of interests. No one interest dominates broad areas of policy, and government can enjoy considerable autonomy; indeed, it is often the dominant partner. Disaggregation and plurality are seen as synonyms in this species of corporate pluralism. There are many divisions within government, civil society is highly fragmented – a fact reflected in the growing number of interest groups – and policy making takes place within a variety of policy networks characterized by close relations between different interests and different sections of government.

The utility of the concept of policy networks is not restricted to those concerned with pluralist theory. It is also relevant to other approaches. The New Right is concerned with the corporate state, professional monopolies and bureaucratic limitations on competition and change – topics with an obvious affinity to the policy networks literature. More formally, Ostrom's (1986, p.460) concept of 'action arenas' with the attendant notions of, for example, roles and resources, offers a *potential* bridge between the currently separate literature on networks and rational choice.

Similarly, policy networks can be deployed within a neo-Marxist approach. For example, regulation theorists argue that Britain is moving towards a post-Fordist economy; for example, it is shifting from mass production to small batch production, from mass consumption to the differentiated consumer (Jessop, 1988; Stoker, 1990). However, these changes occur at different rates and lead to different practices between countries. The theory does not explain these variations. A meso-level concept like policy networks is central to understanding resistance to such changes, and the ways in which political institutions and practices adapt. Policy networks are political structures which filter or mediate the change to post-Fordism.

The key point of these illustrations is not that any one approach is preferable but that the concept of policy networks can be used in conjunction with both different models of the distribution of power and different theories of the state. This diversity demonstrates clearly that the concept of 'policy networks' is a meso-level one which helps to classify the patterns of relationships between interest groups and governments. But it must be used in conjunction with one of the several theories of the state in order to provide a full explanation of the policy process and its outcomes. Such an exhortation is, of course, only a first step. The real challenge is to work out the relationship between the levels of analysis. The case studies in Marsh and Rhodes (1992) identify this problem, but none resolves it.

Conclusions: New Directions

This review of the study of policy networks in Britain points to six areas of potential development: network characteristics, comparison, disaggregation, policy types, multitheoretic research and accountability.

First, there is a danger that the study of policy networks will become, like the study of corporatism, a field bedevilled by arguments over the 'best' definition. However, future developments need not hinge on agreement about definitions. The several dimensions can become a matter of empirical investigation. We described Table 7.3 as a diagnostic tool. It specifies a series of dimensions along which policy networks can vary. The key lies in appraising the extent to which any form of interest intermediation has the characteristics associated with policy networks. In addition, it will be necessary to explore the relationship between these dimensions to determine whether or not they co-vary and in this way develop an empirical typology.

Second, any conclusions drawn from Marsh and Rhodes (1992) suffer from the limitation that the case studies are restricted to policy making in British government. As the GIR research initiative demonstrated, the comparative study of networks is of enormous value and future studies of policy networks should be cross-national. Moreover, the studies of British policy making suggest the form of that comparative research. Ostensibly, British government witnessed a 'revolution' in the 1980s. However, the degree and rate of change varied dramatically between policy areas. We know that policy networks are a source of inertia. We also need to know the conditions under which they can sustain policy innovation. The relationship between policy innovation and policy networks is ripe for comparative investigation.

Third, cross-national studies cannot simply assume that national variations are significant. Sectoral variations may be more important and, in consequence, it is necessary to disaggregate and explore subsectoral variations.

Fourth, it is clear that there are marked variations between policy areas. The cross-national subsectoral comparisons must encompass a variety of policy areas. For example, the research could explore the viability of Ripley and Franklin's (1980, ch.1) typology and the proposition that only relationships in distributive policy arenas can be termed policy networks (ibid., pp.22–3).

Fifth, the meso-level concept of policy networks needs to be located in a number of macro-level theories of the state and the articulation between levels of analysis needs to be specified. In other words, policy networks are only a component part of any explanation of the process and outcomes of policy making. Moreover, there are a variety of competing yet complementary theories and this variety is to be welcomed, provided research is explicitly multitheoretic: that is, it seeks to compare and contrast the strengths and weaknesses of the several theories.

Finally, given that policy networks are a species of private government, it is imperative to devise effective forms of political accountability. We need to identify the conditions under which they can be constrained, contained and even dispensed with. They may be a ubiquitous part of government, but are they an inevitable necessity? Can private government be replaced by responsible government? To describe policy networks is not to condone the oligopoly of the political system.

Note

1   This chapter was written with David Marsh (University of Birmingham) and my thanks to him for letting me reuse it here. Both authors would like to thank the Nuffield Foundation for funding the workshop upon which this chapter is based and the several participants at that workshop for their comments on an initial draft. Another version was presented to the workshop on 'Institutions, Structures and the Intermediation of Interests' at the ECPR Joint Sessions, University of Bochum in April 1990. We are also indebted to the participants of this workshop for their comments. Finally, Rod Rhodes would like to thank Keith Alderman (University of York) for his detailed scrutiny of the manuscript.

8 Analysing Networks: from Typologies of Institutions to Narratives of Beliefs[1]

Introduction

This chapter reviews recent British and other European literature on policy networks and asks two questions: where are we now, and where do we go? The next section of the chapter summarizes current approaches to the study of networks and the attendant debate. In the third section it is argued that these approaches are characterized by the assumptions that networks are given facts from which you can read off individual beliefs and actions; a focus on routines, not change; a tendency to build elaborate typologies; and an emphasis on managing networks. In the fourth section, an alternative approach is proposed, rooted in an antifoundational epistemology. It is suggested that the notions of tradition and narrative are central to understanding networks.

Developments in the Study of Policy Networks

There is a massive literature on policy networks in Britain (for reviews, see Dowding, 1995; Jordan, 1990; LeGales and Thatcher, 1995; Marsh, 1998, ch.1; Marsh and Smith, 1995; Rhodes 1981, ch.5; 1990; 1997a; chs 1 and 2) and in the rest of Europe (see Bogason and Toonen, 1998; Jordan and Schubert, 1992; Kenis and Schneider, 1991). Börzel (1998) usefully distinguishes between approaches which treat networks as interest intermediation and as governance. In the rest of this section, I describe developments in the 1990s employing her headings.

Networks as Interest Intermediation

I take Marsh and Rhodes (1992) as the starting point because it has influenced recent debates (see Börzel, 1998; Dowding, 1995; LeGales and Thatcher, 1995). We define policy networks as a meso-level concept which links the micro level of analysis, dealing with the role of interests and government in particular policy decisions, and the macro level of analysis, which is concerned with broader questions about the distribution of power in modern society. Network analysis stresses continuity in the relations between interest groups and government departments, a process referred to as 'interest intermediation'. Policy networks are sets of resource-dependent organizations. Their relationships are characterized by power-dependence; that is, 'any organisation is dependent on other organisations for resources', and 'to achieve their goals, the organisations have to exchange resources'. So actors 'employ strategies within known rules of the game to regulate the process of exchange'. Relationships are a 'game' in which organizations manoeuvre for advantage. Each deploys its resources, whether constitutional-legal, organizational, financial, political or informational, to maximize influence over outcomes while trying to avoid becoming dependent on the other 'players' (Marsh and Rhodes, 1992, pp.10–11).

Various authors have constructed typologies and lists of the characteristics of policy networks and policy communities (see, for example, Grant *et al.*, 1988; Waarden, 1992; Wilks and Wright, 1987). The typology developed by Marsh and Rhodes, 1992, pp.249–51) is 'a suitable case for deconstruction'. It treats policy network as the generic term. Networks can vary along a continuum according to the closeness of the relationships in them. Policy communities are at one end of the continuum and involve close relationships; issue networks are at the other end and involve loose relationships (see Chapter 7 above, Table 7.1).

There has been much debate about this analysis of policy networks as interest intermediation. For example, Dowding (1995) criticizes it on three grounds. First, he argues that the concept of policy network is used as a metaphor, and is not explanatory. Second, he argues that the approach does not go beyond typology to specify causal relationships – for example, between such network characteristics as density of linkages and policy outcomes. Moreover, in so far as there is an (implicit) explanation, it does not rely on the characteristics of networks to explain actions but on the properties of actors, for example on the resources individuals can deploy, not their nodal position in the network or other structural characteristics. Third, he argues that the analysis of games and bargaining is undeveloped and even confused by the distinctions between micro (or individual), meso (or network) and macro (or state) levels of analysis. These distinctions are not required for 'an analytical theory which produces testable empirical implications under different conditions'. In other words, Dowding would have us adopt a deductive rational actor model covering theories of bargaining and quantitative network analysis (see, for example, Laumann and Knoke, 1987; for critical comments, see Marsh and Smith, 1995).

The debate rolls on. Marsh (1998, pp.12–13, 67–70), Marsh and Smith (1995) and Rhodes (1997a, pp.10–13, 24) criticize Dowding because he focuses on agents and does not explore how the structure of the network affects the process of bargaining. Marsh and Smith (1995) argue that network structures shape the preferences of actors; there is a dialectical relationship between structures and agents. They criticize Dowding for taking refuge in intentionalism and methodological individualism and failing to recognize the structure–agency problem. They argue that, at the micro level, networks comprise strategically calculating subjects whose actions shape policy outcomes. However, the preferences and interests of these actors cannot be assumed. They must be explained by a meso- or macro-level theory. For Marsh and Smith, the future lies in longtitudinal, qualitative, comparative, case studies. In this debate, it is a case of 'ne'er the twain shall meet'. The two sides have irreconcilable differences of both theory and method. I simplify, but the differences are as basic as economics v. sociology, quantitative v. qualitative and deductive v. inductive. There is a similar divergence when analysing networks as governance.

Networks as Governance

The most recent work treats networks as the analytical heart of governance. This literature falls into two broad schools depending on how they seek to explain network behaviour: power-dependence or rational choice. The two approaches are illustrated by, respectively, the work of the British 'Local Governance' and 'Whitehall' research programmes, and the work originating at the *Max-Planck-Institut für Gesellschaftsforschung*. I also discuss an important variation on the power-dependence approach, best illustrated by the 'governance club' at the Erasmus University, Rotterdam, that focuses on managing networks.

Power-dependence   The UK Economic and Social Research Council Research Programmes on 'Local Governance' and 'Whitehall' fuelled much recent research in Britain. At the start of the 'Local Governance' Programme, the system of government beyond Westminster and Whitehall was described as changing 'from a system of local govern*ment* into a system of local govern*ance* involving complex sets of organizations drawn from the public and private sectors' (Rhodes, 1992, p.2). Here 'governance' is a broader term than 'government', with services provided by any permutation of government and the private and voluntary sectors. Complexity arising out of the functional differentiation of the state makes interorganizational linkages a defining characteristic of service delivery. The several agencies must exchange resources if they are to deliver services effectively. All organizations have to exchange resources, employing strategies within known rules of the game to achieve their goals (Rhodes, 1981, ch.5; Stoker, 1998a, p.22). These themes remained prominent throughout the programme (see Stoker, ibid., p.18; 1999c).

The ESRC Whitehall Programme generalized the governance argument from local government to British government as a whole, challenging the conventional wisdom of the Westminster model (Rhodes, 1997a, ch.1). Networks are a common form of social coordination, and managing interorganizational links is just as important for private sector management as for public sector. They are a means of coordinating and allocating resources – a governing structure – in the same way as markets and bureaucracies. So networks are an alternative to, not a hybrid of, markets and hierarchies: 'If it is price competition that is the central co-ordinating mechanism of the market and administrative orders that of hierarchy, then it is trust and co-operation that centrally articulates networks' (Frances, 1991, p.15; see also Powell, 1991).

Other key characteristics include diplomacy, reciprocity and interdependence (Rhodes, 1997b). More important, this use of governance also suggests that networks are *self-organizing*. At its simplest, self-organizing means that a network is autonomous and self-governing. Networks resist government steering, develop their own policies and mould their environments. Indeed I define governance as *self-organizing, interorganizational networks*. These networks are characterized, first, by interdependence between organizations. Changes in the role of the state meant that the boundaries between public, private and voluntary sectors became shifting and opaque. Second, there is continuing interaction between network members, caused by the need to exchange resources and negotiate shared purposes. Third, these interactions are game-like, rooted in trust and regulated by rules of the game negotiated and agreed by network participants. Finally, the networks have a significant degree of autonomy from the state. Networks are not accountable to the state; they are self-organizing. Although the state does not occupy a privileged, sovereign position, it can indirectly and imperfectly steer networks.

The key problem confronting government is, therefore, its reduced capacity to steer. The story of British government as a unitary state with a strong executive is replaced by the story of the hollowing-out of the state by international interdependencies and multiplying internal networks. There is now a differentiated polity with a hollow crown.

The Max-Planck-Institut and actor-centred institutionalism For Renate Mayntz, Fritz Scharpf and their colleagues at the Max-Planck-Institut, policy networks represent a significant change in the structure of government. They are specific 'structural arrangements' which deal typically with 'policy problems'. They are a 'relatively stable set of mainly public and private corporate actors'. The links between network actors serve as 'communication channels and for the exchange of information, expertise, trust and other policy resources'. Policy networks have their own 'integrative logic' and the dominant decision rules stress bargaining and sounding out. So, as with the power-dependence approach, the Max Planck school stresses functional differentiation, the linkages between organizations, and dependence on resources (Kenis and Schneider, 1991, pp.41–3).

The Max Planck school also stress the advantages of networks over markets and hierarchies. Thus networks can avoid not only the negative externalities of markets but also the 'losers' – that is, those who bear the costs of political decisions – produced by hierarchies, because:

> in an increasingly complex and dynamic environment, where hierarchical co-ordination is rendered difficult if not impossible and the potential for deregulation is limited due to the problems of market failure, governance becomes more and more feasible only within policy networks, which provide a framework for efficient non-hierarchical co-ordination of the interests and actions of public and private corporate actors which are mutually dependent on their resources. (Börzel, 1998, p.16)

To explain how policy networks work, Scharpf (1997, chs 2 and 3) combines rational choice and the new institutionalism to produce actor-centred institutionalism. The basic argument is that institutions are systems of rules that structure the opportunities for actors (individual and corporate) to realize their preferences. So 'policy is the outcome of the interactions of resourceful and boundedly rational actors whose capabilities, preferences and perceptions are largely, but not completely, shaped by the institutionalised norms within which they interact' (ibid., p.195).

Networks are one institutional setting in which public and private actors interact. They are informal institutions; that is, informally organized, permanent, rule-governed relationships. The agreed rules build trust and foster communication while also reducing uncertainty; they are the basis of non-hierarchic coordination. Scharpf uses game theory to analyse and explain these rule-governed interactions.

There is much agreement, therefore, that governance as networks is a common and important form of governing structure in advanced industrial societies, but there are different emphases and competing explanations about the way networks affect government and its policies.

Networks as management   The spread of networks and the recognition that they constrain central ability to act has fuelled research on how to manage networks. The 'governance club' of Walter Kickert, Jan Kooiman and their colleagues at the Erasmus University, Rotterdam illustrates this concern (see Kickert, 1993; 1997; Kickert *et al.*, 1997; Klijn *et al.*, 1995; Klijn, 1997; Kooiman, 1993). The basic argument of the 'governance club' is that lack of legitimacy, complexity of policy processes and the multitude of institutions concerned reduce government to only one of many actors. Other institutions are, to a great extent, autonomous; they are self-governing. Government steers at a distance (Kickert, 1993, p.275).

Governance refers to 'the directed influence of social processes' and covers 'all kinds of guidance mechanisms connected with public policy processes' (Kickert, 1997, p.2). Policy networks make public policy. They are '(more or less) stable patterns of social relations between interdependent actors, which take shape around policy problems and/or policy programmes' (p.6). The core of these interorganizational links is power-dependence (Klijn, 1997, p.21). However, the main concern of the Erasmus Rotterdam 'governance club' is with managing networks. Table 8.1 identifies three approaches to network management. I paraphrase their arguments and illustrate the approaches from the British literature on networks. The focus is on the ways in which state actors steer networks and this steering encompasses the *structure* of network relations, the *process* of consensus building and the *outcome* of joint problem solving (Kickert, 1997, p.46).

The instrumental approach is a 'top-down' approach to network steering. Although there are limits on the centre's ability to steer, it still tries to do so. This approach accepts that government occupies a special position and will seek to exercise its legitimate authority, but it also recognizes the constraints imposed by networks. So government departments are the focal organization, using strategies aimed at altering dependency relationships to get effective problem solving. Perri 6 (1997) provides specific examples of this approach in action. To counter functional government he wants, to use his watchwords, holistic, preventive, culture changing and outcome-oriented government (p.10). The key to real progress is integrating budgets and information. A specific example of this approach is the policy initiative on Health Action Zones (NHS Executive EL (97)65, 30 October 1997) which exhorts agencies from the public, private and voluntary sectors to work together to bring better health care to the poor. The instrumental approach assumes the centre can devise and impose tools which will foster integration in and between policy networks to attain central objectives.

The key problem with the instrumental approach is the cost of steering. A central command operating code, no matter how well disguised, runs the ever-present risk of recalcitrance from key actors and a loss of flexibility in

Table 8.1   Approaches to network management

	Instrumental approach	Interactive approach	Institutional approach
Focus	Improving steering conditions	Cooperation	Network arrangements and their impacts
Level of analysis	Focal organization and its set	Interactions of actors (individuals and organizations)	Network structure
View of policy networks	Closed and multi-form object of steering	Horizontal interaction	Product and context of interaction and governance
Characteristics of network management	Strategic steering	Game playing to develop cooperation and prevent blockages	Diplomacy and incremental adaptation of incentive structures, rules and culture of networks
Criteria of evaluation	Effective problem solving	Satisficing policy, consensus	Institutionalized key interests and relationships

Source: Modified from **Kickert** *et al.*, (1997, p.186).

dealing with localized problems. Control deficits are an ever-present unintended consequence of the top-down imposition of objectives.

The interactive approach stresses the dependence of network actors. Goals and strategies develop out of mutual learning; collective action depends on cooperation. Management by negotiation, or diplomacy, replaces hierarchy as the most effective management strategy with its stress on how important it is to sit where the other person is sitting to understand their objectives and to build and keep trust between actors (Rhodes, 1997b). Stoker's (1999b) review of techniques for steering urban governance includes indirect management through cultural persuasion, communication and monitoring as well as direct management through financial subsidies and structural reform. Klijn *et al.* (1995, p.442) distinguish between game management and network structuring. Indirect management through game management includes selectively favouring some actors in the network, mobilizing supporters and their resources, greater expertise in the rules of the game, and managing perceptions to simplify compromise. Ferlie and Pettigrew (1996, pp.88–9) found the National Health Service was embedded in a web of inter-agency alliances which changed the style of NHS management. For example, there was a shift to matrix management styles with chief executive officers increasingly concerned to build and maintain links and institutionalize strategic alliances. Respondents identified the following key networking skills: 'strong interpersonal, communication and listening skills; an ability to persuade; a readiness to trade and to engage in reciprocal rather than manipulative behaviour; an ability to construct long-term relationships' (ibid., p.96). Painter *et al.* (1997, p.238) provide specific advice on game management. They conclude that local authorities should conduct an audit of other relevant agencies; draw a strategic map of key relationships; identify which of their resources will help them to influence these other agencies; and identify the constraints on that influence.

The key problem of the interactive approach is the costs of cooperation. For example, the more actors in a network, the longer it takes to agree, and such delays are costly. Network management is time consuming, objectives can be blurred and outcomes can be indefinite (Ferlie and Pettigrew, 1996, pp.95–6). Decision making is satisficing, not maximizing. Also the interaction approach ignores the context of network relations; for example, the way in which political control can change the perceptions and strategies of local authorities in their dealings with other local agencies.

The institutional approach focuses on the institutional backcloth, the rules and structures, against which the interactions take place. Thus Klijn *et al.* (1995, p.442) suggest that networking strategies involve changing relationships between actors, the distribution of resources, the rules of the game, and values and perceptions. Similarly, Stoker (1999b) itemizes new funding arrangements and creating new agencies as two key ways of altering the structure of network relations. For example, for urban governance alone, he lists eight new agencies (for instance, urban development corporations) which central actors used both as tools to give specific issues a higher profile and to involve a wider range of actors. This approach aims at incremental changes in incentives, rules and culture to promote joint problem solving.

The institutional approach has three key problems. First, incentives, rules and culture are notoriously resistant to change. Second, many mainstream studies of networks show they are closed. They privilege a few actors who equate their sectional interest with the public interest. Third, appointments to the special-purpose agencies are patronage appointments and these bodies are rarely accountable to elected assemblies. As with the instrumental and the interactive approaches, the institutional approach to network management encounters important problems. No one approach is a panacea for central steering in the differentiated polity.

Deconstructing Networks

The foregoing summary of networks in the 1990s sought to present a balanced summary of a continuing debate.[2] The present section confronts the issue: 'How do we know what we know in the study of networks?' I do not summarize other people's criticisms of networks but present my own critique and outline an antifoundationalist way of studying networks as an alternative to the social science approach. The section considers what networks will look like from an antifoundational perspective.

Antifoundationalism provides an alternative epistemology to the positivism informing much mainstream work on networks. Antifoundationalists explicitly reject the idea of given truths whether based on pure reasons or on pure experience. As a result, they typically look suspiciously on any claim to describe neutrally an external reality. They emphasize the constructed nature of our claims to knowledge (Rorty, 1980).

'Constructivist' theories of the human sciences often suggest narratives are the stuff of all the human sciences where narratives are 'as much invented as found', so there is an 'irreducible and inexpungeable element of interpretation' (White, 1978, pp.51, 82).[3] For example, Collingwood (1939; 1993) argues that historians ask questions and answer them with stories to make sense out of 'facts' which in their raw form make no sense at all. He summarizes his position as follows: 'history should be (a) ... an answering of questions; (b) concerned with human action in the past; (c) pursued by interpretation of evidence; and (d) for the sake of human self-knowledge'

(Collingwood, 1993, pp.10–11). And Collingwood insists that knowledge is *'Created,* not *discovered,* because evidence is not evidence until it makes something evident' (Collingwood, 1965, p.99 original emphasis). This approach does not mean there are no 'facts', only that facts are constructed by the historian. The human sciences are constructed and shaped by language, context and the theories used. The resulting interpretation is always incomplete, always open to challenge. Such a conception of the human sciences contrasts markedly with the views commonly found in political science, where the influence of the natural science models is great (Kavanagh, 1991).

Crucially, an antifoundational epistemology in the human sciences still allows for the possibility of judging competing theories or narratives by agreed standards of comparison. Objectivity arises from criticizing and comparing rival webs of interpretation about agreed facts using established rules of intellectual honesty. The key rules are accuracy and openness. Accuracy means using established standards of evidence and reason; so we will prefer one theory over another if it is more accurate, comprehensive and consistent. Openness means taking criticism seriously and preferring positive speculative theories which open new avenues of research and make new predictions supported by the facts. These rules provide the criteria for comparing webs of interpretation or narratives. The clear difference between this approach and conventional approaches to studying government is that all interpretations are provisional. We cannot appeal to a logic of vindication or refutation. Objectivity rests on criteria of comparison. The web of interpretation we select will not be a web which reveals itself as a given truth. Rather, we will select the 'best' interpretation by a process of gradual comparison.[4]

Antifoundationalism has implications beyond the epistemological domain. Neither scholars nor their subjects have pure perceptions or pure reason. Those we study do not have pure experiences or interests. So we cannot read off their beliefs, desires or actions from allegedly objective social facts about them. Rather, they construct their beliefs against the background of a tradition (or episteme, or paradigm) and often in response to dilemmas (or problems, or anomalies). Antifoundationalism encourages us, therefore, to understand explanation in the human sciences through such notions as traditions, narratives, decentring and dilemmas.[5]

Traditions

A tradition is a set of theories or narratives, and associated practices, that people inherit and that form the background against which they form beliefs and perform actions. Traditions are contingent, constantly evolving, and necessarily located in a historical context. Traditions emerge out of specific instances and the relations between them where the instances that make up a tradition are handed on from generation to generation, whether from parent to child in families or elder to apprentice in organizations and networks. Traditions must be composed of beliefs and practices relayed from teacher to pupil and so on. Moreover, because traditions are not fixed and static, it is not possible to identify or construct their particular instances by comparing them with the key features of the tradition.[6] Rather, we can only identify the particular instances that compose any given tradition by tracing the appropriate historical connections back through time (Bevir, 1999).

Narratives

Narratives are the form theories take in the human sciences; they are to the human sciences what theories are to the natural sciences. The point I want to make by evoking narratives is that the human sciences do not offer us causal explanations that evoke physically necessary relationships between phenomena. Rather, they offer us explanations of human affairs that work by relating beliefs, actions and institutions to one another by through the appropriate conditional and volitional connections (Bevir, 1999). Although narratives may follow a chronological order and contain such elements as setting, character, actions and happenings, their defining characteristic is that they explain actions by reference to beliefs and preferences. The human sciences rely, therefore, on narrative structures akin to those found in works of fiction. However, the stories told by the human sciences are not fiction. The difference between the two lies not in the use of narrative, but in the relationship of the narrative structures to our objective knowledge of the world.

Beliefs

To focus on beliefs is to explore the way institutions are created, sustained or modified through the ideas and actions of individuals. Such actor-centred accounts are essential because we cannot read off the ideas and actions of individuals from knowledge of objective social facts about them. Although historians of ideas increasingly emphasize both how social discourses inform individual utterances and how social discourses are embedded in practices and institutions, it remains the case that individuals can exercise their particular reason in given social contexts (Bevir, 1999). This approach will produce a radical emphasis on the capacity of the individual subject to imbue his or her actions with meaning and to redefine that meaning in, for example, organizational dialogue.

Dilemmas

A dilemma arises for an individual or institution when a new idea stands in opposition to an existing idea and so forces a reconsideration. Because we cannot read off the ideas and actions of individuals from objective social facts about them, we can understand how their beliefs and actions, and social practices, change only by exploring the ways in which they conceive of, and respond to, dilemmas. Thus an analysis of change and developments in policy networks and government must take place through a study of the relevant dilemmas. For example, to understand both Thatcherism and New Labour one needs to understand not only that Britain suffered from severe inflation in the 1970s but also the ways in which libertarians, conservatives, Whigs and socialists conceived the origins, nature and solution to such inflation (see Bevir and Rhodes, 1998). Political scientists should explore the ways individuals have developed intellectual traditions to bring about change in the institutions of which they are a part. At some key moments, of course, the process of change is especially dramatic and rapid. Here a focus on key periods and key cases, on dilemmas, provides a way of grappling with the moments that produced change.

This approach to the study of networks differs markedly from current approaches in four main ways. First, the social science approach adopts a positivist epistemology, treating networks as social structures from which we can read off the beliefs, interests and actions of individuals. The network to which an individual belongs allegedly establishes the content of his or her beliefs and interests. In contrast, an antifoundational approach regards networks as enacted by individuals. The beliefs and actions of individuals are not determined by their 'objective' position in an organization or network. Rather, their beliefs and actions construct the nature of the organization or network. An antifoundational approach, therefore, encourages us to explore the ways in which they are made and remade through the activities of particular individuals using, for example, the tools of political ethnography.

Second, current explanations of network changes rely on exogenous, not endogenous, causes. Thus Marsh and Rhodes (1992, p. 149 above and p.261) argue that networks create routines for policy making and change is incremental. They identify four broad categories of change: economic, ideological, knowledge and institutional, and all are external to the network. An antifoundational approach explores how networks are enacted by individual actors. Thus it encourages us to look for the origins of change in the contingent responses of individuals to dilemmas. A dilemma arises for an individual or an institution when a new idea stands in opposition to an existing idea and so forces a reconsideration. By focusing on the individual's responses to dilemmas, exogenous change is built into the heart of networks, with change taking the form of confronting new beliefs and responding to the actions of others.

Third, the network literature is characterized by typologies (see above, pp.138–9 and 162). An antifoundational approach does not treat network dimensions and characteristics as given. It is a commonplace observation that even simple objects are not given to us in pure perceptions but are constructed in part by the theories we hold true of the world. When we turn our attention to complex political objects, the notion that they are given to us as brute facts verges on the absurd. The 'facts' about networks are not 'given' to us but are constructed by individuals in the stories they hand down to one another. The study of networks, therefore, is inextricably bound up with interpreting the narratives on which they are based.

The final characteristic of the network literature is that it is practical, seeking to improve network management. We have seen that there is an extensive literature on this topic. The social science model of networks treats them as given facts; as if they are cars and the researcher is the car mechanic, finding the right tool to effect repairs. An antifoundational approach posits that networks cannot be understood apart from traditions. The individuals whose beliefs, interests and actions constitute a network necessarily acquire the relevant interest and beliefs against the background of traditions. In other words, there is no essentialist account of a network but only the several stories of the participants and observers. So there can be no single tool kit for managing them. An antifoundational approach claims that practitioners learn by telling, listening to and comparing stories.

In short, an antifoundational approach turns the current approaches to networks on their head by insisting that networks are enacted by individuals through the stories they tell one another and cannot be treated as given facts. So 'Where do we go?' How do we develop an antifoundational approach to an understanding of networks?

Reconstructing Networks

I have summarized the current state of the policy networks debate. I have offered my own criticisms of that literature. I now offer a way forward in the analysis of networks and, therefore, of British government. I do so through the notions of traditions, beliefs and dilemmas.

Beliefs and the 'Everyday Maker'

An actor-centred study of a network represents a shift of topos from institution to individual. Current approaches to policy networks focus on the oligopoly of the political marketplace. They stress how networks limit participation in the policy process; decide which issues will be included and excluded from the policy agenda; shape the behaviour of actors through the rules of the game; privilege certain interests; and substitute private government for public accountability.

An actor-centred account of networks makes no such assumptions. It would focus on the social construction of policy networks through the ability of individuals to create meaning. Bang and Sørensen's (1998) story of the 'Everyday Maker' provides an instructive example of an actor-centred account of governance as networks focused on the beliefs and actions of individuals. They interviewed 25 active citizens in the Nørrebro district of Copenhagen to see how they engaged with government. They argue that there is a long tradition of networking in Denmark. They argue Denmark has recently experienced the conflicting trends of political decentralization through governmental fragmentation, which has further blurred the boundaries between public, private and voluntary sectors, and political internationalization, which has moved decision making to the EU (ibid., p.11). They describe this shift from government to 'governance networks' as ideal typical and suggest the governance of Denmark is a paradoxical mixture of government (hierarchy) and governance (networks).

In a system of governance, the 'Everyday Maker' focuses on immediate and concrete policy problems at the lowest possible level. Civic engagement is about: 'balancing relations of autonomy and dependence between elites and lay-actors in recursive, institutional networks of governance within or without the state or civil society' (ibid., p.3). The 'Everyday Maker' has

> a strong self-relying and capable individuality; a perception of politics as the concrete and direct handling of differences, diversity and dispute in everyday life; a notion of commonality as relating to solving common concerns; an acceptance of certain democratic values and procedures in handling not only of high but also of low politics. (Ibid.)

Thus Grethe (a grassroots activist) reflects that she has acquired the competence to act out various roles: contractor, board member, leader. There has been an 'explosion' of 'issue networks, policy communities, ad hoc policy projects and user boards, including actors from "within", "without", "above" and "below" government'. So the task of the 'Everyday Maker' is 'to enter in and do work at one point of entry or another' (ibid., p.15).

Political activity has shifted from 'formal organising to more informal networking' (p.20). And, amidst these networks, 'You do in fact miss local government – a visible local government. They become visible at once when there are hullabaloos ... in ordinary everyday life, they are conspicuous by their absence' (p.21). Politics is no longer about left and right but engaging in what is going on in institutions (p.23). In short, Bang and Sørensen draw a picture of Nørrebro's networks through the eyes of its political activists.

There are some instructive contrasts between Bang and Sørensen's research and an antifoundational account. First, they employ an ideal–typical research method, specifying not only the characteristics of the 'Everyday Maker' but also the maxims which guide their political behaviour. Specific instances are then compared with these ideal–typical formulations. An actor-centred account would not assume the 'Everyday Maker' had these characteristics. Rather, for example, it might use such ethnographic tools as studying individual behaviour in everyday contexts; gathering data from many sources; adopting an 'unstructured' approach (that is, collecting data in a raw form, not to a preconceived plan); focusing on one group or locale; and, in analysing the data, stressing the 'interpretation of the meanings and functions of human action' (paraphrased from Hammersley, 1991, pp.1–2; see also Geertz, 1973, pp.20–21).[7]

Second, the 'Everyday Maker' is a normative ideal. Her behaviour epitomizes civic engagement in Denmark. A note of caution is in order. The 'Everyday Maker' may be an endangered species. Jensen (1998) shows how the democratic experiment in Danish social housing is confounded by the fatalism of tenants and the lack of suitable democratic skills. Normative ideals could lead the researcher to ignore the fatalist for whom networks will have a different meaning.

Third, Bang and Sørensen's account of networks focuses on the beliefs and actions of only one group of actors and does not provide a 'thick description' (Geertz, 1973, ch.1). An actor-centred account implies a micro analysis but does not imply necessarily a 'bottom-up' approach. The analysis is not restricted to any one category of actor. So, to the 'Everyday Maker', we need to add the street-level bureaucrats, who can make and remake policy; services users, whose experiences can differ markedly from the expectations of the service provider; and the beliefs and actions of the political and managerial elite who seek to steer other actors in the network. Actor-centred studies of networks would build a multifaceted picture of they way the several actors understand them. There is no expectation that there will be the one 'true' account. The researcher constructs stories about the way other people understand what they are doing in networks. These stories will conflict but overlap. They will be built out of the several organizational, network and political traditions actors have learnt and constructed as they enact and remake networks in their everyday lives. The researcher constructs and compares webs of meaning.

Finally, Bang and Sørensen note but do not explore the traditions of governance as networks which shape the 'Everyday Maker', and indeed other actors in the networks, a point I return to below.

Traditions and Narratives

One popular social science explanation for the growth of governance posits that advanced industrial societies grow by a process of functional and institutional specialization and the fragmentation of policies and politics (Rhodes, 1988, pp.371–87). For some authors, differentiation is part of a larger context. For example, regulation theory sees it as an outcome of the shift from Fordism to post-Fordism (see also Jessop, 1997, pp.308–15: Stoker, 1998b, pp.126–7; 1999b). In contrast, an antifoundational approach stresses how different governmental traditions understand and respond to governance as networks. Networks are understood through traditions. In addition, networks construct or reconstruct their own traditions. Individuals learn about the network and its constituent organizations through stories of famous events and characters. Traditions are passed on from person to person. They are learnt. Much will be taken for granted as common sense. Some will be challenged; for example, when beliefs collide and have to be changed or reconciled. The several traditions will produce different stories which we will compare. We may prefer one story to another because it is more accurate and open. But that story will still be provisional.

One way of illustrating this approach would be to explore the traditions and narratives that inspire political actors. In this way I could show how governance as networks arises out of the multiple narratives that legislators, bureaucrats and others have come to adopt through a process of modifying traditions to meet specific dilemmas. However, because I do not know their relevant stories, I will fall back on academic accounts of the rise and nature of governance as networks, showing how these accounts reflect different governmental traditions.

Governance as networks is a narrative interpreted through traditions, and in Britain it is possible to identify several traditions; for example, Tory, Liberal, Whig and Socialist (Bevir and Rhodes, 1998). Here I illustrate the argument by looking at the New Right and the New Labour traditions, both of which exercise a powerful influence on the way we currently understand British government.

Henney (1984, pp.380–81), writing in the liberal tradition, sees governance as networks as an example of the corporate state, 'the institutionalised exercise of political and economic power' by the various types of local authority, government, the unions and to a lesser extent business. They 'undertake deals when it suits them; blame each other when it suits them; and cover up for each other when it suits them'. These interactions are conducted 'behind closed doors' and each network builds a 'cultural cocoon' rationalizing their interests with the public interest. They 'institutionalise irresponsibility'. Producers interests rule, OK – only for Henney it is not, and he wants to cut local government down to a manageable size by removing some functions and transferring others to the social market. But the problem of networks as producer capture is not easily resolved. Marketization is the alleged solution, but it fragments service delivery structures, creates the motive for actors (individuals and organizations) to cooperate and, therefore, multiplies the networks and opportunities for producer capture which Henney's reforms seek to counter. Beliefs in the virtues of markets have to confront the defects of quasi-markets and resilience of networks.

The socialist tradition in the guise of New Labour sees governance as networks as a problem of integration. For Perri 6 (1997) government confronts 'wicked problems' which do not fit in with functional government based on central departments and their associated policy networks. Such functional government is costly, centralized, short term, focuses on cure, not prevention, lacks coordination, measures the wrong things and is accountable to the wrong people (ibid., p.26). The solution is holistic government which will span departmental cages. The 12 recommendations include holistic budgets designed around outcomes, not functions; cross-functional outcome measures; integrated information systems (for example, one-stop shops); and culture, value for money and preventive audits (ibid., pp.10–12 and chs 4–7).

This report epitomizes the long-standing Fabian tradition in the Labour Party which sees salvation in administrative engineering. But again the problem of network integration is not easily resolved. Perri 6's proposed reforms have a centralizing thrust. They aim to coordinate the departmental cages, a centralizing measure, and to impose a new style of management on other agencies, a central command operating code. But network structures need a decentralized, diplomatic, negotiating style. Beliefs in 'leaders know best' confront the belief that decentralized structures need indirect or 'hands-off' management.

Governance as networks has important implications for other state traditions. Loughlin and Peters (1997, p.46) distinguish between the Anglo-Saxon (no state) tradition, the Germanic (organic) tradition, the French (Jacobin) tradition, and the Scandinavian tradition which mixes the Anglo-Saxon and Germanic. Thus, in the Germanic tradition, state and civil society are part of one organic whole; the state is a transcendent entity. Its defining characteristic is that it is a *Rechtsstaat*; that is, a legal state vested with exceptional authority but constrained by its own laws. Civil servants are not just public employees, but personifications of state authority. The Anglo-Saxon tradition draws a clearer boundary between state and civil society; there is no legal basis to the state; and civil servants have no constitutional position. The Jacobin tradition sees the French state as the one and indivisible republic, exercising strong central authority to contain the antagonistic relations between state and civil society. The Scandinavian tradition is also 'organic', characterized by *Rechtsstaat*, but differs from the Germanic tradition in being a decentralized unitary state with a strong participation ethic. (In this paragraph, I paraphrase Loughlin and Peters, 1997, pp.46–55; see also Dyson, 1980.)

These traditions underpin different interpretations of governance as networks. To return to the Bang and Sørensen (1998) example, local networks with high participation are a long-standing feature of the Danish governmental tradition. The Nørrebro district of Copenhagen is famous even in this tradition for its activism, which extended to (inconceivable) street riots over Danish membership of the EU. So the 'Everyday Maker' acts in national and local traditions characterized by beliefs in political activism. For the Danish tradition, with its participation ethic, governance as networks poses the issue of how to keep the multiplying networks under democratic control.

In the Germanic tradition, the legal framework sets the boundaries to, and guides, official action. The direct imposition of control is unnecessary. There is a high degree of tolerance for the multi-level networks (*Politikverflechtung*) so common in federal systems. On the other hand, the Jacobin tradition with its assumption of conflict between state and civil society sees networks as a potential threat to state authority unless subject to state control, for example through strong mayoral leadership. In other words, in seeking to interpret and understand governance as networks, we have to ask: whose interpretation, in which tradition? Moreover, I have illustrated an argument. As Loughlin and Peters (1997, p.60) are the first to admit, this depiction of state traditions is broadbrush. Traditions do not exist as, for example, ideal types to which we compare specific instances. A more thorough account must cover the variety and nuances of traditions as learnt. Nonetheless, I have illustrated how traditions shape our understanding of governance as networks, both nationally and cross-nationally.

Dilemmas and the Analysis of Change

As noted earlier, a *dilemma* arises for an individual or institution when a new idea stands in opposition to an existing idea and so forces a reconsideration. Because we cannot read off the ideas and actions of individuals from objective social facts about them, we can understand how their beliefs, actions and social practices change only by exploring the ways in which they think about, and respond to, dilemmas. Thus an analysis of change and developments in government must take place through a study of relevant dilemmas. I build change into the heart of my account of networks by exploring how individual actors respond to dilemmas and reinterpret and reconstruct traditions.

Stoker's (1999a) analysis of the new public management (NPM) in British local government shows how dilemmas stemming from inflation and changing beliefs about public spending led to a new story, not about NPM, but about local governance, illustrating people's contingent responses to dilemmas. Ideally, of course, I should tell the story through the eyes of public managers but their version of the story is not available. So, instead, I use Stoker's accounts of how public managers responded to the dilemma of inflation and reduced public spending; that is, an academic 'constructions of other people's constructions of what they are up to' (Geertz, 1973, p.9).[8]

Inflation had become a major problem for the British economy by the end of the 1970s and it is now widely accepted that the key monetary levers should be interest rates rather than fiscal policy; the supply side of the economy should be considered more significant than demand management; low inflation should be as important a goal of economic policy as low unemployment; and government should develop monetary policy in accord with rule, not discretion, to preserve credibility. These beliefs had direct and immediate consequences for public spending: it was to be cut.

Local authorities are a major vehicle for delivering welfare state services and account for much public spending. They are thus a prime target for any government committed to low inflation and the attendant curbs on public spending. Management reform was one part of the effort to contain public spending. The new public management's rhetoric told a story of economy, efficiency and effectiveness – the '3Es' – which contrasted sharply with the story of the local government officer as professional with clients. In theory the '3Es' would deliver more public services for less money. There was a second strand to NPM: marketization. This term refers to the use of market mechanisms in the delivery of public services, covering contracting out (for example, compulsory competitive tendering of many local government services); quasi-markets in the guise of the purchaser–provider split (for example, in the NHS); and experiments with voucher schemes (for example, nursery education).

Both the '3Es' and marketization generated unintended consequences. Thus Stoker (1999a) identifies several, negative unintended consequences, including fragmentation, loss of accountability and a decline in the public service ethic. More significant for the argument here, he also identifies important unintended benefits. First, NPM disrupted the system. Second, local authorities were increasingly forced to account for their actions in public. Third, these twin pressures produced a sense of crisis which helped to create new policy ideas. The delicious irony is that the new ideas were not those of NPM but of local governance. So local authorities adopt a wider role of concern for the well-being of the locality, work in partnership with many actors and agencies, and focus on the outcomes of services delivered through the partnerships. As Stoker (1999a) concludes:

> It is in some respects ironic that the pressures unleashed by New Management have encouraged local authorities to rethink and redefine their role. The vision of the New Management reformers aimed at a more efficient and customer-oriented service delivery by local authorities has been challenged by a broader vision of a new community governance.

So the number of networks multiplied. Their membership grew and it was drawn from more sectors. Both by intent and as an unintended consequence of reform, the capacity of the centre to steer those networks declined (Rhodes, 1997a, pp.12, 45).

The response to the dilemma of inflation and public spending cuts can be seen in the language used to talk about the management changes. Mackintosh (1999) argues that NPM contains two economic discourses (see Table 8.2). The public trading discourse is the language of corporate management and marketization handed down by the government for years. The public business discourse is a reaction to the perceived limits of NPM. It seeks adaptable, flexible relationships for dealing with several agencies and clients. These changes in management and in language illustrate the contingent nature of the way people responded to the dilemma posed by inflation and the need to curb public spending. There is no objective or rational reason for NPM to evolve into local governance. Individuals can modify the practices they inherit in many ways; there is no one rational, scientific or self-interested response to dilemma

Conclusions

I have identified and described four current approaches to networks. I have summarized their defining characteristics, most notably the propositions that facts are given and you can read off the ideas and actions of individuals from knowledge of objective social facts. I have argued for an antifoundational

Table 8.2 Two economic discourses

Public trading discourse	Public business discourse
Tight contract specification	Incomplete specification
Specified service for a price	Variable service on an agreed budget
Short-term focus	Longer-term focus
Even-handed choice between many contractors	Developing relationship with few contractors
Separation of priority setting and delivery	Association of priority setting with delivery
Emphasis on purchaser–client link	Emphasis on provider–client link
Internal relations take 'exchange value' form	Internal relations take cross-subsidy form
Single principal	Many constituencies

Source: Mackintosh (1999).

approach rooted in interpreting traditions and networks. I have shown how the notions of beliefs, traditions and dilemmas can be used to understand networks in government.

The social science literature on governance as networks identifies and focuses on key changes in government and it poses distinctive, new questions about government, for example about reshaping the state. However, an antifoundational approach to studying governance as networks teaches important additional lessons for both academics and practitioners.

For academics, I argue that there is no essentialist account of networks which can be used either to produce law-like generalizations or to legitimate advice to policy makers. Second, the road to understanding lies in actor-centred accounts focusing on the political ethnography of networks and on narratives that give due recognition to the creative individual, not the techniques of positivist social science. Networks are constructed by individual actors and not created by governments or imposed by the researcher. As researchers, we write constructions about the way other people construct the world.

For practitioners, the key lesson of an antifoundational approach is that there is no single tool kit they can use to steer networks. However, they can learn by listening to and telling stories. The social sciences offer only provisional knowledge, but an awareness of our limits does not render the human sciences useless. If we cannot offer solutions, we can define and redefine problems in novel ways. We can tell the policy makers and administrators distinctive stories about their world and how it is governed (see, for example, Rein, 1976). The language of networks challenges the language of managerialism, markets and contracts. The language of narratives challenges the language of predictive social science.

In short, therefore, I provide a language for redescribing the world, for understanding how several actors construct the meaning of recent government changes. In particular, I challenge the dominant, managerial discourse about networks. Too often the analysis of networks is reduced to managerial skills. In no way do I wish to suggest that learning how to steer networks is unimportant. I do want to suggest, however, that steering networks involves understanding participants' stories as much as more technical means, and the analysis of governance as networks needs an actor-centred exploration of beliefs, traditions and dilemmas. Understanding networks is to do with the changing nature of government and how national traditions interpret such changes.

Notes

1   A special thank you to Mark Bevir (University of Newcastle) with whom I wrote the first draft of this chapter and to Lotte Jensen (University of Copenhagen) who provided a constructive critique.

2   On developments in policy network theory, see Bogason and Toonen (1998) and several recent articles in *Public Administration*: Blom-Hansen (1997), Börzel (1998), Cavanagh *et al.* (1995), Hindmoor (1998), Jordan *et al.* (1994), Kickert (1997), Klijn *et al.* (1995), Painter *et al.* (1997), Taylor (1997).

3   On the constructivist theory of history, see, for example, Collingwood (1939; 1965; 1993), Oakeshott (1983), White (1973; 1978; 1987). For a good introduction, see Jenkins (1995). For a boisterous debate, see the exchange between Marwick (1995) and White (1995).

4   This approach is not relativist, but I do not have the space to develop the argument here. See Bevir (1994; 1999), Bevir and Rhodes (1998), Rhodes (1997a, ch.9).

5   The original framework was clearly rooted solidly in a positivistic social science epistemology. However, it genuflected in the direction of the human sciences approach with its reference to Sir Geoffrey Vickers and the idea of appreciative systems (Vickers, 1968). The term refers to that combination of factual and value judgements which describe the 'state of the world' or 'reality'(see pp.83–4 above and Rhodes, 1986, p.8). It is the individual decision maker's map of the world. Constructing maps of the way decision makers make sense of the world is a defining characteristic of an actor-centred approach to networks.

6   Greenleaf (1983, pp.15–20) provides a well-known analysis of the British political tradition. He posits a dialectic between two opposing tendencies: libertarianism and collectivism. Libertarianism stresses four things: the basic importance of the individual, the limited role of government, the dangers of concentrating power and the rule of law. Its antithesis, collectivism stresses the public good, social justice and the idea of positive government. Greenleaf's opposing tendencies are ahistorical. Although they come into being in the nineteenth century, they remain static after that, acting as fixed catego-

ries, ideal types, into which he forces individual thinkers and texts, even different parts of the one text or different utterances by the one thinker.

7   For a similar recognition that the political ethnography of networks is an instructive approach, see Heclo and Wildavsky (1974), McPherson and Raab (1988), Rhodes (1997a, ch.9).

8   Again, I simply illustrate the argument that the notion of dilemma helps us to understand change. I do not provide a detailed exploration of change in networks. Any such account would need to recognize that individuals have several antidotes to, and coping mechanisms for, challenges to their belief systems. Such challenges can take the form of responding to different beliefs or to the actions of others and any response will be affected by the salience of those beliefs and actions for the several parties. Also, understanding changes needs an understanding of the way in which beliefs are constructed, both in the complex patterns of social interaction and in the handed-down traditions.

References

Agger, R.E., Goldrich, D. and Swanson, B.E. (1964), *The Rulers and the Ruled*, New York: Wiley.

Albrow, M. (1973), 'The Study of Organisations: Objectivity or Bias?', in G. Salaman and K. Thompson (eds), *People and Organisations*, London: Longmans.

Aldrich, H.E. and Pfeffer, J. (1976), 'Environments of Organisations', in A. Inkeles (ed.), *Annual Review of Sociology, II*, Palo Alto, Cali.: Annual Review Inc.

Anderson, W. (1960), *Intergovernmental Relations in Review*, Minneapolis: University of Minnesota.

Ashford, D. (1974), 'The Effects of Central Finance on the British Local Government System', *British Journal of Political Science*, 4: 305–22.

Ashford, D. (1977), 'Are Britain and France Unitary?', *Comparative Politics*, 9: 483–99.

Association of County Councils *et al.* (1979), *Review of Central Government Controls Over Local Authorities*, London: ACC, ADC and AMA.

Bachrach, P. and Baratz, M.S. (1962), 'Two Faces of Power', *American Political Science Review*, 56: 947–52.

Bachrach, P. and Baratz, M.S. (1963), 'Decisions and Nondecisions: an analytical framework', *American Political Science Review*, 57: 632–42.

Bailey, M. (1979), *Oilgate*, London: Coronet Books.

Bang, H.P. and Sørensen, E. (1998). 'The Everyday Maker: a New Challenge to Democratic Governance', paper to the ECPR Workshops, 26th Joint Sessions, University of Warwick, 23–28 March.

Bardach, E. (1977), *The Implementation Game*, Boston: MIT Press.

Barker, A. (1978), *Central–Local Government Relationships in Britain as a Field of Study: A commentary and research register*, London: SSRC.

Barrett, S. and Fudge, C. (eds) (1981), *Policy & Action: Essays on the Implementation of Public Policy*, London, Methuen.

Barrett, S. and Hill, M. (1982), 'Report to the SSRC Central–Local Government Relationships Panel on the "Core" or Theoretical Component of the Research on Implementation' (Report to SSRC, mimeo).

Bauer, R.A. and Gergen, K.J. (1968), *The Study of Policy Formation*, New York: The Free Press.

Becquart-Leclerq, J. (1978), 'Relational Power and Systemic Articulation in French Local Polity', in L. Karpik (ed.), *Organisation and Environment: theory, issues and reality*, London: Sage.

Beer, S.H. (1973), 'The Modernisation of American Federalism', *Publius*, **3** (2): 49–95.

Beer, S.H. (1976), 'The Adoption of General Revenue Sharing', *Public Policy*, **24**:127–95.

Beer, S.H. (1978), 'Federalism, Nationalism and Democracy in America', *American Political Science Review*, **72**: 9–21.

Beer, S.H. (1980), 'British Pressure Groups Revisited: Pluralistic Stagnation from the Fifties to the Seventies', *Public Administration Bulletin*, **32**: 5–16.

Bell, D. (1976), *The Coming of Post-Industrial Society*, Harmondsworth: Penguin.

Bendix, R. (1956), *Work and Authority in Industry*, New York: Wiley.

Benson, J. (1982), 'Networks and Policy Sectors: A Framework for Extending Inter-organisational Analyses', in D. Rogers and D. Whetton (eds), *Inter-organisational Co-ordination*, Ames, Iowa: Iowa State University Press.

Benson, J.K. (1975), 'The Inter-organisational Network as a Political Economy', *Administrative Science Quarterly*, **20**: 229–49.

Berne, E. (1968), *Games People Play*, Harmondsworth: Penguin.

Bevir, M. (1994), 'Objectivity in History', *History and Theory*, **33**: 328–44.

Bevir, M. (1999), *The Logic of the History of Ideas*, Cambridge: Cambridge University Press.

Bevir, M. and Rhodes, R.A.W. (1998), 'Narratives of "Thatcherism" and the Dilemmas of British Government', *West European Politics*, **21** (1): 97–119.

Birch, A.H. (1955), *Federalism, Finance and Social Legislation*, Oxford: Clarendon Press.

Birch, A.H. (1964), *Representative and Responsible Government*, London: Allen & Unwin.

Birch, A.H. (1966), 'Approaches to the Study of Federalism', *Political Studies*, **14:** 15–23.

Birch, A.H. (1977), *Political Integration and Disintegration in the British Isles*, London: Allen & Unwin.

Birley, D.T. (1970), *Education Officer and His World*, London: Routledge & Kegan Paul.

Birnbaum, P. (1976), 'Power Divorced from its Sources: a critique of the exchange theory of power', in B.M. Barry (ed.), *Power and Political Theory*, New York: Wiley.

Birrell, D. (1978), 'The Centralisation of Local Government Functions in Northern Ireland – an appraisal', *Local Government Studies*, **4** (4): 23–37.

Blackburn, R. (1972), 'The New Capitalism', in R. Blackburn (ed.), *Ideology in Social Science*, London: Fontana/Collins.

Blackstone, T. (1971), *A Fair Start: the provision of pre-school education*, London: Allen Lane, The Penguin Press.

Blau, P.M. (1964), *Exchange and Power in Social Life*, New York: Wiley.

Blau, P.M. and Scott, W.R. (1963), *Formal Organisations*, London: Routledge & Kegan Paul.

Blom-Hansen, J. (1997), 'A "New Institutional" Perspective on Policy Networks', *Public Administration*, **75**: 669–93.

Boaden, N. (1971), *Urban Policy Making*, London: Cambridge University Press.

Boddy, M. and Fudge, C. (eds) (1984), *Local Socialism*, London: Macmillan.

Bogason, P. and Toonen, T.A.J. (eds) (1998), *Comparing Networks*, Special issue of *Public Administration*, **76** (2).

Börzel, T.J. (1998), 'Organizing Babylon: on the different conceptions of policy networks', *Public Administration*, **76**: 253–73.

Boyle, E., Crosland, A. and Kogan, M. (1971), *The Politics of Education*, Harmondsworth: Penguin.

Bramley, G. and Stewart, M. (1981), 'Implementing Public Expenditure Cuts', in S. Barrett and C. Fudge (eds) (1981), *Policy & Action: Essays on the Implementation of Public Policy*, London, Methuen.

Bridges, Lord (1971), 'Portrait of a Profession', in R.A. Chapman and A. Dunsire (eds), *Style in Administration*, London: Allen & Unwin.

Brier, A.P. (1970), 'The Decision Process in Local Government: a case study of fluoridation in Hull', *Public Administration*, **48**: 153–68.

Brittan, S. (1975), 'The Economic Contradictions of Democracy', *British Journal of Political Science*, **5**: 129–59.

Bulpitt, J.G. (1980), 'Territorial Politics in the United Kingdom: an analytical prospectus', mimeo, Department of Politics, Warwick University.

Bulpitt, J.G. (1983), *Territory and Power in the United Kingdom*, Manchester, Manchester University Press.

Burkhead, J. (1974), 'Federalism in a Unitary State: regional economic planning in England', *Publius*, **4** (2): 39–61.

Burns, T. (1969), 'On the Plurality of Social Systems', in T. Burns (ed.), *Industrial Man*, Harmondsworth: Penguin.

Burns, T. (1974), 'On the Rationale of the Corporate System', in R. Marris (ed.), *The Corporate Society*, London: Macmillan.

Burns, T. (1977), *The BBC: Public Institution and Private World*, London: Macmillan.

Carnell, F.G. (1961), 'Political Implications of Federalism in New States', in U.K. Hicks *et al.* (eds), *Federalism and Economic Growth in Underdeveloped Countries*, London: Allen & Unwin.

Cavanagh, M., Marsh, D. and Smith, M. (1995), 'The Relationship Between Policy Networks at the Sectoral and Sub-sectoral Levels', *Public Administration*, **73**: 627–33.

Cawson, A. (1982), *Corporatism and Welfare*, London: Heinemann.

Cawson, A. and Saunders, P. (1983), 'Corporatism, Competitive Politics and Class Strength', in R. King (ed.), *Capital and Politics*, London: Routledge & Kegan Paul.

Central Policy Review Staff (1977), *Relations Between Central Government and Local Authorities*, London: HMSO.

Chandler, A. (1962), *Strategy and Structure*, Cambridge, Mass.: MIT Press.

Chandler, J.A. (1991), *Local Government Today*, Manchester: Manchester University Press.

Chester, D.N. (1951), *Central and Local Government*, London: Macmillan.

Chester, Sir Norman (1981), *The English Administrative System 1790–1810*, Oxford: Clarendon Press.

Child, J. (1973), 'Organisation Structure, Environment and Performance: the role of strategic choice', in G. Salaman and K. Thompson (eds), *People and Organisations*, London: Longmans.

Clark, T.N. (1974), 'Community Autonomy in the National System: federalism, localism and decentralisation', in T.N. Clark (ed.), *Comparative Community Politics*, New York: Halsted Press.

Clegg, S. (1975), *Power, Rule and Domination*, London: Routledge & Kegan Paul.

Clegg, S.R. (1990), *Modern Organisations. Organisation Studies in the Post-modern World*, London: Sage.

Clegg, T. (1982), 'Social Consumption, Social Investment and the Dual State: the case of transport policy in the Paris region', paper to the PSA Annual Conference, University of Kent, Canterbury.

Coates, D. (1984), 'Food Law', in D. Lewis and H. Wallace (eds), *Polices into Practice*, London: Heinemann.

Cochrane, A. (1993), *Whatever Happened to Local Government?*, Buckingham: Open University Press.

Cockburn, C. (1977), *The Local State*, London: Pluto Press.

Collingwood, R.G. (1965), *Essays in the Philosophy of History*, Austin, Texas: University of Texas Press.

Collingwood, R.G. (1978) [1939], *An Autobiography*, with a new introduction by Stephen Toulmin, Oxford: Oxford University Press.

Collingwood, R.G. (1993), *The Idea of History*, rev. edn, Oxford: Oxford University Press.

Committee of Inquiry into Local Government Finance (Layfield) (1976), *Report*, Cmnd 6453, London: HMSO.

Committee on the Management of Local Government (Maud) (1967), Volume 1, *Report*, London: HMSO.

Cox, A. (1981), 'Corporatism as Reductionism: the analytic limits of the Corporatist thesis', *Government and Opposition*, **16** (1): 78–95.

Crenson, M.A. (1971), *The Unpolitics of Air Pollution*, Baltimore: Johns Hopkins Press.

Cripps, F. and Godley, W. (1976), *Local Government Finance and its Reform*, Cambridge: Department of Applied Economics.

Crispin, A. (1976), 'Local Government Finance: assessing the central government's contribution', *Public Administration*, **54**: 45–61.

Cross, J.A. (1954), 'The AMC: a study of its structure', unpublished MA thesis, University of Manchester.

Cross, J.A. (1974), *The Principles of Local Government Law*, London: Sweet & Maxwell.

Crossman, R.H.S. (1975), *The Diaries of a Cabinet Minister, Volume 1, Minister of Housing*, London: Jonathan Cape/Hamish Hamilton.

Crouch, C. (1977), *Class Conflict and the Industrial Relations Crisis*, London: Heinemann.

Crouch, C. (1979), *The Politics of Industrial Relations*, Glasgow: Fontana/ Collins.

Crozier, M. (1972), 'The Relationship between Micro and Macro Sociology', *Human Relations*, **25**: 239–51.

Crozier, M. (1973), 'The Problem of Power', *Social Research*, **40**: 220–21.

Crozier, M. (1976), 'Comparing Structures and Comparing Games', in G. Hofstede and M.S. Kassem (eds), *European Contributions to Organisation Theory*, Assen/Amsterdam: Van Gorcum.

Crozier, M. and Friedberg, E. (1977), *L'acteur et le système*, Paris: Edition du Seuil.

Crozier, M. and Thoenig, J.C. (1976), 'The Regulation of Complex Organised Systems', *Administrative Science Quarterly*, **21**: 547–70.

Cunningham, C. (1992), 'Sea Defences: A Professionalised Network?', in D. Marsh and R.A.W. Rhodes (eds), *Policy Networks in British Government*, Oxford: Oxford University Press.

Cyert, R.M. and March, J.G. (1963), *A Behavioral Theory of the Firm*, Englewood Cliffs, NJ: Prentice-Hall.

Dahl, R.A. (1969), 'The Concept of Power', in R. Bell, D.V. Edwards and R.H. Wagner, (eds), *Political Power: a reader in theory and research*, New York: The Free Press.

Davis, K.C. (1969), *Discretionary Justice*, Baton Rouge: Lousiana State University Press.

Dearlove, J. (1973), *The Politics of Policy in Local Government*, London: Cambridge University Press.

Dearlove, J. (1979), *The Reorganization of Local Government*, Cambridge: Cambridge University Press.

Dell, E. (1960), 'Labour and Local Government', *Political Quarterly*, **31**: 333–47.

Deutsch, K.W. *et al.* (1957), *Political Community and the North Atlantic Area*, Princeton: Princeton University Press.

Douglas, J. (1976), 'The Overloaded Crown', *British Journal of Political Science*, **6**: 483–505.

Dowding, K. (1991), *Rational Choice and Political Power*, Aldershot: Edward Elgar.

Dowding, K. (1995), 'Model or Metaphor? A Critical Review of the Policy Network Approach', *Political Studies*, **43**: 136–58.

Drucker, H.M., Dunleavy, P., Gamble, A. and Peele, G. (eds) (1983), *Developments in British Politics*, London: Macmillan.

Dunleavy, P. (1980a), 'Theories of the State and Society and the Study of Central–Local Relations', in G.W. Jones (ed.), *Central–Local Relations in Britain*, Farnborough: Saxon House.

Dunleavy, P. (1980b), *Urban Political Analysis*, London: Macmillan.

Dunleavy, P. (1981), *The Politics of Mass Housing in Britain, 1945–1975*, Oxford: Clarendon Press.

Dunleavy, P. (1984), 'The Limits of Local Government', in M. Boddy and C. Fudge (eds) (1984), *Local Socialism*, London: Macmillan.

Dunleavy, P. and O'Leary, B. (1987), *Theories of the State*, London: Macmillan.

Dunleavy, P. and Rhodes, R.A.W. (1983), 'Beyond Whitehall', in H.M. Drucker, P. Dunleavy, A. Gamble and G. Peele (eds), *Developments in British Politics 1*, London: Macmillan.

Dunleavy, P. and Rhodes, R.A.W. (1986), 'Government Beyond Whitehall', in H.M. Drucker, P. Dunleavy, A. Gamble and G. Peele (eds), *Developments in British Politics 2*, London: Macmillan.

Dunleavy, P. and Rhodes, R.A.W. (1988), 'Government Beyond Whitehall', in H.M. Drucker, P. Dunleavy, A. Gamble and G. Peele (eds), *Developments in British Politics 2*, rev. edn, London: Macmillan.

Dunsire, A. (1981), 'Central Control over Local Authorities: a cybernetic approach', *Public Administration*, **59**: 173–88.

Dyson, K.H.F. (1980), *The State Tradition in Western Europe*, Oxford: Martin Robertson.

Elazar, D. *et al.* (1969), *Co-operation and Conflict in American Federalism*, Ill.: Peacock.

Elcock, H. (1994), *Local Government: policy and management in local authorities*, London: Routledge.

Elkin, S.L. (1975), 'Comparative Urban Politics and Inter-organisational Behaviour', in K. Young (ed.), *Essays on the Study of Urban Politics*, London: Macmillan.

Emerson, R.M. (1962), 'Power–Dependence Relations', *American Sociological Review*, **27**: 31–41.

Emery, F.E. (ed.) (1969), *Systems Thinking*, Harmondsworth: Penguin.

Emery, F.E. and Trist, E.L. (1965), 'The Causal Texture of Organisational Environments', *Human Relations*, **18**: 21–32.

Emery, F.E. and Trist, E.L. (1969), 'Socio-Technical Systems', in F.E. Emery (ed.), *Systems Thinking*, Harmondsworth: Penguin.

Etzioni, A. (1960), 'Two Approaches to Organizational Analysis: a critique and a suggestion', *Administrative Science Quarterly*, **5**: 257–78.

Etzioni, A. (1968), *The Active Society*, New York: The Free Press.

Evan, W.M. (1966), 'The Organisation-Set: toward a theory of inter-organisational relations', in J.D. Thompson (ed.), *Approaches to Organisational Design*, Pittsburgh: University of Pittsburgh Press.

Evan, W.M. (1976), *Inter-organisational Relations*, Harmondsworth: Penguin.

Expenditure Committee (1977), 'Supplementary Memorandum by Society of Local Authority Chief Executives on Unnecessarily Detailed Control by Government Departments', Eleventh Report from the Expenditure Committee, *The Civil Service, Volume II, Minutes of Evidence*, HC 535, London: HMSO.

Ferlie, E. and Pettigrew, A. (1996), 'Managing Through Networks: some issues and implications for the NHS', *British Journal of Management*, **7**: 81–99.

Fesler, J.W. (1965), 'Approaches to the Understanding of Decentralisation', *Journal of Politics*, **27**: 536–66.

Finer, S. E. (1957), *The Life and Times of Sir Edwin Chadwick*, London: Methuen.

Flynn, R. (1983), 'Co-optation and Strategic Planning in the Local State', in R. King (ed.), *Capital and Politics*, London: Routledge & Kegan Paul.

Fox, A. (1973), 'Industrial Relations: a social critique of pluralist ideology', in J. Child (ed.), *Man and Organisation*, London: Allen & Unwin.

Frances, J. (1991), 'Introduction', in G. Thompson, J. Frances, R. Levačič and J. Mitchell (eds), *Markets Hierarchies and Networks: the co-ordination of social life*, London: Sage.

Friend, J.K. (1976), 'Planners, Policies and Operational Boundaries: some recent developments in Britain', *Policy and Politics*, **5** (1): 25–44.

Friend, J.K. (1977), 'The Dynamics of Policy Change', *Long Range Planning*, **10**, February: 40–47.

Friend, J.K. and Jessop, W.N. (1969), *Local Government and Strategic Choice*, London: Tavistock.

Friend, J.K., Power, J. and Yewlett, C.J.L. (1974), *Public Planning: the intercorporate dimension*, London: Tavistock.

Fudge, C. and Barrett, S. (1981), 'Reconstructing the field of Analysis', in S. Barrett and C. Fudge (eds), *Policy and Action*, London: Methuen.

Galbraith J.K. (1972), *The New Industrial State*, 2nd edn, London: Deutsch.

Galbraith, J.K. (1973), *Economics and the Public Purpose*, Boston: Houghton Mifflin.

Geertz, C. (1973). *The Interpretation of Cultures*, New York, Basic Books.

Glaser, B.G. and Strauss, A. (1967), *The Discovery of Grounded Theory*, New York: Aldine.

Goldsmith, M. and Rhodes, R.A.W. (1986), *Register of Research and Research Digest on Central–Local Government Relations in Britain*, London: ESRC.

Goodwin, M. (1982), 'The Local State and the Local Provision of Welfare', paper to the PSA Annual Conference, University of Kent, Canterbury.

Grant, W.P., Paterson, W. and Whitson, C. (1988), *Government and the Chemical Industry: A Comparative Study of Britain and West Germany*, Oxford: Clarendon Press.

Green, L.P. (1959), *Provincial Metropolis*, London: Allen & Unwin.

Greenleaf, W.H. (1983), *The British Political Tradition. Volume 1. The Rise of Collectivism*, London: Methuen.

Griffith, J.A.G. (1966), *Central Departments and Local Authorities*, London: Allen & Unwin.

Gross, E. (1969), 'The Definition of Organisational Goals', *British Journal of Sociology*, **20**: 277–94.

Gyford, J. and James, M. (1983), *National Parties and Local Politics*, London: Allen & Unwin.

Haas, E.B. (1964), *Beyond the Nation State*, Stanford: Stanford University Press.

Habermas, J. (1971), *Toward a Rational Society*, London: Heinemann.

Hallstein, W. (1972), *Europe in the Making*, London: Allen & Unwin.

Hammersley, M. (1991), *Reading Ethnographic Research. A Critical Guide*, Harlow, Essex: Longman.

Hampton, W. (1981), 'Who Calls the Tune: Review Article', *Public Administration Bulletin*, No. 36, 63–6.

Hanf, K. (1978), 'Introduction', in K. Hanf and F. Scharpf (eds), *Interorganisational Policy Making*, London: Sage.

Hanf, K. and Scharpf, F.W. (eds) (1978), *Inter-organisational Policy Making*, London: Sage.

Harris, R. and Shipp, P.J. (1977), *Communications Between Central and Local Government in the Management of Local Authority Expenditure*, Coventry: Institute for Operational Research.

Hartley, O.A. (1971), 'The Relationship Between Central and Local Authorities', *Public Administration*, **49**: 439–56.

Haywood, S. and Alaszewski, A. (1980), *Crisis in the Health Service*, London: Croom Helm.

Heclo, H. (1978), 'Issue Networks and the Executive Establishment', in A. King (ed.), *The New American Political System*, Washington, DC: American Enterprise Institute.

Heclo, H. and Wildavsky, A. (1974), *The Private Government of Public Money*, London: Macmillan.

Henney, A. (1984), *Inside Local Government. The Case for Radical Reform*, London: Sinclair Browne.

Hepworth, N. (1977), 'Local Government and Central Control', *Public Administration*, **55**: 11–16.

Hepworth, N.P. (1976), *The Finance of Local Government*, 3rd edn, London: Allen & Unwin.

Hickson, D.J., Hinings, C.R., Lee, C.A., Schneck, R.E. and Pennings, J.M. (1971), 'A Strategic Contingencies' Theory of Intra-organisational Power', *Administrative Science Quarterly*, **16**: 216–29.

Hill, D. (1982), 'Review' of Rhodes (1981), *Public Administration*, **60**: 111–12.

Hill, F. (1966), 'The Partnership in Theory and Practice', *Political Quarterly*, **37**: 169–79.

Hindmoor, A. (1998), 'The Importance of Being Trusted: transaction costs and policy network theory', *Public Administration*, **76**: 25–44.

Hodges, M. (1972), 'Introduction' in M. Hodges (ed.), *European Integration*, Harmondsworth: Penguin.

Hogwood, B. (1979), 'Analysing Industrial Policy: a multi-perspective approach', *Public Administration Bulletin*, No. 29: 18–42.

Hogwood, B. (1982), 'Introduction', in B. Hogwood and M. Keating (eds), *Regional Government in England*, Oxford: Clarendon Press.

Hogwood, B. and Keating, M. (eds) (1982), *Regional Government in England*, Oxford: Clarendon Press.

Hogwood. B.W. (1979), 'The Tartan Fringe', *Studies in Public Policy*, No. 34, Glasgow: University of Strathclyde.

Hood, C.C. (1976), *The Limits of Administration*, London: Wiley.

Houlihan, B. (1983), 'Conceptualising Central–Local Relations', paper to the PSA Annual Conference, University of Newcastle.

Hull, C. and Rhodes, R.A.W. (1977), *Intergovernmental Relations in the European Community*, Farnborough: Saxon House.

Hunt, A. (ed.) (1977), *Class and Class Structure*, London: Lawrence & Wishart.

Isaac-Henry, K. (1970), 'The Politics of Comprehensive Education in Birmingham 1757–1967', unpublished M. Soc. Sc. Thesis, University of Birmingham.

Isaac-Henry, K. (1974), 'Local Authority Associations and Local Government Reform', *Local Government Studies*, **1** (3): 1–12.

Isaac-Henry, K. (1978), 'The Association of Municipal Corporations and the County Councils Association – a study of influences and pressures on reorganisation 1945–72', mimeo, Birmingham Polytechnic.

Isaac-Henry, K. (1980), 'The English Local Authority Associations', *Public Administration Bulletin*, No. 33: 21–41.

Jenkins, K. (1995), *On 'What is History?'*, London: Routledge.

Jensen, L. (1998), 'Cultural Theory and Democratizing Functional Domains: the case of Danish Housing', *Public Administration*, **76**: 117–39.

Jessop, R. (1979), 'Corporatism, Parliamentarism and Social Democracy', in P.C. Schmitter and G. Lehmbruch (eds), *Trends Towards Corporatist Intermediation*, London: Sage.

Jessop, R. (1980), 'The Transformation of the State in Post-war Britain', in R. Scase (ed.), *The State in Western Europe*, London: Croom Helm.

Jessop, R. (1988), 'Conservative Regimes and the Transition to post-Fordism', *Essex Papers in Politics and Government*, no. 47.

Jessop, B. (1990), 'Regulation Theories in Retrospect and Prospect', *Economy and Society*, **19**: 153–216.

Jessop, B. (1997), 'The governance of complexity and the complexity of governance: preliminary remarks on some problems and limits of economic guidance', in A. Amin and J. Hausner (eds), *Beyond Market and Hierarchy: interactive governance and social complexity*, Cheltenham: Edward Elgar.

Johnson, N. (1973), *Government in the Federal Republic of Germany*, Oxford: Pergamon.

Jones, G.W. (1977), *Responsibility and Government*, London: London School of Economics and Political Science.

Jones, G.W. (1979), 'Central–Local Relations, Finance and the Law', *Urban Law and Policy*, **2**: 25–6.

Jones, G.W. (ed.) (1980), *New Approaches to the Study of Central–Local Government Relations*, Aldershot: Gower.

Jordan, A.G. (1981), 'Iron Triangles, Woolly Corporatism and Elastic Nets', *Journal of Public Policy*, **1**: 95–123.

Jordan, G. (1990), 'Sub-governments, Policy Communities and Networks. Refilling the Old Bottles?', *Journal of Theoretical Politics*, **2**: 319–38.

Jordan, G. and Schubert, K. (eds) (1992), *Policy Networks*, Special issue of *European Journal of Political Research*, **21** (1 and 2).

Jordan, M., Maloney, W. and McLaughlin, A. (1994), 'Characterising Agricultural Policy Making', *Public Administration*, **72**: 505–26.

Jowell, J. (1973), 'The Legal Control of Administrative Discretion', *Public Law*, Autumn: 178–220.

Judge, D., Stoker, G. and Wolman, H. (eds) (1995), *Theories of Urban Politics*, London: Sage.

Karpik, L. (1978), 'Preface', in L. Karpik (ed.), *Organisation and Environment: theory, issues and reality*, London: Sage.

Katz, D. and Kahn, R.L. (1966), The *Social Psychology of Organizations*, New York: Wiley.

Kaufman, F.X., Majone, G. and Ostrom, V. (eds) (1986), *Guidance, Control and Evaluation in the Public Sector*, Berlin: de Gruyter.

Kavanagh, D. (1991), 'Why Political Science Needs History', *Political Studies*, **39**: 479–95.

Keith-Lucas, B. (1962), 'Poplarism', *Public Law*, Spring: 52–80.

Keith-Lucas, B. and Richards, P.G. (1978), *A History of Local Government in the Twentieth Century*, London: Allen & Unwin.

Kenis, P. and Schneider, V. (1991), 'Policy Networks and Policy Analysis: Scrutinizing a New Analytical Toolbox', in B. Marin and R. Mayntz (eds) (1991), *Policy Networks: Empirical Evidence and Theoretical Considerations*, Frankfurt am Main: Campus Verlag.

Keohane, R. and Nye, J. (1977), *Power and Interdependence*, Boston: Little, Brown.

Kesselman, M. (1967), *The Ambiguous Consensus*, New York: Alfred A. Knopf.

Kickert, W.J.M. (1993), 'Complexity, Governance and Dynamics: Conceptual Explorations of Public Network Management', in J. Kooiman (ed.), *Modern Governance*, London: Sage.

Kickert, W.J.M. (1997), 'Public Governance in the Netherlands: an alternative to Anglo-American "managerialism"', *Public Administration*, **75**: 731–52.

Kickert, W.J.M., Klijn, E-H. and Koppenjan, J.F.M. (eds) (1997), *Managing Complex Networks: Strategies for the Public Sector*, London: Sage.

King, A. (1975), 'Overload: Problems of Governing in the 1970s', *Political Studies*, **23**: 162–74.

King, A. (1978), 'The American Policy in the Late 1970s: Building Coalitions in the Sand', in A. King (ed.), *The New American Political System*, Washington, DC: AEI.

King, R. (1983), 'The Political Nature of the Local Capitalist Association', in R. King (ed.), *Capital and Politics*, London, Routledge & Kegan Paul.

King, R. (ed.) (1983), *Capital and Politics*, London: Routledge & Kegan Paul.

Klijn, E-H. (1997). 'Policy Networks: an overview', in W.I.J. Kickert, E-H. Klijn and J.F.M. Koppenjan (eds), *Managing Complex Networks: Strategies for the Public Sector*, London: Sage.

Klijn, E.H., Koopenjan, J. and Termeer, K. (1995), 'Managing Networks in the Public Sector', *Public Administration*, **73**: 437–54.

Klonglan, G.E., Warren, R.D., Winkelpleck, J.M. and Paulson, S.K. (1976), 'Interorganizational Measurement in the Social Services Sector: differences by hierarchical level', *Administrative Science Quarterly*, **21**: 675–87.

Kooiman, J. (ed.) (1993), *Modern Governance*, London: Sage.

La Porte. T.R. (1974), *Organised Social Complexity: challenge to politics and policy*, Princeton: Princeton University Press.

Landau, M. (1969), 'Redundancy, Rationality and the Problem of Duplication and Overlap', *Public Administration Review*, **39**: 346–58.

Laumann, E. and Knoke, D. (1987), *The Organisational State*, Wisconsin: University of Wisconsin Press.

Laumann, E.O., and Pappi, F.U. (1976), *Networks of Collective Action*, New York: Academic Press.

Lawrence, P.R., and Lorsch, J.W. (1967), *Organisations and Environment*, Boston: Graduate School of Business Administration, Harvard University.

Lee, J.M., Wood, B. with Solomon B.W. and Walters, P. (1974), *The Scope for Local Initiative*, London: Martin Robertson.

LeGales, P. and Thatcher, M. (eds) (1995), *Les réseaux de politique publique. Débat autour des policy networks*, Paris: Editions L'Harmattan.

Lehmbruch, G. and Schmitter, P. (eds) (1980), *Patterns of Corporatist Policy Making*, London: Sage.

Levine, S. and White P.E. (1961), 'Exchange as a Conceptual Framework for the Study of Inter-organisational Relationships', *Administrative Science Quarterly*, **5**: 583–601.

Lindberg, L.N. (1963), *The Political Dynamics of European Economic Integration*, Stanford: Stanford University Press.

Lindberg, L.N. and Scheingold, S.N. (1970), *Europe's Would-be Polity*, Englewood Cliffs, NJ: Prentice-Hall.

Litwak, E. and Hylton, L.F. (1962), 'Inter-organisational Analysis: a hypothesis on co-ordinating agencies', *Administrative Science Quarterly*, **7**: 395–415.

Livingston, W.S. (1956), *Federalism and Constitutional Change*, Oxford: Clarendon Press.

Long, N. (1958), 'The Local Community as an Ecology of Games', *American Journal of Sociology*, **64**: 251–61.

Loughlin, J. and Peters, B.G. (1997), 'State Traditions, Administrative Reform and Regionalization', in M. Keating and J. Loughlin (eds), *The Political Economy of Regionalism*, London: Frank Cass.

Lowi, T.J. (1969), *The End of Liberalism*, New York: Norton.

Lowi, T.J. (1978), 'Europeanization of America: From United States to United State', in T.J. Lowi and A. Stone (eds), *Nationalizing Public Policies in America*, London: Sage.

Lukes, S. (1974), *Power: A Radical View*, London: Macmillan.

Maass, A. (1959), *Area and Power*, Glencoe, Ill.: The Free Press.

Mackenzie, W.J.M. (1961), *Theories of Local Government*, Greater London Papers No. 2, London: London School of Economics and Political Science.

Mackenzie, W.J.M. (1976), 'Pressure Groups in Britain', in R. Rose (ed.), *Studies in British Politics*, 3rd edn, London: Macmillan.

Mackintosh, M. (1999), 'Two Economic Discourses in the New Management of Local Governance: "public trading" and "public business"', in G. Stoker (ed.), *The New Management of Local Governance: Audit of an Era of Change in Britain*, London: Macmillan.

Madgwick, P. and James, M. (1980), 'The Network of Consultative Government in Wales', in G.W. Jones (ed.), *Approaches to the Study of Central–Local Government Relations*, Farnborough: Saxon House.

March, J.G. and Olsen, J.P. (1989), *Rediscovering Institutions: The Organisational Basis of Politics*, New York, The Free Press.

Marsh, D. (1983), *Pressure Politics*, London: Junction Books.

Marsh, D. (1992), 'Youth Employment Policy 1970–1990: Towards the Exclusion of the Trade Unions', in D. Marsh and R.A.W. Rhodes (eds), *Policy Networks in British Government*, Oxford: Oxford University Press.

Marsh, D. (ed.) (1998), *Comparing Policy Networks*, Buckingham: Open University Press.

Marsh, D. and Chambers, J. (1981), *Abortion Politics*, London: Junction Books.

Marsh, D. and Grant, W. (1977), 'Tripartism: Myth or Reality?', *Government and Opposition*, **12**: 195–211.

Marsh, D. and Rhodes, R.A.W. (eds) (1992), *Policy Networks in British Government*, Oxford: Oxford University Press.

Marsh, D. and Smith, M. (1995), 'The Role of Networks in an Understanding of Whitehall: towards a dialectical approach', paper to the PSA Annual Conference, University of York, 18–20 April.

Martin, R.C. (1965), *The Cities and the Federal System*, London: Athlone Press.

Martlew, C. (1983), 'The State and Local Government Finance', *Public Administration*, **61**: 127–47.

Marwick, A. (1995) 'Two Approaches to Historical Study: The Metaphysical (Including 'Postmodernism') and the Historical', *Journal of Contemporary History*, **30**: 5–35.

May, R.J. (1969), *Federalism and Fiscal Adjustment*, Oxford: Clarendon Press.

May, R.J. (1970), 'Decision Making and Stability in Federal Systems', *Canadian Journal of Political Science*, **3**: 73–87.

Mayntz, R. and Scharpf, F.W. (1975), *Policy-making in the German Federal Bureaucracy*, Amsterdam: Elsevier.

McFarland, A. (1979), 'Recent Social Movements and Theories of Power in America', paper to the Annual Meeting of the American Political Science Association, Washington, DC, 31 August.

McFarland, A. (1987), 'Interest Groups and Theories of Power in America', *British Journal of Political Science*, **17**: 129–47.

McPherson, A. and Raab, C. (1988), *Governing Education*, Edinburgh: Edinburgh University Press.

Merkl, P.H. (1959), 'Executive–Legislative Federalism in West Germany', *American Political Science Review*, **53**: 732–41.

Metcalfe, L. (1978), 'Policy Making in Turbulent Environments', in K. Hanf and F.W. Scharpf (eds), *Inter-organisational Policy Making*, London: Sage.

Michels, R. (1962) [1915], *Political Parties*, New York: Collier Books.

Miliband, R. (1969), *The State in Capitalist Society*, London: Weidenfeld & Nicolson.

Mills, M. (1992), 'The Case of Food and Health and the Use of Networks', in D. Marsh and R.A.W. Rhodes (eds), *Policy Networks in British Government*, Oxford: Oxford University Press.

Mindlin, S.E. and Aldrich, H. (1975), 'Inter-organisational Dependence: a review of the concept and re-examination of the findings of the Aston Group', *Administrative Science Quarterly*, **20**: 382–92.

Mitchell, A. (1974), 'Clay Cross', *Political Quarterly*, **45**: 165–78.

Mitchell, J.C. (1969), 'The Concept and Use of Social Networks', in J.C. Mitchell (ed.), *Social Networks in Urban Situations*, Manchester: Manchester University Press.

Mohr, L. (1973), 'The Concept of Organisational Goal', *American Political Science Review*, **67**: 470–81.

Nichols, T. (1969), *Ownership, Control and Ideology*, London: Allen & Unwin.

O'Toole, L. (1997), 'Treating Networks Seriously: Practical and Research Based Agendas in Public Administration', *Public Administration Review*, **57** (1): 45–52.

Oakeshott, M. (1983), *On History and Other Essays*, Oxford: Oxford University Press.

Olsen, J.P. (1991), 'Political Science and Organisation Theory: Parallel Agendas but Mutual Disregard', in R.M. Czada, and A. Windhoff-Héritier (eds), *Political Choice. Institutions, Rules and the Limits of Rationality*, Boulder, Colo.: Westview Press.

Ostrom, E. (1986), 'A Method of Institutional Analysis', in F.X. Kaufman, G. Majone and V. Ostrom (eds), *Guidance Control and Evaluation in the Public Sector*, Berlin: de Gruyter.

Ostrom, V. (1974), *The Intellectual Crisis in American Public Administration*, Alabama: Alabama University Press.

Page, E. (1978), 'Why Should Central–Local Relations in Scotland be different to those in England?', *Public Administration Bulletin*, No. 28, December: 51–72.

Page, E. (1982), 'Central Government Instruments of Influence on Local Authorities', unpublished PhD thesis, Strathclyde University: Glasgow.

Painter, C., Rouse, J. and Isaac-Henry, K. (1997), 'Local Authorities and Non-elected Agencies: strategic responses and organisational networks', *Public Administration*, **77**: 225–45.

Panitch, L. (1980), 'Recent Theorisations of Corporatism: reflections on a growth industry', *British Journal of Sociology*, **31**: 159–87.

Parry, G. and Morriss, P. (1974), 'When is a Decision not a Decision?', in I. Crewe (ed.), *The British Political Sociology Yearbook, 1, Elites in Western Democracy*, London: Croom Helm.

Parsons, T. (1969), 'On the Concept of Political Power', in R. Bell, D.V. Edwards and R.H. Wagner (eds), *Political Power: a reader in theory and research*, New York: The Free Press.

Pentland, C. (1973), *International Theory and European Integration*, London: Faber & Faber.

Perri 6 (1997), *Holistic Governance*, London: Demos.

Perrow, C. (1970), *Organizational Analysis*, London: Tavistock.

Perrow, C. (1972a), *The Radical Attack on Business*, New York: Harcourt Brace Jovanovich.

Perrow, C. (1972b), *Complex Organizations*, Glenview, Ill.: Scott, Foresman.

Perrow, C. (1979), *Complex Organizations*, 2nd edn, Glenview, Ill.: Scott, Foresman.

Peterson, J. (1992), 'The European Technology Community', in D. Marsh and R.A.W. Rhodes (eds), *Policy Networks in British Government*, Oxford: Oxford University Press.

Pettigrew, A.M. (1973), *The Politics of Organisational Decision Making*, London: Tavistock.

Pickvance, C.G. (1976), *Urban Sociology: Critical Essays*, London: Tavistock.

Plant, R. (1983), 'The Resurgence of Ideology', in H. Drucker, P. Dunleavy, A. Gamble and G. Peele (eds), *Developments in British Politics*, London: Macmillan.

Pollock, L. and McAllister, I. (1980), *A Bibliography of United Kingdom Politics: Scotland, Wales and Northern Ireland*, Studies in Public Policy, Volume III, Glasgow: University of Strathclyde.

Polsby, N. (1979), 'Empirical Investigations of Mobilisation of Bias in Community Power Research', *Political Studies*, **37**: 527–41.

Poulantzas, N. (1973), *Political Power and Social Classes*, London: New Left Books.

Powell, W. (1991), 'Neither Market Nor Hierarchy: network forms of organisation', in G. Thomson, J. Frances, R. Levačič and J. Mitchell (eds), *Markets, Hierarchies and Networks: the co-ordination of social life*, London: Sage.

Pressman, J. and Wildavsky, A. (1973), *Implementation*, Berkeley/Los Angeles: University of California Press.

Pross, P. (1986), *Group Politics and Public Policy*, Toronto: Oxford University Press.

Pugh, D.S. and Hickson, D.J. (1976), *Organizational Structure in its Context*, Farnborough: Saxon House.

Pugh, D.S., and Hinings, C.R. (1976), *Organizational Structure: extensions and replications*, Farnborough: Saxon House.

Quade, E. (1976), *Analysis for Public Decisions*, 2nd edn, New York: American Elsevier.

Ranson, S., Hinings, C.R. and Greenwood, R. (1980), 'The Structuring of Organizational Structures', *Administrative Science Quarterly*, **25**: 1–17.

Read, M. (1992), 'Policy Networks and Issue Networks: The Politics of Smoking', in D. Marsh and R.A.W. Rhodes (eds), *Policy Networks in British Government*, Oxford: Oxford University Press.

Reagan, M.D. (1972), *The New Federalism*, New York: Oxford University Press.

Redcliffe-Maud, Lord J. and Wood, B. (1974), *English Local Government Reformed*, London: Oxford University Press.

Regan, D.E. (1977), *Local Government and Education*, London: Allen & Unwin.

Rein, M. (1976), *Social Science and Public Policy*, Harmondsworth: Penguin.

Rhodes, G. (1976), 'Local Government Finance 1918–1966', in Committee of Inquiry into Local Government Finance, Appendix 6, *The Relationship Between Central and Local Government*, London: HMSO.

Rhodes, R.A.W. (1978), 'The Rationality of Ambiguous Confusion: rules, strategies and prizes in British central–local relations', Report to the SSRC Panel on Research into Central and Local Government, London.

Rhodes, R.A.W. (1979), 'Ordering Urban Change: corporate planning in the government of English cities', in J. Lagroye and V. Wright (eds), *Local Government in Britain and France*, London: Allen & Unwin.

Rhodes, R.A.W. (1981), *Control and Power in Central–Local Government Relationships*, Farnborough: Gower.

Rhodes, R.A.W. (1984), 'Continuity and Change in British Central–Local Relations: the "Conservative" threat, 1979–83', *British Journal of Political Science*, **14**: 311–33.

Rhodes, R.A.W. (1986), *The National World of Local Government*, London: Allen & Unwin.

Rhodes, R.A.W. (1988), *Beyond Westminster and Whitehall*, London: Unwin-Hyman; reprinted Routledge, 1992.

Rhodes, R.A.W. (1990), 'Policy Networks: A British Perspective', *Journal of Theoretical Politics*, **2** (3): 292–316.

Rhodes, R.A.W. (1991), 'Now Nobody Understands the System: The Changing Face of Local Government', in P. Norton (ed.), *New Directions in British Politics?*, Aldershot: Edward Elgar.

Rhodes, R.A.W. (1992) 'Beyond Whitehall: researching local governance', *Social Sciences*, No. 13, November: 2.

Rhodes, R.A.W. (1996), 'The New Governance: governing without Government', *Political Studies*, **44**: 652–67.

Rhodes, R.A.W. (1997a), *Understanding Governance*, Buckingham: Open University Press.

Rhodes, R.A.W. (1997b), 'It's the mix that matters: from marketisation to diplomacy', *Australian Journal of Public Administration*, **56**: 40–53.

Rhodes, R.A.W. (1997c), 'Shackling the Leader? Coherence, capacity and the hollow crown', in P. Weller, H. Bakvis and R.A.W. Rhodes (eds), *The Hollow Crown: countervailing trends in core executives*, London: Macmillan.

Rhodes, R.A.W. (1998), 'Different roads to unfamiliar places: UK experience in comparative perspective', *Australian Journal of Public Administration*, **57** (4): 19–31.

Rhodes, R.A.W. (1999), 'Governance and Public Administration', in J. Pierre (ed.), *Debating Governance*, Oxford: Oxford University Press.

Ribbins, P.M. and Brown, R.J. (1979), 'Policy Making in English Local

Government: the case of secondary school reorganisation', *Public Administration*, **57**: 187–202.

Richards, P.G. (1973), *The Reformed Local Government System*, London: Allen & Unwin.

Richardson, J. and Jordan, A.G. (1979), *Governing Under Pressure*, Oxford: Martin Robertson.

Riker, W.H. (1964), *Federalism: Origin, Operation, Significance*, Boston: Little, Brown.

Riker, W.H. (1969), 'Six Books in Search of a Subject or Does Federalism Exist and Does it Matter?', *Comparative Politics*, **2**: 135–46.

Ripley, R.B. and Franklin, G. (1980), *Congress, The Bureaucracy and Public Policy*, 2nd edn, Homewood, Ill: Doresy.

Robson, W.A. (1966), *Local Government in Crisis*, London: Allen & Unwin.

Rockart, J.F. and Short, J.E. (1991), 'The Networked Organisation and the Management of Interdependence', in M.S. Scott (ed.), *The Corporation of the 1990s*, Oxford: Oxford University Press.

Rogers, D. and Whetton, D. (eds) (1982), *Inter-organisational Co-ordination*, Ames, Iowa: Iowa State University Press.

Rorty, R. (1980), *Philosophy and the Mirror of Nature*, Oxford: Blackwell.

Rose, R. (1976), 'The United Kingdom as a Multi-National State', in R. Rose (ed.), *Studies in British Politics*, 3rd edn, London: Macmillan.

Rose, R. (1978), 'Ungovernability: Is there Fire Behind the Smoke?', *Studies in Public Policy*, No. 16, Glasgow: University of Strathclyde.

Rose, R. (1982), *Understanding the United Kingdom*, London: Longmans.

Royal Commission on Local Government in England (Redcliffe-Maud) (1969), *Report*, Cmnd 4040, London: HMSO.

Royal Commission on Local Government in Scotland 1966–69 (Wheatley) (1969), *Report*, Cmnd 4150, Edinburgh: HMSO.

Ryan, A. (1970), *The Philosophy of the Social Sciences*, London: Macmillan.

Sampson, A. (1974), *The Sovereign State*, London: Coronet Books.

Sampson, A. (1976), *The Seven Sisters*, London: Coronet Books.

Saunders, P. (1980), *Urban Politics*, London: Hutchinson.

Saunders, P. (1981), *Social Theory and the Urban Question*, London: Hutchinson.

Saunders, P. (1982), 'Why Study Central–Local Relations?', *Local Government Studies*, **8** (2): 55–66.

Saunders, P. (1986), 'Reflections on the dual state thesis: the argument, its origins and its critics', in M. Goldsmith and S. Villadsen (eds), *Urban Political Theory and the Management of Fiscal Stress*, Aldershot: Gower.

Saward, M. (1992), 'The Civil Nuclear Network in Britain', in D. Marsh and R.A.W. Rhodes (eds), *Policy Networks in British Government*, Oxford: Oxford University Press.

Sawyer, G.F. (1969), *Modern Federalism*, London: Watts.

Scarrow, H. (1971), 'Policy Pressures by British Local Government: the case of regulation in the public interest', *Comparative Politics*, 4: 1–28.

Scharpf, F.W. (1977), 'Public Organisation and the Waning of the Welfare State', *European Journal of Political Research*, 5: 339–62.

Scharpf, F.W. (1978), 'Inter-organisational Policy Studies: issues, concepts and perspectives' in K. Hanf and F.W. Scharpf (eds), *Inter-organizational Policy Making*, London: Sage.

Scharpf, F.W. (1997), *Games Real Actors Play. Actor Centred Institutionalism in Policy Research,*. Boulder, Colo.: Westview Press.

Scharpf, F.W., Reissert, B. and Schnabel, F. (1978), 'Policy Effectiveness and Conflict Avoidance in the Intergovernmental Policy Formation', in K. Hanf and F.W. Scharpf (eds), *Inter-organisational Policy Making*, London: Sage.

Scharpf, F.W., Reissert, B. and Schnabel, F. (1976), *Politikverflechtung*, Kronberg: Scriptor.

Schmitter, P. (1979), 'Still the Century of Corporatism?', in P.C. Schmitter and G. Lehmbruch (eds), *Trends Towards Corporatist Intermediation*, London: Sage.

Schmitter, P. (1980), 'Reflections on where the theory of neo-corporatism has gone and where the praxis of neo-corporatism may be going', in G. Lehmbruch and P. Scmitter (eds), *Patterns of Corporatist Policy Making*, London: Sage.

Schmitter, P. and Lehmbruch, G. (eds) (1979), *Trends Towards Corporatist Intermediation*, London: Sage.

Selznick, P. (1949), *TVA and the Grass Roots*, Berkeley/Los Angeles: University of California.

Sharkansky, I. (ed.) (1970), *Policy Analysis in Political Science*, Chicago: Markham.

Sharp, Dame E. (1962), 'The Future of Local Government', *Public Administration*, 40: 375–86.

Sharpe, L.J. (1970), 'Theories and Values of Local Government', *Political Studies*, 18: 153–74.

Sharpe, L.J. (1979), 'Modernising the Localities: local government in Britain and some comparisons with France', J. Lagroye and V. Wright (eds), *Local Government in Britain and France*, London: Allen & Unwin.

Sharpe, L.J. (1984), 'Functional Allocation in the Welfare State', *Local Government Studies*, 10 (1): 27–45.

Sherwood, F.P. (1967), 'Devolution as an Organisational Strategy', in R.T. Daland (ed.), *Comparative Urban Research*, Beverley Hills, California: Sage.

Shonfield, A. (1965), *Modern Capitalism*, London: Oxford University Press.

Silverman, D. (1970), *The Theory of Organisations*, London: Heinemann.

Simeon, R. (1972), *Federal–Provincial Diplomacy: the making of recent policy in Canada*, Toronto/Buffalo: University of Toronto Press.

Simon, H.A. (1960), *The New Science of Management Decision*, New York: Harper and Row.

Skinner, B. and Langdon, J. (1974), *The Story of Clay Cross*, Nottingham: Spokesman Books.

Smith B.C. (1976), *Policy Making in British Government*, London: Martin Robertson.

Smith, B.C. (1980), 'The Measurement of Decentralisation', in G.W. Jones (ed.), *Central–Local Relations in Britain*, Farnborough: Saxon House.

Smith, B.C. and Stanyer, J. (1976), *Administering Britain*, London: Fontana/Collins.

Smith, B.L.R. and Hague, D.C. (eds) (1971), *The Dilemma of Accountability in Modern Government*, London: Macmillan.

Smith, M. (1992), 'The Agricultural Policy Community: Maintaining a Closed Relationship', in D. Marsh and R.A.W. Rhodes (eds), *Policy Networks in British Government*, Oxford: Oxford University Press.

Social Science Research Council (1979), *Central–Local Government Relationships*, London: SSRC.

SOLACE (Society of Local Authority Chief Executives) (1980), *The Local Government Bill: an appraisal prepared by SOLACE in collaboration with INLOGOV*, London: SOLACE.

Stanyer, J. (1976), *Understanding Local Government*, London: Fontana/Collins.

Stewart, J.D. (1972), *Management in Local Government*, London: Charles Knight.

Stewart, J.D. (1980), 'From Growth to Standstill', in M. Wright (ed.), *Public Spending Decisions*, London: Allen & Unwin.

Stewart, J.D. (1983), *Local Government: the Conditions of Local Choice*, London: Allen & Unwin.

Stoker, G. (1990), 'Regulation Theory, Local Government and the Transition from Fordism', in D. King and J. Pierre (eds), *Challenges to Local Government*, London: Sage.

Stoker, G. (1991), *The Politics of Local Government*, 2nd edn, London: Macmillan.

Stoker, G. (1995), 'Intergovernmental Relations', *Public Administration*, **73**: 101–22.

Stoker, G. (1998a), 'Local Governance', *International Social Science Journal*, No. 155, March: 17–28.

Stoker, G. (1998b), 'Theory and Urban Politics', *International Political Science Review*, **19**: 119–29.

Stoker, G. (1999a), 'Introduction: the Unintended Costs and Benefits of New Management Reform for British Local Government', in G. Stoker (ed.), *The New Management of Local Governance: Audit of an Era of Change in Britain*, London: Macmillan.

Stoker, G. (1999b), 'Urban Political Science and the Challenge of Urban Governance', in J. Pierre (ed.), *Debating Governance*, Oxford: Oxford University Press.

Stoker, G. (ed.) (1999c), *The New Management of Local Governance: Audit of an Era of Change in Britain*, London: Macmillan.

Stones, R. (1992), 'International Monetary Relations, Policy Networks and the Labour Government's Policy of Non-Devaluation 1954–67', in D. Marsh and R.A.W. Rhodes (eds), *Policy Networks in British Government*, Oxford: Oxford University Press.

Strauss, A., Schatzman, L., Ehrlich, D., Bucher, R. and Sabshin, M. (1963), 'The Hospital and its Negotiated Order', in E. Friedson, (ed.), *The Hospital in Modern Society*, New York: Macmillan.

Sundquist, J.D. (1969), *Making Federalism Work*, Washington, DC: The Brookings Institution.

Swaffield, J.C. (1970), 'Local Government in the National Setting', *Public Administration*, **48**: 307–15.

Swann, B. (1972), 'Local Initiative and Central Control', *Policy and Politics*, **1**: 55–63.

Tarrow, S. (1977), *Between Centre and Periphery*, New Haven, Yale University Press.

Taylor, A. (1997), '"Arm's Length but Hands On". Mapping the New Governance. The Department of National Heritage and Cultural Policies in Britain', *Public Administration*, **75**: 441–66.

Taylor, J.A. (1979), 'The Consultative Council on Local Government Finance: a critical analysis of its origins and development', *Local Government Studies*, **5** (3): 7–36.

Terreberry, S. (1968), 'The Evolution of Organisational Environments' *Administrative Science Quarterly*, **13**: 590–613.

Thoenig, J-C. (1978a), 'Pouvoir d'état et pouvoirs locaux', *Pouvoirs*, **4**: 25–37.

Thoenig, J-C., (1978b), 'State Bureaucracies and Local Government in France', in K. Hanf and F.W. Scharpf (eds), *Inter-organisational Policy Making*, London: Sage.

Thompson, J.D. (1967), *Organisations in Action*, New York: McGraw-Hill.

Thompson, J.D. and McEwen, I. (1958), 'Organisational Goals and Environment: goal-setting as an interaction process', *American Sociological Review*, **23**: 23–31.

Toffler, Alvin (1971), *Future Shock*, London: Pan Books.

Touraine, A. (1974), *The Post Industrial Society*, London: Wildwood House.
Truman, D.B. (1951), *The Governmental Process*, New York: Alfred A. Knopf.
Tuite, M., Chisholm, R. and Radnor, M. (1972), *Inter-organizational Decision Making*, Chicago: Aldine.
Turk, H. (1970), 'Inter-organizational Networks in Urban Society', *American Sociological Review*, **35**: 1–19.
Turk, H. (1977), *Organizations in Modern Life*, San Francisco: Jossey-Bass.
Vickers, Sir Geoffrey (1965), *The Art of Judgement*, London: Methuen.
Vickers, Sir Geoffrey (1972), *Freedom in a Rocking Boat*, Harmondsworth: Penguin.
Vile, M.J.C. (1961), *The Structure of American Federalism*, Oxford: Clarendon Press.
Vile, M.J.C. (1973), *Federalism in the United States, Canada and Australia*, Research Paper 2 to the Commission on the Constitution, London: HMSO.
Waarden, F. van (1992), 'Dimensions and Types of Policy Networks', *European Journal of Political Research*, **21**: 29–52.
Walker, D.B. (1974), 'How Fares Federalism in the Mid-Seventies?', *The Annals*, No. 416, November: 17–31.
Wallace, H. (1984), 'Implementation Across National Boundaries', in D. Lewis and H. Wallace (eds), *Policies into Practice*, London: Heinemann.
Wallace, W., Wallace, H. and Webb, C. (1977), *Policy-Making in the European Communities*, London: Wiley.
Warren, R., Rose, S. and Bergunder, A. (1974), *The Structure of Urban Reform*, Lexington, Mass.: Heath.
Weick, K.E. (1979), *The Social Psychology of Organizing*, 2nd edn, Reading, Mass.: Addison-Wesley.
West Midlands Study Group (1956), *Local Government and Central Control*, London: Macmillan.
Westergaard, J. (1977), 'Class, Inequality and Corporatism', in A. Hunt (ed.), *Class and Class Structure*, London: Lawrence & Wishart.
Wheare, K.C. (1946), *Federal Government*, London: Oxford University Press.
White, H. (1973), *Metahistory*, Baltimore, Johns Hopkins Press.
White, H. (1978), *Tropics of Discourse*, Baltimore: Johns Hopkins Press.
White, H. (1987), *The Content of the Form*, Baltimore: Johns Hopkins University Press.
White, H. (1995), 'Response to Arthur Marwick', *Journal of Contemporary History*, **30**: 233–46.
Wildavsky, A. (1975), 'A Bias Towards Federalism', University of California, Berkeley, Graduate School of Public Policy.

Wilensky, H. (1970), 'The Professionalisation of Everyone', in O. Grusky and G.A. Miller (eds), *The Sociology of Organisations*, New York: The Free Press.

Wilks, S. (1989), 'Government–Industry Relations', *Public Administration*, **67**, 329–39.

Wilks, S. and Wright, M. (1987), 'Conclusion Comparing Government–Industry Relations: States, Sectors and Networks', in S. Wilks and M. Wright (eds), *Comparative Government–Industry Relations*, Oxford: Clarendon Press.

Wilson, D. and Game, C., with Leach, S. and Stoker, G. (1994), *Local Government in the UK*, London: Macmillan.

Winkler, J.T. (1976), 'Corporatism', *European Journal of Sociology*, **17**: 130–31.

Winkler, J.T. (1977), 'The Corporatist Economy: theory and administration', in R. Scase (ed.), *Industrial Society: Class, Cleavage and Control*, London: Allen & Unwin.

Wistow, G. (1992), 'The Health Service Policy Community: Professionals Pre-eminent or under Challenge?', in D. Marsh and R.A.W. Rhodes (eds), *Policy Networks in British Government*, Oxford: Oxford University Press.

Wood, B. (1976), *The Process of Local Government Reform 1966–74*, London: Allen & Unwin.

Worms, J.P. (1966), 'Le Préfet et ses notables', *Sociologie du Travail*, **8**: 249–75.

Wright, D.S. (1974), 'Intergovernmental Relations: an analytical overview', *The Annals*, No. 416, November: 1–16.

Wright, D.S. (1978), *Understanding Intergovernmental Relations*, North Scituate, Mass.: Duxbury Press.

Wright, D.S. (1988), *Understanding Intergovernmental Relations*, 3rd edn, North Scituate, Mass.: Duxbury Press.

Wright, D.S. and Peddicord, T.E. (1975), *Intergovernmental Relations in the United States: selected books and documents on Federalism and National–State–Local Relations*, Philadelphia: Center for the Study of Federalism, Temple University.

Wright, M. (ed.) (1980), *Public Spending Decisions*, London: Allen & Unwin.

Wright, M. (1989), 'Contextualising Policy Networks in the Comparative Analysis of Industrial Policy', paper to the Conference on Policy Networks: Structural Analysis of Public Policy Making, *Max-Planck-Institut für Gesellschaftsforschung*, Cologne, 4–5 December.

Young, K. (1977), 'Values in the Policy Process', *Policy and Politics*, **5**: 1–22.

Young, K. and Mills, L. (1980), *Understanding the Assumptive Worlds of Government Actors: issues and approaches*, London: SSRC.

Yuchtman, E. and Seashore, S.E. (1967), 'A System Resource Approach to Organizational Effectiveness', *American Sociological Review*, **32**: 891–903.

Subject Index

National Government Environment 125, 133, 134
Negotiation, *see* bargaining
Networks xii–xvii *passim*, 24, 25, 37, 42, 46, 50–54 *passim*, 81, 93–7 *passim*, 114, 127, 128, 129–34, 137–83n
  Characteristics 129
  Definition 129, 138
  Types 138–40
Non-decisions, *see* mobilization of bias

Organizational Environment 35–6, 39–40, 48, 52–3, 66, 68, 79–80
Organizational Power 39–53, 55, 91, 100–1
Organization Goals 37–9, 43, 52–4, 56n, 74, 82–4, 88–90, 95
Organization Structure 39, 43
Overload, *see* ungovernability

Pluralist Theory xiv, 49–50, 55n, 92, 94, 98, 100–3 *passim*, 124, 156–8 *passim*
  Neo-pluralism 118–9, 122, 157 *see also* post-industrial society
Policy Communities 4, 10, 18, 30, 90, 93–105 *passim*, 120–31 *passim*, 133–8 *passim*, 140–42 *passim*, 145, 147, 154, 162, *see also* technocrats
Policy Implementation xiv, 51–2, 88–9
Policy-making xv, 51–4, 67, 74, 117, 119, 120, 134, 144, 156, 158, 172, *see also* decision-making
Post-Fordism xiii, xviiin, 175
Post-industrial society,
  Theory of xii, 8–11, 51, 54, 74, 99–100
Power-dependence, model of xii, xiii, xv, 4, 12, 79–82, 105–6, 118, 124, 133, 162, 163, 165
Process of Exchange 84–7, *see also* bargaining, dependence and internal political process

Professions,
  Technocrats 9–11, 70–1, 74, 99–100, 127
  Topocrats 70–1, 74, 99–100, 126, 127
Public Expenditure Survey Committee (PESC) 25, 28
Public Interest Groups 70, 94–7 *passim*, 100, 103, 104, 106

'Quangos' 6, 98

Rate Support Grant (RSG) 18, 32n
Rational Choice xii, 163, 165
Redcliffe-Maud Report 14
Resources 27, 31, 36–8 *passim*, 41, 44, 46–8, 51, 54, 66–7, 73, 78–87 *passim*, 91–2, 102–3, 105–8n *passim*, 113, 115–7 *passim*, 121, 131, 133, 138, 141, 144, 162, 164
  Constitutional-legal 80–2 *passim*
  Financial 80–2 *passim*, 106
  Hierarchical 80
  Informational 80–1
  Political 29, 67, 73, 80–1
  Power as 47–8, 91
Rules of the Game 44–5, 48–51, 54, 57, 64, 69–74 *passim*, 78, 84–6, 91–2, 101–2, 106, 126, 131, 162, 164
  Structural/hegemonic power 114, 121

State Theory xii, xviin, xiii
  Dual State xviin, 122–5, 133
  Regulation State xiii, xviiin, 175
Steering xiv, 164, 166, 168, 182
Strategies 24, 43–4, 46–8, 54, 57, 64, 72, 74, 78, 86–7, 115–6, 126
Systems Theory 36–8, 40, 52

Technocrats, *see* professions
Technostructure 9, 30
Territorial Politics 112, 113, 127
Topocrats, *see* professions
Tradition 161, 170–1, 173, 176–8, 181, 182, 183n
TUC 8, 150, 155

Also by R.A.W. Rhodes

(with C Hull), *Intergovernmental Relations in the European Community*. (Farnborough: Saxon House, 1977; reprinted, Gower paperback, 1983).

Public Administration and Policy Analysis. (Farnborough: Saxon House, 1979, reprinted Gower, 1981)

Social Science Research Council (Committee member and co-author), *Central–Local Government Relations: A Panel report to the Research Initiatives Board*. (London: SSRC, 1979).

Control and Power in Central–Local Government Relations. (Aldershot: Gower and Brookfield VT: Ashgate Pub., 1981, reprinted 1983 and 1986, Japanese translation, 1987; Second edition with a new Preface and 3 additional chapters Aldershot: Ashgate 1999).

(with I. Budge, D. McKay *et al.*), *The New British Political System: Government and Society in the 1980s*. (London and New York: Longman, 1983; reprinted 1984; revised edition, 1985). New edition as: *The Changing British Political System: Into the 1990s*. (London and New York: Longman 1988).

The National World of Local Government. (London and Winchester, Mass: Allen and Unwin, 1986).

Beyond Westminster and Whitehall: The Sub-Central Governments of Britain (London and Winchester, Mass: Unwin-Hyman/Allen and Unwin, 1988; corrected edition with new Preface and bibliographical addendum, London: Routledge, 1992).

(with Bruno Dente, Marco Cammelli and others), *Reformare la Pubblica Amministrazione*. (Torino: Edizioni della Fondazione Giovanni Agnelli, 1995).

Understanding Governance. (Buckingham and Philadelphia: Open University Press, 1997).

Edited by R.A.W. Rhodes

Training in the Civil Service. (London: Joint University Council for Social and Public Administration, 1977).

(with V. Wright), *Tensions in the Territorial Politics of Western Europe*. (London: Frank Cass, 1987).

(with D. Marsh), *Policy Networks in British Government*. (Oxford: Clarendon Press, 1992).

(with D. Marsh), *Implementing Thatcherite Policies: audit of an era*. (Buckingham and Philadelphia: Open University Press, 1992).

(with P. Dunleavy), *Prime Minister, Cabinet and Core Executive*. (London: Macmillan, and New York: St Martins Press, 1995).

(with H. Bakvis, P. Weller), *The Hollow Crown*. (London: Macmillan, 1997).

United Kingdom, Volumes 1 and 2. (Aldershot: Ashgate 1999).

(with B. G. Peters and V. Wright), *Administering the Summit*. (London: Macmillan, 1999).

Transforming British Government. Volume 1. Changing Institutions. Volume 2. Changing Roles and Relationships. (London: Macmillan, 2000).